SHAPING THE CITY

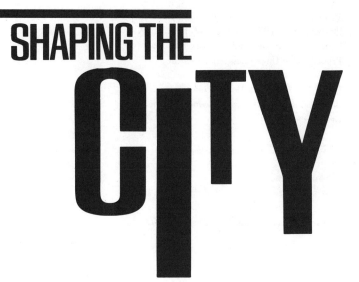

Roger K. Lewis

The AIA Press,
Washington, D.C., 1987

Contents

The AIA Press, 1735 New York Avenue, N.W., Washington, D.C. 20006.

Design by Watermark Design Office. Body and display type set in Bodoni by Unicorn Graphics.

90 89 88 87   7 6 5 4 3 2 1

ISBN 0-913962-88-0

Library of Congress Cataloging-in-Publication Data

Lewis, Roger K.
  Shaping the city.

  Articles from the author's column in the Washington Post.
  Includes index.
  1. Architecture—Washington (D.C.) 2. Washington (D.C.)—Buildings, structures, etc.   I. Title.
NA735.W3L49   1987   720′.9753   87-1358
ISBN 0-913962-88-0 (pbk.)

Preface

Shaping the City began on Saturday, September 8, 1984, as a weekly column in the *Washington Post*. During previous months, I had thought about, discussed with others, and drafted an outline for a series of columns, plus a few sample articles about the history of Washington, D.C. The *Post*'s real estate editor at the time, Albert Crenshaw, expressed interest in running them.

We did not know who might read such a column or how long it might continue. However, we had agreed that the column would be aimed at the general public. It would be didactic and expository, describing, explaining, and commenting upon the form of cities and their buildings. We also believed that fairly complex and arcane subjects could be discussed—and made interesting—if they were clearly presented. Therefore, part of the mission was to demystify some of the theories and practices associated with architecture, urban design, and real estate development.

Each article was conceived as a freestanding essay, yet connected topically to other articles, sometimes in a running series. Thus, readers of this book, depending on their interests, can roam freely through its contents, starting and stopping where they please. Although Washington, D.C., is the principal source of examples illustrating ideas treated here, most themes are generic and universal, of interest, it is hoped, to readers anywhere. Accordingly, some columns have been edited to emphasize concepts more than specific sites.

Shaping the City does not convey massive amounts of data or opinions. Nor is it an exhaustive reference or critical tome. Instead, it aspires to sensitize readers to a multitude of real-world phenomena directly affecting or constituting the physical environment. It seeks to provide a framework for making thoughtful judgments, as much by posing questions as offering answers.

Why does a building, a neighborhood, or an entire city look the way it does? Why is one person's architecture another person's real estate venture? What influences the design, investment, and construction decisions made by architects, planners, developers, financial institutions, governments, and individual citizens who determine why, when, and how urban and suburban environments are built?

Attitudes about cities and architecture depend on who you are, on your goals and values. Most readers fall into one or more of the following groups, each with its own special viewpoints:

- Designers—primarily planners, architects, landscape architects, and engineers,
- Owners and developers of real estate who initiate and carry out construction,
- Lenders and investors who provide equity and debt capital to finance building,
- Officials of government agencies and politicians responsible for managing cities, for building public infrastructure, and for public welfare,
- Users of the built environment—citizens who occupy, visit, conduct trade, pass through, or merely observe the city and its buildings.

Architects see buildings as opportunities to explore and express design ideas. They may seek esthetic rather than economic payoffs. For them, the ideal client is a patron providing the opportunity to create a form of art through building. Some architects may take a longer, more historical view than their clients, anticipating or recalling stylistic images and trends evolving over decades or even centuries. Still others treat buildings as technological artifacts, purposeful machines believed to be inherently beautiful.

Real estate developers and investors, on the other hand, primarily seek to make a return on the equity they risk. To them, buildings are business enterprises, economic "black boxes" yielding, they hope, short-term financial benefits as well as long-term rewards. They expect architects and engineers to provide designs that are buildable and conform to projected budgets, schedules, space and functional requirements, and marketing criteria. Only then can buildings fulfill their ultimate investment purpose: attracting tenants who pay rents that exceed operating and debt service costs.

Lenders see buildings as generators of mortgage loans that comprise assets in their portfolios. Using depositors' capital, they think of buildings as forms of collateral and security for loans, not as architecture per se. Underwriting standards, not esthetic standards, are what matter most to them.

Acknowledgments

Government agencies and officials may view buildings as sources of tax revenue, providers of employment, business catalysts or, negatively, as additional loads on already overburdened public facilities and services. Politicians may see a project as adding prestige both to the city and to the politicians who advocated the project. Many government employees are preoccupied by their regulatory mandate, mostly through enforcement of zoning laws and building codes.

To tenants and other users of buildings, matters of comfort, security, convenience, utility, location, and leasing may be of first priority. The soundness of the mortgage loan, the financial return to investors, or the winning of design awards may be secondary or of no importance.

Individual citizens have different points of view depending on where they live and work, the paths they travel, and the cultural perspectives they bring to bear. Some care about preserving old buildings while others hardly take notice. Some care about façades while others, indifferent to façades, care much more about the shops, office space, restaurants, or apartments behind them.

Shaping the City tries to recognize and respect the disparity of viewpoints about habitats that everyone nevertheless must share. At the same time, it attempts to relate esthetic, economic, functional, technological, and social concerns to paint a holistic picture. By understanding better the conditions and forces that interact to shape the environment, readers perhaps will see the city's fabric and its architecture in a new light.

Neither this book nor the columns on which it is based would exist were it not for the encouragement of Albert Crenshaw, former real estate editor at the *Washington Post*. Being a practitioner and teacher of architecture, not a journalist, I am especially grateful for his initial editorial guidance and critiques.

I am likewise grateful to Ken Bredemeier, Al Crenshaw's successor, for his continuing support. He has further encouraged me to explore new topics, express opinions, and illustrate observations for the *Post*'s diverse readership.

The University of Maryland and its School of Architecture are owed a debt of gratitude. Their policies regarding faculty research, writing, and consulting gave me the time to produce a weekly column while I continued teaching and practicing. Some of the issues, ideas, and references found in *Shaping the City* came from the school's classrooms or the books in its library.

Finally, I want to thank sincerely the many people—colleagues, friends, members of my family and, above all, readers—who generously took the time to communicate with me, affirming their interest, voicing approval, suggesting topics, or correcting errors. Knowing that someone is reading, learning from, and perhaps enjoying what I have written is the greatest incentive to these endeavors and an indispensable source of satisfaction.

For Ellen and Kevin

1.

Shaping a City
Creating America's Capital

Founding a Capital City

The "look" of Washington, D.C., and its very existence, are the result of historical compromise and human perseverance. In fact, were it not for its politically expedient geographic location somewhere near the center of gravity of the original 13 colonies, the nation's capital might not be here at all.

Faced with a deplorable summer climate, lack of urban amenities, and questionable commercial potential, it is a wonder that Congress and Washington's early citizens stuck it out.

Historian Samuel Eliot Morison described the city as it appeared in 1800 this way:

"Pennsylvania Avenue, studded with stumps and alder bushes, led from the Capitol through a morass to the White House. . . . Two miles further west lay Georgetown, a comfortable little Maryland town that afforded officials an agreeable change from each other's society. The red clay soil of the District became dust in dry weather and liquid cement in every rain, after which swarms of mosquitoes spread malaria.

"Several fine groves of tulip trees were the only features of natural beauty within the city site; Jefferson's one recorded wish for despotic power was to save these trees from the inhabitants, who proceeded to fell them for firewood."

A complaining diplomat dubbed the capital "The City of Magnificent Distances."

A half-century earlier, colonists had chosen the sites of Georgetown and Alexandria to establish river-oriented trading centers. They surveyed and subdivided the towns' lands, which were connected to the hinterlands of Maryland and Virginia by a developing network of roads. Town plans were made pragmatically, with little debate about how to fashion a new settlement. Handling matters of defense, access, transportation, dwelling, and urban government was well understood.

The layouts and architectural form of these new port settlements derived from familiar and accepted 17th- and 18th-century English urban precedents for making simple, rectangular patterns of blocks, streets, public spaces, and buildings. The ample supply of land guaranteed that settlement could expand as the need arose, with the most valuable commercial property being adjacent to the port and main roads.

The early builders of Georgetown and Alexandria could not have foreseen development much beyond that required to meet immediate, local demands. They were not overly concerned with issues of imagery, monumentality, or master planning, but were instead driven primarily by economic, social, and survival pressures typical of the Colonial period. Perhaps they consciously rejected most notions of grandiose architecture or urban utopia, seeing them as inappropriate imports alien to the American landscape.

At the end of the 18th century, Washington was no more than a few isolated, rural settlements on the way to somewhere else north or south. The new republic's politically expedient decision to locate its capital between the Anacostia and Potomac rivers, unlike the earlier settlers' decisions to create the port of Georgetown and Alexandria, required a new consensus and a new set of design conventions. Impromptu building and ad hoc land subdivision would be inadequate for this unprecedented and, it was hoped, soon-to-be-magnificent settlement on the Potomac.

The efforts of George Washington, Thomas Jefferson, and the imaginative French engineer, Major Pierre L'Enfant, resulted in Washington's seminal city plan. First drafted in 1791, it consisted of a rectangular grid of streets 90 feet wide and variably spaced, all oriented north-south (numbered streets) or east-west (lettered streets). The grid stretched northward from the Potomac River and its eastern branch to Boundary Street (later Florida Avenue) and westward to Georgetown. It was punctuated by open squares and circles from which radiated a series of diagonal avenues 160 feet wide, cutting across the grid.

The anchors of L'Enfant's plan, in addition to the landscape and rivers, were the Capitol, sited atop Jenkin's Heights ("a pedestal waiting for a monument"), the President's House, the Mall, and the Washington Monument. Great vistas along the avenues, and from the squares and circles, would provide an appropriate sense of grandeur. Further, the plan attempted to relate to existing topography and roads, even as its rational geometry imposed a totally new and grandiose order.

Whereas previous historical urban precedents in the colonies had been English and vernacular in spirit, those for the new capital were clearly Continental and baroque, legacies of France and Italy.

But imposing this grand vision on a muddy, shrub-covered site bounded by forest and marshland would prove to be a formidable task. For years, it remained a place where people came, transacted the government's business, and fled. Even after the Capitol's first wing and the President's House were constructed, government officials retreated hastily from the infant city the moment Congress adjourned, and few stayed in town for the hot, steamy summers.

New Washington seemed both artificial and inhospitable. The necessities that invented it had been poetic and political, not economic, making it unique among American cities. For all its aspirations, its growth potential and desirability as a place to reside permanently were far from evident. It remained a sparsely populated village whose future promise depended on a paper concept.

In fact, Congress had intended to finance new public buildings through selling lots, but the dismal lack of sales forced the city's commissioners to finance construction through loans guaranteed by Congress. The first American example of the ideal planned city—a city of intent, symbol, and ceremony—appeared to be in jeopardy.

The War of 1812 and the burning of the Capitol by the British in 1814 threatened to dampen further the nation's hopes for its new capital. With many considering abandoning this 10-mile square on the Potomac as the seat of government, there was little preoccupation with issues of land-use planning, zoning, density (except for the lack of it), or the availability and cost of real estate. Unregulated growth, land speculation, and the provision of public services—trash collection, paving and maintenance of streets, utilities, police and fire protection, and transportation—would not become issues until much later in the century.

September 15, 1984

A City Grows . . .
Despite the Mud

Washington, D.C., was conceived in the 18th century to be a great, new urban seat of government. Yet it remained a village for several decades of the 19th century.

It is hard to know exactly when Washington became a viable city. But between 1814 and 1860, the District of Columbia, having relinquished its acreage in Virginia, achieved critical mass. Congress had persevered in its commitment to make Washington the undeniable national capital despite skepticism, miserable weather, mosquitoes, mud, and burning by the British.

Growth was spurred by the need to serve, lobby, or report on those who governed. The Chesapeake and Ohio Canal was built in the belief that D.C. could become a great trading port for America's heartland. Hotels, rooming houses, residences, stores, and restaurants randomly filled block after block of L'Enfant's plan, sometimes obscuring it.

The sale, subdivision, and development of property was unregulated, the price, size, shape, and use of lots being determined by free-market forces. And the Mall, the "Grand Avenue" of L'Enfant's plan, was grazed by cattle and bisected by the sewage-filled Washington canal connecting the C & O to the Anacostia River.

Washington's unique pattern of streets became a network of muddy roadways. Although streets and public spaces were the responsibility of the federal government, Congress did little to plan or improve thoroughfares, leaving this to local citizens and developers who usually could not afford to grade and pave properly L'Enfant's 160-feet-wide avenues or 90-feet-wide streets.

During the Civil War, the District became an administrative and military beehive. After 1865, freed slaves and others migrated to the city by the thousands to look for new opportunities. Unfortunately, many remained unemployed, ill housed, and underfed, occupying ramshackle dwellings in alleys or on federal property.

Postwar demographic pressures had become overwhelming. From 1800 to 1850, the District's population had grown from 14,000 to 50,000. By 1870, it had reached 132,000! Clearly, while the Union had been restored to order, the capital's order was faring poorly.

Laissez-faire optimism and expansion typical of 19th-century America had produced a distinctly schizophrenic urban landscape, the result of L'Enfant's visionary, orderly plan being infilled haphazardly by ad hoc private construction on blocks subdivided into smaller and smaller lots, punctuated periodically by monumental federal buildings.

The expanded, massive Treasury Building east of the White House typified the situation. Sited there impulsively one morning by an impatient Andrew Jackson, this neoclassical edifice rudely interrupted L'Enfant's intended visual and symbolic connection along Pennsylvania Avenue between the President's House and the Capitol. The Old Patent Office, now the American Art/Portrait Gallery Building, was built at Seventh and G Streets in 1836, just before the Treasury. Its location had been intended for a church.

The city had also sprawled rapidly. New housing appeared east of the Capitol, to the northwest along Massachusetts Avenue and K Street, and farther north at Meridian Hill

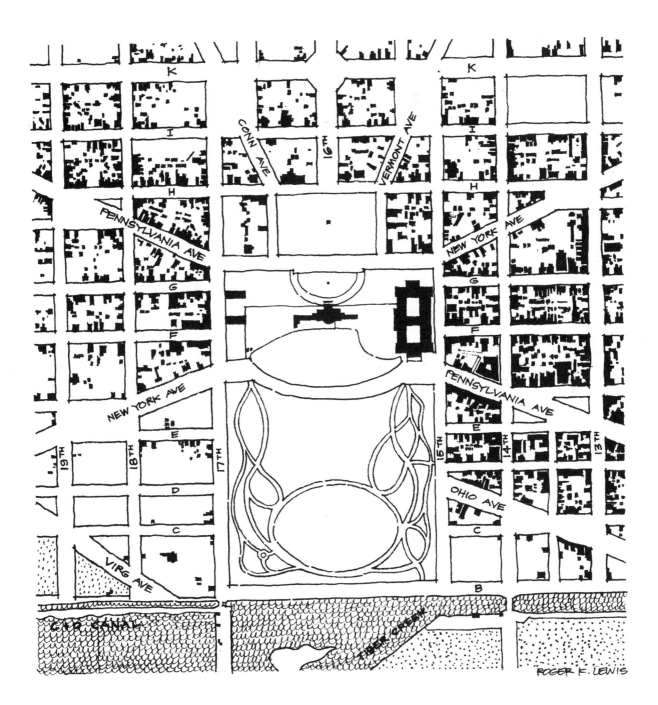

and Mt. Pleasant. Alley occupancy kept increasing, and Washingtonians began to realize that their city, no longer a village, needed schools, sewers, a water supply system, and paved streets. A city of slums, social unrest, disease, swamps, and rampant land speculation was overpowering the city of aspiration.

In 1868, Mayor Sayles Bowen changed the city's paving standards, laying 15 miles of sidewalks and 4 miles of sewer. Nevertheless, in 1870, there were still 200 miles of unpaved streets, and even more without sewers or drainage. Much of Washington's property remained marshland and subject to periodic flooding. South of the White House the Ellipse of today remained a swamp.

Physical problems were accompanied by political ones. Congress, alarmed by the behavior and corruption attributed to the local governing officials, was equally worried about the implications of universal suffrage, which, in D.C., implied enfranchising a fast-growing black population. Its response in 1871 was to abolish, for a century to come, local self-government in the District of Columbia. The city charter form of government was superseded by a congressionally appointed governor, council, and board of public works.

This new form of government, created by the Territorial Act, ushered in a "new era," and with it came rowhouse developer Alexander Shepherd. Shepherd was appointed to the board of public works, over which he quickly gained control, and in the short span of three years, he proceeded to transform Washington. Earning the title "Boss" Shepherd, he spent millions of dollars for sewers, grading and paving streets, water mains, and trees.

Unfortunately, Shepherd's zeal and willingness to ride roughshod over his opponents were not offset by equally compelling technical expertise or esthetic sensitivity. His "comprehensive" plans could not await detailed or accurate surveys or the assurance of funding. He intended to urbanize totally the Washington landscape from the Mall to P Street, from New Hampshire Avenue to New Jersey Avenue, whatever the costs.

With little advance public notice, street levels were completely revised for drainage, new bridges installed, hills cut, and valleys filled. Even streets lined with vacant lots and few buildings were improved for future growth. Street railways were extended, street lighting added, and more land acquired and subdivided by developers to the north and northwest. In 1872, over 1,200 new structures were built.

To Shepherd and many others, Washington's cachet was its individual public edifices and wide streets, not its overall form or potential network of public spaces and parks capable of cementing the separate parts into a whole. In fact, streets, alleys, and public space accounted for 54 percent of Washington's developed area, according to one study, compared with 29 percent in Philadelphia, 35 percent in New York City, and 25 percent in Paris.

Shepherd was convinced that his comprehensive plans would foster real estate activity and increase property values. But booms are frequently followed by busts. In 1873 and 1874, panics, bankruptcies, and economic depression set in. Investigations and hearings led Congress once again to change its mind about how to rule D.C.; the territorial government was dissolved and replaced by three presidentially appointed commissioners.

Boss Shepherd, condemned for his bulldozing tactics and freewheeling fiscal strategy, departed his Connecticut Avenue mansion and headed for Mexico, leaving an indelible mark upon the city.

By 1879, there were 150,000 permanent residents in the District, mostly because of the federal government, whose employees numbered 7,800 in 1880 and 23,000 in 1890, a nearly threefold increase in 10 years.

The nation's capital had become a city, but not the commercial port envisioned a half-century earlier. The C & O canal, constructed with such painstaking optimism, would never make Washington a "continental emporium" or trading center. Washington's fate was tied to the growth of government and the real estate market, and little else.

September 22, 1984

Washington Matures

Historian Constance McLaughlin Green has declared that "the economic history of Washington during the last years of the 19th century becomes a story of real estate."

Between 1879 and 1901, new office buildings and stores went up on F Street while new housing appeared in the "suburbs" of Kalorama Heights, Chevy Chase, and Cleveland Heights. In 1887, nearly 2,500 new buildings were constructed, and land that sold for 8 cents per square foot in 1882 was selling for 40 cents per square foot. Real estate dealers proliferated like never before.

The federal government continued expanding and building. The new State, War, and Navy Building stood west of the White House, constructed in 1872 during the Shepherd era. Designed in French Second Empire style as the world's largest office building, its appeal to Victorian tastes offended many neoclassicists. Further, it echoed the siting error of the Treasury east of the White House as it interrupted the New York Avenue vista. The Old Pension Building at 5th and G Streets, and the Old Post Office at 12th and Pennsylvania, continued the romantic, late Victorian departure from classicism.

A new esthetic consciousness, plus a modicum of social consciousness, seems to have arrived along with the real estate expansion. Washington's poor and growing black population continued to live invisibly in substandard alley dwellings. In 1881, two-thirds of the houses in D.C. had no sewer connections, and virtually none of the alleys were sewered. Congress was moved to pass a law in 1892 that prohibited dwellings in alleys less than 20 feet wide and without sewers, water lines, and overhead lighting. This was followed by an act in 1897 requiring all dwellings to have sewer connections.

In 1888, citing the growth of "inharmonious subdivisions" to the north and northwest of the city, Congress passed a law requiring developers to lay out subdivisions in conformance with the existing D.C. street plan. This was perhaps the first attempt to introduce any significant land-use regulation in the District of Columbia.

During the 1880s, pursuing further the goals advocated earlier by Boss Shepherd, the District continued its efforts to drain wetlands and control both flooding and mosquito breeding. Marshes were filled, and Potomac Park and the Tidal Basin were created.

Residents of Washington had begun to appreciate the value of preserving and maintaining open space, a unique and readily perceived characteristic of D.C. that contrasted with the denser fabric of other cities. They must have understood that such open space "might ultimately contribute more to Washington's appearance . . . than a formless proliferation of individually handsome buildings," observes historian Green. So inspired, Congress acquired Rock Creek Park in 1890, and its 1893 Highway Act called for streets and parkways to be designed by qualified landscape architects.

11

Control of urban growth was being exercised at last. Much of the impetus for aggressively taking hold of the city's physical future was provided by the 1893 Columbian Exposition in Chicago, an ensemble of monumental, neoclassically inspired, pristine white buildings baroquely fronting on equally grand plazas.

The 400th anniversary of America's discovery by Columbus dramatically signaled the onset of the turn-of-the-century "city beautiful" movement in America. Not only did the exposition engender a new urban design awareness, but it also contributed to the rediscovery and accelerated reimportation of Beaux-Arts classicism in architecture.

Washington continued growing, and stepped up its beautifying. At the end of the century, Boundary Street had become Florida Avenue, and bridges were being designed to span Rock Creek at both Massachusetts and Connecticut Avenues. Even then, it was evident that the Northwest precincts were the favored recipients of public works embellishments, as opposed to Anacostia, the Southwest and Navy Yard areas, Capitol Hill or the Northeast.

Some 65,000 saplings, and new electric street lighting, with much of the wiring underground, lined avenues and streets. Telephone and telegraph services were becoming widely available, as well as intercity rail service. Unfortunately, the Baltimore and Potomac railroad depot occupied a site stretching across the Mall at 6th Street. Although convenient, its placement, noise, and smells were obviously contrary to L'Enfant's intentions.

The construction of the 14-story, 160-foot-high, Moorishly decorated, yellow-brick Cairo hotel above Scott Circle catalyzed passage of the 1899 Heights of Buildings Act, limiting the height of private structures so that they would not stand taller than the capital city's significant public edifices, particularly the Capitol Building. Indeed, over a century earlier, Thomas Jefferson had favored a height limitation comparable to Paris, where houses are "low & convenient, & the streets light and airy."

In 1910, Congress passed a new ordinance limiting the height of buildings in D.C. to the width of the street or avenue on which buildings front, plus 20 feet. Washington's image as a horizontal rather than vertical city was strongly reaffirmed and codified, notwithstanding the objections voiced by proponents of free enterprise and unbridled capitalism. Building height restrictions were to be one of the most powerful economic and architectural form determinants in creating Washington's look—along with the powerful Board of Trade, founded in 1889.

With the calendar flipped over into the 20th century and esthetic awareness at its peak, Senator James McMillan embarked upon developing a new physical plan for the nation's capital. To establish a Parks Commission in 1901, McMillan appointed architects Daniel Burnham and Charles McKim, sculptor Augustus St. Gaudens, and landscape architect Frederick Law Olmsted's son, Frederick Law Olmsted Jr., to be commissioners.

Although it had no financial or construction authority, the commission was charged with recommending a general plan for all of the District. Instead, the commissioners chose to focus on clarifying and completing the essential elements of L'Enfant's original plan, particularly the open space system linking the Capitol Building, the Mall, the White House, and Potomac and Rock Creek parks.

The McMillan Park Commission plan is, for the most part, what we see implemented today. It convinced Congress and the railroad to abandon the 19th-century depot site on the Mall in favor of a new, monumental Union Station, a building clearly foreshadowed by the Columbian Exposition. The picturesquely romantic gardens of the Mall gave way to a series of treed "allees," flanked on the north and south by imposing museums and terminated on the west end by the Lincoln Memorial, in turn linked to Virginia by Memorial Bridge. An enclave of new federal office buildings north of the Mall would constitute the Federal Triangle; at Lafayette Square, north of the White House, additional federal buildings were planned.

Here at last was city beautiful, city classicist, city administrative, and city affluent all merged into one. Little time was wasted carrying out the plan. By 1908, Congress had authorized the construction of Union Station, the District Building on 14th Street, the Central Library at 8th and K Streets, the House of Representatives and Senate office buildings, the Department of Agriculture building, the National Museum (later the National Museum of Natural History), and the Army War College at Arsenal Point. By 1909, the depot and tracks had finally been removed from the Mall.

L'Enfant's concept was blossoming. Washington's building and the business of government continued growing, but so was its poor and powerless population. The Maryland and Virginia suburbs, previously rural domains for the affluent escaping the city's swelter, were soon to be developed. The 19th-century national capital was becoming a 20th-century international one.

September 29, 1984

The City Begins to Sprawl

Born in the 18th century, its adolescence spent in the 19th, the nation's capital reached adulthood only with the arrival of the 20th century's complexities.

Washington 80 years ago was small in comparison to Baltimore, Philadelphia, New York, or Boston. To many, it was still a provincial big town with a terrible climate and an excess of politicians, a place to pass through and look at briefly on the way to newly developing Florida.

But new technological, political, economic, and demographic forces were destined to give Washington its eventual fleshy, grown-up city form: the automobile and telephone; phenomenal expansion of government accelerated by new ideas about the interventionist role of the federal government and by the necessities of war; the optimism of the roaring twenties, the New Deal of the depressed thirties; Washington's relative economic stability, expansion of business, and increasing population; and with mobility, enduring employment, and airconditioning, the discovery that Washington was a livable city.

In 1918, at the end of World War I, there were approximately 120,000 federal civilian employees in Washington. In 1943, halfway through World War II, the number reached 285,000.

Overall, D.C.'s population rose from 487,000 in 1930 to 663,000 in 1940, primarily because of New Deal activity. Prior to 1930, the number of federal workers had actually decreased, but the general D.C. population rose steadily as commercial activity and in-migration increased during the twenties. By 1940, the Washington metropolitan area population hit 1 million.

Congress and local citizens realized earlier in the century that things were going to change even more rapidly than before. Without proper planning and management, Washington might return to some of the physical conditions deplored in the 19th century. And the pressure to take the short-term, expedient approach was difficult to resist in the face of real estate developers or government agencies motivated only by their own immediate needs and points of view.

The L'Enfant and McMillan conceptions had demonstrated the value of making and adhering to long-range plans. Thus, the establishment of both new laws and planning bodies, whose mission was to direct the city's physical growth, seemed indispensable:

1910—Fine Arts Commission permanently established and new Height of Buildings Act passed.
1920—Zoning ordinance adopted, separating residential, commercial, and industrial uses of land and stipulating further height and area limits.
1926—National Capital Park and Planning Commission created and Public Buildings Act passed, authorizing construction of the Federal Triangle.
1930—Shipstead-Luce Act passed, granting the Fine Arts Commission authority to review all new development adjoining public parks and government buildings.

However, the rational acts of government have historically failed to keep pace with the forces of technology, politics, economics, and demography. Accordingly, as railroads had dramatically transformed the scale and landscape of continents, the automobile was to transform the scale and form of cities.

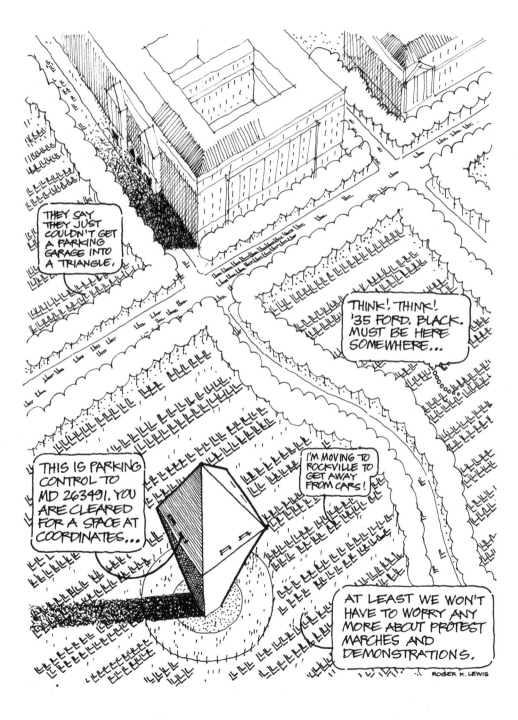

Streetcar and bus lines provided some mass transit potential, theoretically diminishing the need for personal means of conveyance. But Washington's commitment to relatively low density, even downtown, made suburban development and sprawl inevitable. So while rowhousing followed streetcar lines northward and eastward from downtown, new roads and automobile-oriented subdivisions proliferated in other areas, created by developers and designers who correctly anticipated the future.

Whole neighborhoods materialized—Shannon & Luchs built Burleith, west of Wisconsin Avenue, in the mid-twenties. Waverly Taylor built Foxhall Village, west of Georgetown, between 1925 and 1930. Northwest of Cleveland Park, Wesley Heights and Spring Valley were laid out, but with roads conforming more naturally to the terrain, resulting in sometimes radical distortions of the Washington street grid network.

Between 1900 and 1930, after construction of bridges spanning Rock Creek Park, mansion building along Massachusetts Avenue and apartment building along Connecticut Avenue firmly reinforced these areas as "special." However, Georgetown had not yet been "gentrified," and Capitol Hill, Southwest, Foggy Bottom, and close-in Northwest were being further abandoned to tenancy by those unable to take advantage of the new mobility.

The inexpensive farmlands of Maryland and Virginia were being discovered and suburbanized by the automobile and the detached home of the American dream. Crossing the Potomac—at 14th Street, Memorial Bridge, Key Bridge at Georgetown, and Chain Bridge—made the formerly rural northern Virginia counties readily accessible. By 1925, the metropolitan area stretched from Fairfax to Rockville to Hyattsville.

Meanwhile, the federal government never stopped building. The National Museum was completed in 1910, the first Mall building erected in accordance with the McMillan plan. The Freer Gallery and the Lincoln Memorial were subsequently constructed. In the thirties, after some debate about its location, the Jefferson Memorial was built. It formed the southern terminus of the cross-Mall, north-south axis visually linking the Memorial to the White House and off-axis Washington Monument.

The Federal Triangle project, conceived by the McMillan Commission at the beginning of the century, began finally in 1926, supported enthusiastically by Secretary of Commerce Herbert Hoover. Guided by Treasury Secretary Andrew W. Mellon and planner Edward H. Bennett, it involved demolition and rebuilding of the area bounded by Pennsylvania and Constitution Avenues between 15th Street on the west and 6th Street, the apex of the triangle, on the east.

Historian Frederick Gutheim points out that "the triangle area was the large squalid slice of land that had accumulated an infamous reputation in the 19th century as a haven for the city's criminal element, and included the area known as Murder Bay." Only the Romanesquely styled Old Post Office, built in 1899, had been sited in this blighted lowland subject to periodic flooding. The classically inspired Federal Triangle, comprised mostly of office buildings, was one of Washington's first slum clearance projects and foreshadowed things to come.

But despite such continuing efforts to complete the symbolic and functional monumental core of Washington, the government's policies were inexorably shifting. Pragmatism and the new mobility had engendered thoughts of dispersal. Geographic concentration of the government in proximity to the White House or Capitol seemed both unnecessary and undesirable. Parking in the center of Washington had become nightmarish, since few buildings had parking garages. Every available foot of curb space and open space, paved or otherwise, was filling with cars.

According to historian Gutheim, "A traffic study performed in 1934 . . . revealed that 'the proportion of people in Washington who use private automobiles or taxicabs is over twice the average reported from six other cities,' a larger proportion than Los Angeles." Between 1920 and 1930, auto registrations in the District increased 400 percent!

As the thirties ended and war clouds gathered, World War I temporary buildings still occupied parts of the Mall. Citizens, mostly black, were still crowded into countless, substandard alley dwellings. Neighborhoods embarrassingly near the White House and Capitol were deteriorating.

World War II would represent a six-year hiatus in coping with urban problems as the capital dealt with the problems of global war. But it was only a postponement.

October 6, 1984

Removal and Renewal... Today's D.C.

After World War II, D.C. began focusing on inner-city renewal. But to many less-than-affluent citizens, "reee-newal" sounded an awful lot like "reee-moval."

Prior to the war, political Washington pursued what historian Frederick Gutheim describes as the "multicentered regional city" strategy of dispersal of federal facilities.

The Pentagon, completed in 1941, typified the trend, having been erected on the site of the old Washington Municipal Airport between Arlington National Cemetery and the new National Airport. Originally to be housed a couple of blocks west of the White House, the War Department literally occupied the Arlington site following intra-agency battles in the late thirties concerning who would be where.

Farther out, New Deal interest in economic and social reform had led to the construction of cooperatively owned Greenbelt. Optimistic supporters saw it as planned utopia, an idyllic escape to the purity of nature and open space, away from the congestion of the city. Critics saw it as rampant socialism and a threat to American free enterprise. In fact, its greatest impact may have been introducing the "garden apartment" to suburbia.

During the war, some building occurred despite shortages of materials. McLean Gardens was built in 1942 west of Cleveland Park. The National Capital Park and Planning Commission (NCPPC) and the National Capital Housing Authority developed housing for low-income civilians in Anacostia, at the Navy Yard, and near Union Station. Such sites were picked ostensibly because of their proximity to low-level employment centers.

Nevertheless, by war's end, housing and redevelopment pressures had reached crisis proportion and promised to worsen in the face of postwar GI needs. Already overcrowded D.C. neighborhoods—Foggy Bottom, Southwest, parts of Northwest, and Capitol Hill—had deteriorated further. Many agreed that new economic and planning mechanisms were needed to cope with growing urban problems.

The result was the 1945 D.C. Redevelopment Act. It authorized the NCPPC to designate areas for redevelopment and to adopt plans for approval by the D.C. Commissioners. The Redevelopment Land Agency was formed in 1946 to acquire redevelopment properties. Stated simply, these bodies were charged with slum clearance.

Not much happened until 1949. Funding had been very limited previously, but the historic 1949 National Housing Act provided the impetus and dollars for new urban and suburban America. It financed redevelopment and public housing. Low-interest, long-term mortgage insurance programs, first devised in the thirties, expanded. Having started with Greenbelt, the government was promoting residential suburbia for the mobile middle class while simultaneously aspiring to rebuild the inner city.

The next two decades in Washington, as in many cities, were characterized by highway building, comprehensive planning efforts, and urban renewal. While new roads and new subdivisions were devouring farmland as fast as Federal Housing Administration and Veterans Administration mortgages could be endorsed, so-called blight was being attacked downtown.

Before Redevelopment

After Redevelopment

Southwest Washington represents most graphically what occurred during the fifties and sixties. Families, mostly poor, were displaced and forced into overcrowded conditions elsewhere in the city. Only a few had the means to return to their redeveloped neighborhood. The property they once occupied was cleared, its value written down below acquisition costs, and its use upgraded by construction of new administrative, commercial, and residential structures for a decidedly more affluent population. Elevated freeways swept by overhead, following the example of the Whitehurst in Georgetown.

Redevelopers had economic and locational logic on their side. Southwest formed the Mall's Independence Avenue edge and was a stone's throw from the Capitol. It could yield new tax revenues and be safe to walk through. Notions of neighborhood preservation for local citizens held little sway against the planning, architectural, economic, and political theories dominating the landscape of the fifties and sixties.

Southwest was totally transformed. Blocks of modern midrise, lowrise, and townhouse dwellings were constructed. Federal agency office buildings marched southward from the Mall. The Forrestal and L'Enfant Plaza complexes appeared with their pavement-covered subterranean worlds, and an ambiguously defined Potomac River waterfront completed the picture.

Along the Mall, the Smithsonian continued implementing the McMillan Commission plan. It built the National Museum of American History, the Hirshhorn Museum and Sculpture Garden, and the National Air and Space Museum to join its other cultural landmarks. In the 1970s, the National Gallery of Art, originally built in 1941, added its East Building.

As Southwest and the Mall took shape, other areas were changing. Preservation and development efforts around Lafayette Square were followed by the still proceeding redevelopment of Pennsylvania Avenue between the Capitol and the White House.

Across the river, Crystal City and Rosslyn, visually linked to D.C., had sprouted up in defiance of Washington's building height tradition. These Arlington minidowntowns comprise offices, hotels, and apartment buildings through which people can parade either underground or overhead.

The proliferation of attorneys, trade associations, lobbyists, accountants, and others interested in being near the center of power led to an unprecedented surge in office and hotel development. The business district expanded rapidly westward along K and other streets, eventually encompassing the West End. Bumping up against Rock Creek Park, office builders leapfrogged into lower Georgetown while reversing eastwardly toward 11th Street and the new Convention Center. However, traditional downtown department store trade continued its exodus.

To the north, postwar commercial rezoning was bringing downtown uptown along Massachusetts, Connecticut, and Vermont Avenues, often contrary to the wishes of residents. Closer to the Capitol, new administrative and hotel building was appearing around Judiciary Square and Union Station. Capitol Hill, like Georgetown earlier, was being "gentrified." And subsidized housing kept rising in near Northwest and Anacostia, following patterns established in earlier decades.

Outside the District, the automobile tenaciously controlled the environment. The Capital Beltway, the nation's first complete circumferential highway, opened in 1964. Envisioned in Harland Bartholomew's 1950 plan as a means to facilitate the pattern of dispersal started in the thirties, it quickly became metropolitan area "main street."

New travel and settlement patterns emerged near interchanges or along radial roads. Preference for suburbia produced new shopping centers, office and industrial parks, and endless commercial strips in surrounding Prince George's, Montgomery, Fairfax, and Arlington counties. Going downtown became optional.

Back in the city, in the hope of alleviating traffic congestion and eliminating more freeway construction, a subway system was planned and built thanks to regional co-operation between D.C. and county, state, and federal governments. Metro brings commuters to and from downtown along essentially radial paths. Travel along other paths, or to Georgetown, requires bus, bicycle, or car.

Seen from a metropolitan perspective, Metro's map clearly shows that the urban core of D.C. is "downtown." For more than 3 million people, many of whom live in suburbs that could be part of any city, it is a blessing that the heart of Washington so clearly retains a unique shape, a physical coherence, and an architectural significance lacking in most urban and suburban environments. For this, Washingtonians (and all Americans) are indebted to L'Enfant's plan. Like the Constitution, its timeless principles have guided and accommodated nearly two centuries of unforeseen growth and change with amazing success.

October 13, 1984

Flying Into Washington . . . An Overview

Fly into Washington's National Airport from the northwest, along the Potomac River, while sitting on the left side of the airplane. On a clear spring day, you will experience a most dramatic, lump-in-the-throat approach to the nation's first planned city.

Acoustically unfortunate for those below the flight path, the entrance is a revealing and inspiring one for flyers. From this vantage point, the eye can quickly comprehend the unique shape of the capital city. Banking to the left at a thousand feet, you can grasp its compositional rationale in overview.

Approaching the community of Cabin John, Maryland, you see an overwhelmingly verdant landscape, a tapestry of trees punctuated by rooftops and office or apartment buildings jutting up inside, outside, and around the Capital Beltway. The pattern of residential neighborhoods separated by fingers of wooded parkland becomes evident. The George Washington Parkway and the historic C & O Canal flanking the Potomac lie below.

Moving downriver, you spot the Washington National Cathedral sitting high above Cleveland Park and the city's Northwest quadrant. It serves as a Gothically styled architectural and spiritual landmark. Far to the east of the Cathedral rises the Shrine of the Immaculate Conception at Catholic University. From many points in the District, these two churches rival the Capitol as landmark buildings. In fact, when approaching downtown D.C. by car from the northeast along New York Avenue, you see all three of these buildings, along with the Washington Monument.

As the plane nears Georgetown, the northern and western sections of downtown come into view. On the right in Virginia, the pilot can see suburban McLean and Arlington crisscrossed by a network of roads that defy navigational comprehension by any nonresident, while Rosslyn rises threateningly ahead.

The rectangular pattern of streets and housing in Georgetown is clearly visible among dense canopies of leaves. In new Georgetown between the river and M Street, the dominant material is brick and the dominant color red. The minority colors are grays, browns, and beiges with which brick and wood buildings have been painted.

Red brick prevails in the West End as well. But in Foggy Bottom and the business sections north and south of K Street, red brick, though back in style, is still subordinate to the variety of Modernist materials—glass, stone, metals, precast concrete—that characterized nonregional, commercially inspired architecture of the last 30 years.

The behemoths of Watergate and the Kennedy Center loom over the Potomac River and help suggest the transition from the red brick to white marble sectors of Washington. Meanwhile, the pilot, having avoided Rosslyn, can see Arlington National Cemetery, the Pentagon, and a mind-boggling tangle of highways that somehow resolves itself as they converge on the Potomac River bridges.

Just before landing, L'Enfant's Washington comes fully into view. The reds, browns, and beiges have given way to the white, gray, and green of Washington's governmental core; the mélange of materials to the north and west has yielded to the marble, granite, and limestone of monumental downtown.

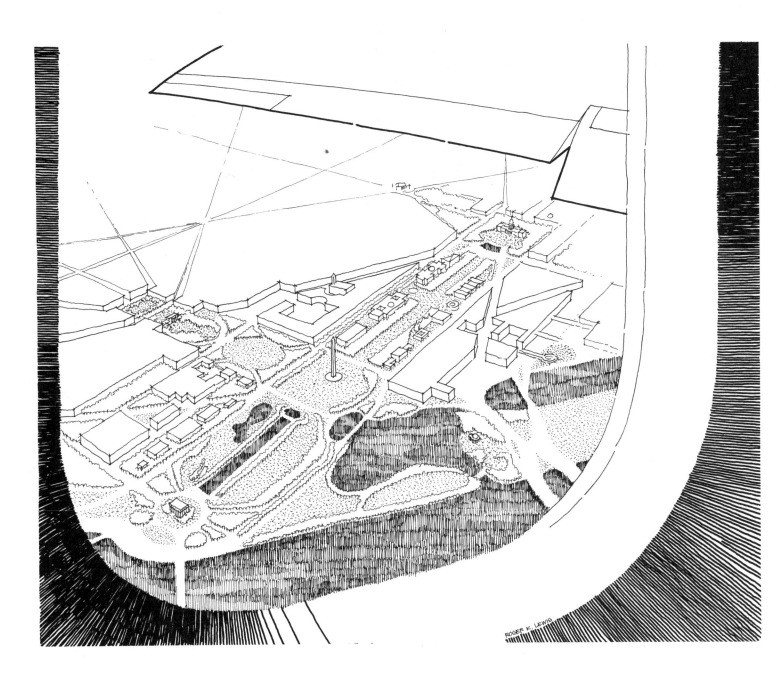

ROGER K. LEWIS

That it can all be taken in and recognized so quickly is a special attribute of this city. There is a disarming simplicity and clarity to the scheme. The organization of this symbolic landscape is not obscured, even at ground level.

The long east-west axis between the Capitol and the Lincoln Memorial is reinforced by the elements of the Mall—its parallel rows of trees, graveled pathways, drives, flanking museums, the Washington Monument, and Reflecting Pool. The romantic, curvilinear gardens north of the Reflecting Pool intensify awareness of this axial relationship. If you look beyond the Capitol, you see RFK Stadium at the terminus of East Capitol Street where the axis intercepts the Anacostia River.

Opposing this axis is the shorter north-south axis established by the White House and Lafayette Park, the South Lawn and Ellipse, the slightly off-axis obelisk (which flags the crossing of the axes) and the Jefferson Memorial at the edge of the Tidal Basin. Especially wonderful is the way in which this irregularly shaped adjunct to the river, bordered by blossoming cherry trees, penetrates into the organized geometry of the core, as if it were assertively biting off a piece of the Mall in order to make East Potomac Park.

Further contemplation reveals that these perceivable relationships are created by broad expanses of shaped lawns and discernible geometric figures inscribed on the ground, which interact with the freestanding buildings and monuments marking the axes. Other buildings lining Constitution and Independence Avenues, and 15th and 17th Streets, help define the edges of these great spaces. You know that it has been designed, that there is a logic behind it all.

You trace the diagonal avenues—Virginia, Pennsylvania, Connecticut, New York, Vermont, Massachusetts, Maryland—lined by buildings and slicing through the grid of streets just as L'Enfant had planned. Squares, circles, plazas, and parks cloaked in green are everywhere. Looking north, you can follow the marvelous intrusion that Rock Creek Park makes upon the city as it twists and undulates its way toward Maryland.

With the plane losing altitude, you see the city increasingly as façades in elevation and less as roofs in plan. Devoid of highrise buildings, D.C. is a "mat" city woven sometimes tightly and sometimes loosely. This characteristic seems exemplified by the tile-roofed Federal Triangle wedged between the Mall and Pennsylvania Avenue. Except for the fortunately preserved Old Post Office and the National Archives, the buildings of the Federal Triangle look as if they were meticulously cut out from a monolithic, horizontal slab of material that was then painted red on top.

Washington clung to its building height tradition in deference to the memorable silhouettes of its symbolic buildings and monuments. Thus, it differentiated itself sharply from other American cities where skyscrapers have engulfed urban cores and have themselves become the new monuments and landmarks.

So in sum, what do we have in Washington, D.C.? Physically and perceptually, it is a low city, a green and spacious city, a river-fronting city, a city with a center whose form is recognizable and measurable. Like a great house with a great room and a great hearth, Washington has its grand, central place around which people can work, conduct business, dwell, and recreate. Even suburbanites who rarely venture downtown subconsciously sense its distant presence and availability. You only have to visit cities like Los Angeles, Houston, or New York to understand the difference.

But beyond function and form, there is conceptual and symbolic significance. Not only does the heart of Washington offer a sense of place, but it also represents ideas and events. We see its form, yet intellectually and emotionally we feel something more.

We see monuments to Lincoln and Jefferson and Washington, but we also think about the Declaration of Independence, the Constitution and Bill of Rights, the Emancipation Proclamation, liberty, democracy, war, and peace. Up the avenues in business or residential districts, down-the-avenue sighting of the Capitol dome or Washington Monument may pull thoughts momentarily away from personal affairs, an arresting visual reminder of where you are and what it might mean.

L'Enfant's Washington is the nation's village green, its town square, a place to remember the past, to celebrate the present, and to plan the future.

October 20, 1984

2.

Streetscapes
Shaping the Public Realm

The Intimate Streets of Georgetown

Why do some urban streets, spaces, and places become animated, active, and memorable, while others seem lifeless, formless, or inhospitable—no matter what the style or quality of the architecture around them might be like?

When a building in the city is designed and built, it is much more than just another journal entry in historians' accounts of periods and styles, in the architect's list of projects built, or in the owners' ledgers of income and expense. While individual buildings have their own separate identity and internal life, they interact with other buildings and spaces around them to constitute some larger environmental experience.

But city building spans dozens of decades, an inevitably piecemeal process characterized by great diversity in architectural styles, ownership, and building intentions. How then can any sort of ultimate coherence result?

Visualize Washington, its different neighborhoods and special precincts. Your recollection may focus sometimes on individual buildings easily remembered, and sometimes on the character of a space— a street, circle, or plaza—contained and shaped by a collection of buildings, no one of which dominates. Occasionally, both spaces and buildings together achieve equal presence, as exemplified by the Mall and its monumental edifices.

In commercial areas away from downtown, urban-scaled public space-making, if it occurs at all, is almost always subordinate to the making of freestanding object buildings—office blocks, shopping strips, fast-food outlets, gas stations, retail malls— surrounded by landscapes of parked cars, lawns, trees, and shrubs. Here, formed spaces are typically limited to sidewalks between storefronts and car bumpers, entry lobbies, and the interior atrium spaces of shopping centers.

The phenomenon of streetscape dominating individual buildings is perhaps clearest in places like Georgetown where some combination of location, accessibility, population density, mixed activity, and architecture have produced a "there" there.

Most Washingtonians know there is something unique about Georgetown, in addition to its history, that makes it so image-rich, active, perpetually busy, crowded, traffic-jammed, yet spatially coherent and memorable (not to mention pricey in its real estate values).

Look first at its location. It fronts on the Potomac River and adjoins the central business district to the east. Key Bridge brings Virginians to and from its west end at M Street, which in turn connects to the western terminus of Pennsylvania Avenue. Wisconsin Avenue, beginning at the K Street river edge, bisects Georgetown and heads upland through affluent Northwest, Bethesda, and on to Rockville. P and Q Streets serve as additional east-west links to downtown.

Despite the still incredibly shortsighted omission of Metro subway service to Georgetown, this centrally located part of Washington remains reasonably accessible by car, bus, or on foot. More important, within Georgetown the pedestrian reigns, not the automobile.

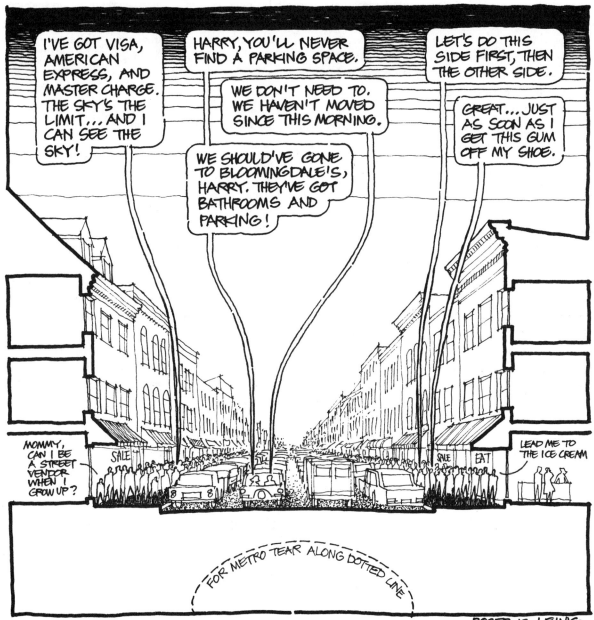

Georgetown's street alignments and widths are based on the original 18th-century grid. Building setback lines are at or close to the sidewalk line. Narrow streets, lined snugly by closely spaced or party-wall buildings, offer pedestrians a sense of enclosure and intimacy lacking in most urban streetscapes dedicated primarily to accommodating great volumes of traffic.

The typical three- to five-story height of Georgetown's buildings, usually a bit less than the width of the street space (the distance between façades on opposite sides of the street), further enhances awareness of the street's potential as a public room. Although individual structures are rich in scale-imparting details that continually arrest the eye—steps, railings, porches, shutters, patterns of masonry, windows, trim—the façades nevertheless work together to form a continuous, comfortably high wall holding and shaping the street space.

Take note of the multiple roles played by the exterior walls of buildings. From the interior, they are the enclosing façades of individual rooms, but from the exterior, they must represent the whole building. In turn, they are somehow obliged to participate in making the street-wall continuum—and all while controlling the passage of light, heat, wind, and water.

Georgetown's narrow streets and frequently clogged traffic make it easier for pedestrians to take over the streetscape, crossing from one side to another between waiting cars or at crosswalks. Walking on one side, you can readily shout and communicate with someone on the other side. You can also see what is displayed in shop windows across the street, something not possible on most downtown commercial streets.

Georgetown's vitality derives not only from its sidewalks—they are not overly wide—but also from the proximity of storefronts to sidewalks and street curbs along Wisconsin and M, the two major shopping streets. These critical dimensions and juxtapositions establish immediate and unavoidable visual contact between pedestrians, and between pedestrians, motorists, and merchandise. No deep arcades redundantly line the sidewalk.

Everyone, including people sitting in cars inching along only a few feet away, engages in window shopping and people watching. Wide, brightly lit shop windows and doorways aggressively present the merchants' stylish goods and celebrate invitingly the ambience of the spaces behind them. Walking in Georgetown is like a visit to a street museum of consumption and indulgence. M Street and Wisconsin Avenue are the exterior, urban analogue of suburbia's interior, enclosed mall.

What else brings people to Georgetown in preference to other places in the city, places with bigger buildings, more parking, and wider streets? Besides Georgetown's chic shops or the chance to partake of the "esprit de carnival" outdoors, there is eating, drinking, and socializing. Restaurants offering from haute cuisine to fast food abound, along with numerous bars and taverns open after midnight.

And many, many people live in Georgetown. Most live on quaint residential streets, but many live in apartments above stores and in more recently developed mixed-use structures such as Georgetown Park. There are also hotels, offices and office buildings, schools, and a major university.

Thus, Georgetown is a city in microcosm, a fairly dense urban village with reasons for people being there all the time, not just Monday through Friday, lunchtime, weekends, or nights. The intense intermixing of the village's activities and land uses, coupled with the physical form of its streetscape environment and historical, architectural charm, gives Georgetown its unusual vitality, notwithstanding horrendous traffic and parking problems.

Georgetown is, of course, exceptional. But it illustrates well the importance of reinforcing the streetscape and the pathways of pedestrians along street edges with many, varied activities (including dwellings) housed in well-proportioned buildings. In a city, such buildings must connect directly and actively with the sidewalk-street environment to serve both tenants and passersby. You need only look again at L'Enfant Plaza or Rosslyn, across the Potomac in Virginia, to realize that these "designed" environments are missing something.

It is, of course, easier to describe or imagine an idealized streetscape than to build one. Coping with constraints imposed by location, market forces, zoning, government regulations, safety requirements, traffic, parking, land values, and financing makes the task very difficult. However, there is no lack of real-life models here, in other American cities, and in urban settlements around the world. They have much to teach us.

March 9, 1985

Where Buildings Meet Sidewalks

In architecture school, teachers of design ask students to focus particular attention on the bottom story or two of buildings and their integration with the pedestrian environments around them. How can we humanize and animate this special realm where buildings meet the ground to form the streetscape?

When you walk by or approach and enter urban buildings, you become increasingly aware of their constituent materials, textures, details, entries, and interior content. Only from the sidewalk vantage point is a building's complexion intimately revealed, warts and all.

A building edging the sidewalk engages your interest and invites interaction as you draw near if its base is porous, not opaque. Buildings that present blank, solid, impenetrable walls to pedestrian passersby do little to animate urban streetscapes. Washington, D.C., has many such inscrutable structures, the FBI Building on Pennsylvania Avenue being the most illustrious.

Architects frequently connect buildings to the pedestrian realm with colonnaded arcades, presumed to yield porosity and openness. Downtown and suburban Washington are full of office buildings whose bottom one or two stories are recessed behind the dominant exterior wall plane at the building setback line. Leaving the structural columns in place creates the colonnade and covered sidewalk behind it. This design tactic has become so conventional and clichéd that we almost take it for granted, yet it can lead to questionable results.

Arcades may redundantly widen sidewalks already sufficiently wide. While this allows space for street vendors, it distances storefronts and shop display windows even farther from the principal pathways of pedestrians and from the street.

On the north sides of buildings, deep arcades never receive sun and remain eternally in shade. Excessively high arcades may offer minimal protection from the descending elements or the summer sun. At night, recessed storefronts share less light with the sidewalk and street. If lights are out in ground-floor establishments, arcades can be dark and ominous, especially when they have low ceilings.

For centuries, continuous colonnaded arcades have encircled freestanding buildings or have wrapped around courtyards within buildings. They have enclosed, either partially or completely, plazas, squares, and gardens framed by several buildings. Visualize atria and courtyards within ancient residences, or the great piazzas of Saint Peter's in Rome and San Marco's in Venice.

Colonnaded arcades provided ways to walk from one place to another. They were connective as well as decorative. Such connecting links not only made sheltered paths of travel between origin and destination, but they also unified otherwise separated structures, creating visual, spatial, and symbolic ties.

Today, however, if you look along any of the principal streets in D.C.'s downtown business district, you see series of disjointed, stop-and-start arcades at the bases of one infill building after another. Many lead nowhere—except to connect the party wall on the left to the one on the right when abutted by buildings without arcades.

BEFORE

APTER

ROGER K. LEWIS

Many colonnaded arcades are not spaces where you would choose to promenade. Pedestrians normally stick to the open sidewalk well outside of arcades and often at a considerable distance from shop windows and doors. Even during inclement weather, the stop-and-start nature of arcades within a block may force you to weave intermittently in and out of façades and in and out of the rain.

Arcade heights and depths vary randomly. In some buildings, the arcade depth is much less than its height, perhaps only a few feet deep, barely enough for one or two people to walk between column and wall. In these cases, the arcade seems vestigial and without purpose. Why have it at all?

Washington's amply wide sidewalks permit great variety in the treatment of main entrances to buildings and subordinate entrances to stores, banks, and restaurants. Canopies, awnings, or other porchlike elements can reach out into and over the public sidewalk, signaling and celebrating the place and act of moving from outside to in-

side, from public to private domains. These gestures seem particularly appropriate, since we often view buildings from oblique angles rather than straight on.

An urban building's entrance need not be gigantic or overwhelming, but it should be visible, well marked, and inviting. Entrance loggias or canopies extending a symbolic hand of welcome to the street have an interior presence as well. An entrance is also an exit, a two-way connector between inside and outside, the portal to the street when viewed from within.

The recessed arcades lining the fronts of so many buildings do not always serve well as porches or loggias to connect inside to outside. Many are no more than buffer or insulating spaces. Most pedestrians approach such buildings by walking along the principal sidewalk and then veering in toward the entry doors, experiencing the colonnaded arcade for a few seconds, the time required to cross its depth obliquely or perpendicularly.

Washington, with its wide sidewalks and not-too-high buildings, could easily accommodate arcades similar to those found in Paris, Rome, and other cities around the world. Many streets of such cities are lined by arcades that extend over the public

sidewalk to within a few feet of the curb. Just enough space remains between curb and column line for open car doors, parking meters, utility poles, street trees, and façade maintenance.

Arcades may be only one story high without occupied building space above. The building proper stays behind the property line. Some arcades run continuously along streets from corner to corner. They also turn corners or penetrate and march into the interior of blocks where courtyards, atria, or shopping galleries may be located.

Arcade roofs can be solid and opaque, or they can have varying degrees of transparency and translucency through the use of finely scaled trellises, glass skylights, or domes. In some cases, flat roofs become outdoor terraces or roof gardens for occupants of second or third floors, depending on the height of the arcade below and the activities within the building.

Properly designed arcades can accommodate outdoor eating and sidewalk cafés, passengers waiting for buses or taxis, street vendors, commercial signage, lighting, visible and legible street addresses, vegetation, as well as pedestrians. At the same time, building owners and commercial tenants retain use of valuable square footage at the ground-floor level, abutting the principal path of movement at the building setback line.

To design and build such arcades in Washington would require modified zoning regulations, coupled with appropriate design guidelines. These would ensure that each building in a zone designated for public sidewalk arcades provided its share of the street arcade in a way compatible with (though not necessarily identical to) adjacent buildings and arcades.

Even now, sidewalks are appropriated and used for some of these purposes, but without the sheltering and linking arcades. Along Capitol Hill's commercial streets, or Connecticut and Pennsylvania Avenues, or 19th Street, you can readily observe and participate in these activities. Sometimes, awnings or umbrellas aid space-making and signal points of access and festivity.

Active sidewalk and street life is one of the wonderful amenities cities offer. Urban architecture, in addition to looking good, must enhance this life and be part of it.

March 16, 1985

The Art of Omission... Public Squares

In creating a work of art, knowing what to omit is no less important than knowing what to include. Sometimes, it is the voids, blank spaces, or meaningful pauses woven into artful compositions that acquire the greatest significance.

The same is true of cities. Their potentially continuous, uninterrupted fabric of streets, blocks, and buildings is enriched by periodic perforation, distortion, and subtraction. Omitting buildings or parts of buildings, or arranging buildings to surround or shape a space, introduce needed exceptions into urban street/block patterns.

Washington has many such spaces—the Mall, squares, plazas, and circles—responsible for much of the city's visual character. What makes these public spaces, formed and functioning in so many different ways, worthwhile omissions?

Squares and plazas offer relief, a chance to pause, slow down, stop, and relax. Like great outdoor rooms lined by buildings and roadways, they allow people to gather and intense activity to occur. Urban wildlife—squirrels, countless pigeons, an occasional seagull, dozens of other species of birds—and colorful vegetation remind us that the natural and built environments are inseparable and interdependent.

Some urban spaces—like miniparks covered by grass, shrubs, trees, and walkways—invite people to take leisurely strolls, eat picnic-style, sunbathe, voice protest, celebrate events, or just sit and talk. On a pleasant spring day, Farragut Square, bounded by I, K, and 17th Streets N.W., best illustrates this kind of space and activity, as does Lafayette Square north of the White House.

Other spaces, mostly paved with brick, stone, or concrete, are only punctuated by landscaping. Here, if conditions are right, people can also meet, sit and talk, eat, ice skate in winter, or watch the world go by. With its pool, steps, benches, food kiosk, umbrellas, and outdoor furniture, Pershing Park at 15th Street and Pennsylvania Avenue N.W. magnetically attracts downtown workers and tourists whenever weather permits.

Some squares and plazas are primarily visual amenities, places to look at from an adjoining building window or nearby street. They may be gardens, more decorative than functional, and rarely used for intense pedestrian activities. Often, they act as forecourts or visual settings for buildings along their edges or for monuments set within them. Hamilton Place, south of the Treasury Building at 15th and E Streets N.W., is one such space.

Some squares and plazas are sacred and ceremonial, spatial symbols of commemoration or sites for recurring ritual. Marked by elements—fences, planting, statues, and controlled paths—that give clues to their sanctity, their compositional geometry may be formal, balanced, and carefully tailored to suggest that random intrusions would upset and spoil their stability and serenity. The spaces south of the White House and adjoining the Capitol's west front seem to inspire such feelings.

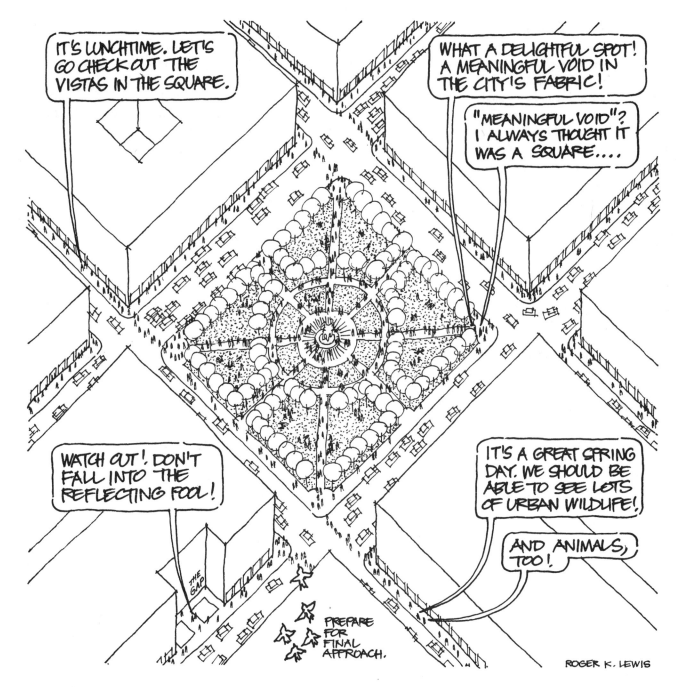

Squares and plazas may be part of a planned processional sequence and experience en route from one place to another, particularly from exterior to interior. Entrance plazas or courtyards can be created by setting back or carving out segments of buildings. From street and sidewalk, one proceeds into and across the courtyard or plaza, then enters the building. Many federal edifices have been sited or shaped to achieve this sense of procession, which also heightens perceived building monumentality.

Sometimes, however, building entrance plazas prove unnecessary, especially along commercial streets. Overscaled, under-populated gaps in the street-wall continuum serve only to reduce usable floor area. Maintaining the building-line façade wall and enriching the building's sidewalk engagement through appropriate storefront and entrance designs might be preferable.

Urban open spaces facilitate views for those traveling through or near them, and for inhabitants of surrounding buildings. The façades of an entire block may be seen at once. Vistas along streets radiating from or adjacent to squares and plazas are dramatically improved because of increased viewing angles and viewing depths. You can frequently see the tops of other structures, both near and far, silhouetted against the sky beyond the immediately abutting buildings.

Well-conceived urban squares and plazas help to orient us and tell us where we are in the city. Being exceptions in the urban fabric, they stick in our memories more easily than dozens of streets, each of whose shape and character might be pleasant but undistinguished.

Any good open space in the city is really an amalgamation of evocative and memorable images—the form and proportions of the space itself, the character of surrounding buildings, the shape and texture of the ground plane, the views into and out of the space, and the activities associated with it. If a space is inadequately defined or contained by buildings and landscape, if its edges "leak" excessively, or if its form is unmeasurable and obscure, then its image may be compromised.

Ambiguity in purpose, plus inaccessibility, makes some urban spaces seem residual, like leftover square footage belonging to no one. Such spaces may become nothing more than yard areas or satisfiers of zoning requirements. If there is no reason to use urban spaces, they remain empty and lifeless. Or they may be transformed into parking lots, as has happened within the Federal Triangle.

With enough activity at street level, almost any square or plaza, regardless of its shape, can be animated. But it must also be visible and accessible, an inviting stopping place for the urban traveler. Out-of-the-way, difficult-to-reach spaces have little chance of attracting streetscape activities or pedestrians. L'Enfant Plaza remains dead much of the time, even though it is a perfectly well-proportioned space, because few people go by it. And its locus of public activity is underground, leaving the plaza to vehicles.

Most good squares and plazas are crossroads, of which Washington's traffic circles are an extreme example. Circle interiors are landscaped islands totally surrounded by paving and automobile circulation. They are easier to see than to be in, since getting to the interior on foot can be life-threatening. Lively Dupont Circle—ringed by trees, the great marble fountain at its center—is a notable exception because of its location at the crossing of so many major streets in a neighborhood rich in activity.

Like the squares of Franklin, Farragut, Mt. Vernon, or McPherson, the circles—Thomas, Westmoreland, Logan, or Washington—act as memorable spatial landmarks within the grid/avenue pattern. We tolerate their inefficiency as traffic facilitators because they and their encompassing buildings are unique place-makers.

Throughout history, and in most cultures, designers have always used courtyards, squares, and plazas as primary elements in urban design. Who cannot help but love the wonderful piazzas and piazzettas of Rome, Florence, or Venice, the squares of Paris and London, or the intimate, irregularly shaped spaces between blindingly white buildings on Grecian hillsides?

But these loved places, these significant voids, are typically filled with pedestrians who participate in the daily and nightly theater of the streetscape. Without the need to shop, travel, socialize, work, recreate, dine, or dwell in these urban spaces and their architectural entourage, they would become derelict and meaningless.

March 23, 1985

The Ceremonial Street

Every village, town, and city should have at least one special, ceremonial street. Many do not.

Like so many other urban phenomena, the concept of the ceremonial street is ancient. Roman towns and cities routinely dedicated certain streets to ritual procession, public celebration, and ceremony. Along such streets and at their end points were temples, government buildings, arenas, and squares befitting and reinforcing the nature of the street itself.

Later, Renaissance and baroque planners of cities in Italy, France, Spain, and northern Europe created secularly inspired grand boulevards leading to monuments, triumphal gates, plazas, or seats of government, as well as to cathedrals.

Older cultures in Indochina, China, and Japan likewise created special streets and sacred precincts intended for collective ceremony and ritualized procession.

Both European and Asian designers usually relied on grand compositional strategies for laying out such streets and spaces. Legible plan geometries, often based on circles and squares, and spatial relationships, often axial, would connote intuitively the uniqueness of these ceremonial routes.

But a different tradition took root in America. Powerful, uncoordinated mercantile forces shaped most cities and towns once a grid pattern was chosen. The character of streets was influenced primarily by transportation efficiency and convenience, land speculation, and zoning predicated on segregation of land uses. Local jurisdictions were reluctant to impose grand master plans on a free and independent real estate market, especially in light of changing political interests.

Thus, few American cities have ceremonial avenues like Paris's Champs Elysées, Berlin's Unter den Linden, or Washington's Pennsylvania Avenue. Such avenues have to be invented, designed, cultivated, and maintained. They do not occur by accident. They are not inevitable byproducts of laissez-faire capitalism.

What specifically makes a street grand and ceremonial? And does it matter if cities like Houston, Baltimore, Newark, Los Angeles, or Phoenix do not really have such streets?

Washington's Pennsylvania Avenue, as originally envisioned by L'Enfant, connected the President's House with the houses of Congress. The connection was to be symbolic as well as functional and experiential. L'Enfant sensed the need for something significant—a monument, an important public building or plaza—at the ends of such streets.

Pennsylvania Avenue between the White House and Capitol is straight, and few world-class ceremonial streets curve. This is because people moving along straight streets can see the street space fully in extended perspective, with their eye led axially toward real and meaningful visual destinations. When streets curve or bend, vistas shorten and destinations disappear.

ROGER K. LEWIS

Another characteristic of ceremonial streets, typified by a revitalized Pennsylvania Avenue, is an appropriately generous and well-proportioned cross section. Street widths must be sufficient to allow long perspective views up or down the street's length. Further, sidewalks and roadways must be ample to accommodate large numbers of people in the course of promenading, celebrating, or demonstrating.

The ceremonial, processional image of such streets can be enhanced by lining them with regionally appropriate trees and with lighting standards of suitable scale and style. Benches and kiosks should be part of the procession. Walkway surfaces may be paved with special materials—granite, slate, marble or brick—as opposed to just concrete or asphalt.

Elegantly designed esplanades can occupy the centers of such roads, providing additional space for streetscape vegetation. Esplanades may also increase safety not only by separating traffic but also by offering pedestrians crossing the road a relatively safe, temporary haven at midstream. Visually, esplanades add another set of parallel lines to the perspective framework and axial vista within the streetscape.

A ceremonial street should be lined with buildings whose height and mass are appropriate to the street's width. If buildings are too low or too far apart, the street space will lack containment and "leak" out visually. On the other hand, if buildings are too tall, visible sky area may be excessively diminished, leaving the street space shady and somber much of the time.

Pennsylvania Avenue's cross section seems to manifest reasonable ratios between height and width—the latter is somewhat less than twice the former. If the buildings were twice as high or the avenue half as wide, the street space would probably seem too constricted. Conversely, if the buildings were half as high or the avenue twice as wide, the street's proportions would seem suburban.

The evolving grandeur of Pennsylvania Avenue could not have been achieved without public design and development intervention. Near the end of the 19th century, there was little that was grand about Pennsylvania Avenue. Its character and the structures flanking it had been built mostly through unfettered, independent commercial entrepreneurship.

In this century, fortunately, the federal and city governments decided that, for purposes of historical intent and good urban design, Pennsylvania Avenue should be the capital's and the nation's primary ceremonial street. Its form would be mandated, its architecture carefully controlled.

Today, though still unfinished, Pennsylvania Avenue is lined by commercial and governmental buildings. There are vast federal agencies in neoclassical edifices, elegant new and old hotels, shops and shopping arcades, restaurants, privately built office buildings, Washington's city hall, a theater, museums, and Canada's chancery. There will even be some housing for those who can afford it.

Pennsylvania Avenue's buildings have had to respect and abide by legally adopted comprehensive plans. As a result, architectural design must conform to special standards regulating building setbacks, bulk, height, and esthetic quality (judgment calls by enlightened commissions). And some buildings aspire to elevating commonplace, daily activities—shopping, walking, eating, working—to the level of ceremony, enhancing the avenue's overall sense of being a ceremonial place.

Added to all of this are periodic open spaces and plazas straddling or adjacent to the street. Such spaces augment ceremonial and celebrational opportunities by interrupting (but, one hopes, without destroying) the linear, façade-flanked perspectives up and down the avenue. They too contribute both daily and occasional special rituals to the collective rituals of the street as a whole.

Pennsylvania Avenue is the site of one of the city's and the nation's most significant ceremonial events, the Presidential Inaugural Parade, occurring every four years. The avenue also is used regularly for countless other parades, marches, and demonstrations whose purposes you may or may not agree with.

No matter what causes you support or for whom you cast your presidential vote, you must admit that it is nice to have a majestic, ceremonial street that can accommodate everybody. Again, no city should be without one.

May 17, 1986

Seeing Through
the Windshield

Like it or not, your perception of cities like Washington, D.C., is strongly influenced by where automobiles can go.

You see relatively little of the city on foot. The local neighborhoods in which you live, work, and shop may be explored as a pedestrian, but your larger geographical framework of familiarity is most likely determined by the pattern of streets and highways on which you drive.

Remember, too, that your *perception* of Washington—what forms as a result of what you actually see and remember from experience—and your *conception* of Washington—what you understand intellectually to be its shape (based primarily on maps and other graphic representations)—are not the same.

Sometimes, what is perceived, even though an incomplete view of the whole, gives sufficient clues to allow you to grasp the concept, or idea of the whole. Drive through parts of Washington. Experience its grid of streets, diagonal avenues, circles, squares, monuments, rivers, bridges, and parks. While you may have seen only two or three percent of the city, you can still formulate in your mind's eye a reliable and meaningful visual picture of L'Enfant's conceptual strategy.

Try to do likewise driving in the planned community of Columbia, Maryland, where finding specific locations, particularly private residences, can be an agonizing challenge. Columbia's network of meandering roadways, although leading you occasionally past sometimes memorable buildings, places, or landmarks, does not allow you to comprehend fully the concept underlying the town's plan. Yet Columbia's plan was rational and organized on paper. It has a major commercial center, subcenters, separate residential villages, schools, parks, and industrial zones. There are primary, secondary, and tertiary roadways. Nevertheless, the idea of the whole escapes you.

Many subdivisions and communities are like Columbia. Their geometries lack comprehensible orientation, points of visual and geometric reference, conceptual as well as perceptual order. Their layouts are often derived from specific, localized considerations with roads engineered to follow contour lines and topography. Minimizing cut and fill, while maximizing numbers of lots, may have been the dominant conceptual planning force.

The late Kevin Lynch, a well-known city planner who taught at Massachusetts Institute of Technology, wrote that a city is seen and understood by inhabitants through memories of specific urban images: certain roads, roadway patterns, and streetscapes; landmark buildings, statues, or towers; and special places and views containing elements attracting conscious or subconscious attention. He recognized that adults—like children enchanted by places, spaces, and objects that seem vivid, unforgettable, magic, and sacred—also need the enchantment and guidance of stable, familiar landmarks.

What is seen from roadways is critical to imparting a sense of place. Views at the ends of streets, even if distant, or where roads bend are special. Intersections offer unique opportunities for creating landmark events, as do bridge crossings, cul-de-sacs, crests and dips, and access ramps.

Consider the various Beltway exits. These cloverleafs are sometimes marked by nearby buildings—the steep A-frame church at Georgia Avenue comes to mind—but many seem to be bland, featureless, indistinguishable places. Sometimes landmark buildings may loom in the distance—like the axially sited Mormon Temple, the brick highrise at Route 1 in Beltsville, or the Capital Centre in Largo—providing clues as to where you are, but without being immediately adjacent to interchanges.

Lynch and other planners also observed that people travel in very personalized "urban realms." These geographic realms are shaped by the paths and places that people use and occupy, their actual city space.

For example, suppose you live in Reston or Bowie and work at Tyson's Corner or the Federal Triangle. Record your day-to-day travels and create a map of your geographical realm—home to office to lunch to office to home, with occasional trips to shops and stores, to recreational centers, to restaurants, or to visit friends. Soon you have drawn a perceptual map whose spatial characteristics are very different from the conceptual map of Washington carried in your mind and glove compartment.

Likewise, a map of your spouse's or roommate's realm would be different from yours. A teenager's realm—linking home, school, the shopping mall, the local drugstore, and perhaps Georgetown—would be different still. And a child's realm would be focused almost entirely on territory within a few hundred feet or yards of home, except for what he or she might be able to observe peering out the car window.

Think about your driving habits, the familiar routes you follow almost instinctively to get from point to point in your realm. Some routes may seem to belong to you alone. How often do you speculate that your car would know the way, with or without you driving? Recall the uncertainty and discomfort experienced when obliged to take an unfamiliar route.

Because there are as many perceived realms and routes as there are citizens, the existence of common landmarks, familiar streets, and comprehensible, ordered roadway patterns seems particularly desirable. Such environmental clues constitute a constant frame of reference on which to map personal realms of travel and occupancy.

The baffling roadway patterns of Northern Virginia, like parts of D.C. and Montgomery and Prince George's counties, provide minimal reference frames. Intersections are visually interchangeable, with roads sometimes radiating in several directions with no particular orientation. Significant or memorable landmarks are hard to identify. Layers of utility poles and wires, commercial signs, traffic signals, and parked cars tend to homogenize the streetscape even more.

Traveling radially along Columbia Pike, Arlington Boulevard, or Lee Highway is navigationally straightforward, if not esthetically uplifting. But moving by car in almost any other direction can be confusing and time consuming. Concentrating on your dog-eared map, your automobile's controls, hard-to-read street signs, and building addresses leaves little opportunity for enjoyment of streetscape views. Despite dozens of trips through Arlington, it remains a roadway puzzle.

It is hard to beat the grid. From ancient Roman camps to the undulating streets of San Francisco to midtown Manhattan to Capitol Hill, street grid patterns seem compelling and fitting. Grids can accommodate exceptions, distortions, directional shifts, dimensional changes, and other superimposed geometries. Gridded blocks can be merged or further subdivided. Grids can flow up and down over hills and through valleys. Grid lines do not even have to be straight; they can curve and turn. Systematic, they are nevertheless incredibly flexible.

Most important, people can relate to such street patterns. Newcomers can find their way and know where they are most of the time. They can see up or down streets to distant landmarks or, looking right and left, catch glimpses of parallel views and landmarks punctuating crossing streets. And they can readily extrapolate their localized experience to formulate a more global conception of their community.

Thus, networks of roads and implicit roadway views are essential determinants of city imagery. Entailing more than civil engineering efficiency or romantic picturesqueness, such road networks and the land parcels they create can exhibit a conceptual order whose geometric composition can be sensed and remembered.

Kevin Lynch and his colleagues were right. A city's image is defined in large measure by what you see from its roads. Fortunately, L'Enfant knew this too.

April 13, 1985

The Ubiquitous Strip

Streets and highways flanked by disconnected buildings floating in seas of parking—the ubiquitous commercial "strip"—exist in virtually every community in the United States.

Such roadway environments are remarkably consistent in character. Unmistakable in purpose, they are universally interchangeable. If you were dropped suddenly into the middle of a typical commercial strip somewhere, you probably would not know if you were near Buffalo, Atlanta, St. Louis, Denver, Los Angeles, or Washington, D.C. Only the climate might provide a clue to your whereabouts.

Commercial strip development has ancient precedents. Dedicating certain districts or streets to commercial activity helped shape Greek and Roman settlements centuries ago. Cities and towns throughout history typically have concentrated trading activities in markets sited along major thoroughfares or at their intersections.

The logic of concentrating commerce and trade along important roads has always been compelling. Expedient for transporting and displaying goods, it simplified travel for traders and their customers. Geographic proximity of associated markets and products facilitated comparison shopping. When something was needed, citizens knew exactly where to look for it while benefiting from a range of competing choices.

Concentrating commercial trading along certain streets also kept commerce separate from what many saw as incompatible land uses. Active and successful trade obviously depended on intense daily public interaction between all elements of a population, both local and "foreign." It also created more noise, congestion, and refuse, all the more reason to locate it along busy streets and intercity highways.

In America, this traditional land-use logic prevailed as automobiles proliferated and suburbia sprawled. Thus, the commercial strip was an inevitable American phenomenon. Land seemed in endless supply, along with the concrete and asphalt needed to pave it. Automobiles and expanding road networks made everything accessible, no matter how remote. Once inside the car, the shopper could go anywhere, so long as there was a place to park. Therefore, why not create commercial strip highways, potentially stretching for miles, the new shopping street for the age of mobility? This would be just an updated version of the venerable American Main Street.

Following the advent of zoning in the 1920s, much of the land abutting regional highways was zoned for commercial use. In turn, accessible acreage was subdivided into road-fronting parcels, which could be developed piecemeal by their respective owners. Design limitations were minimal, if they existed at all. Frequently, zoning did little more than prescribe minimum amounts of parking (usually based on building occupancy and floor area) and maximum building sizes. Regulations rarely addressed site planning or architectural issues.

These circumstances, coupled with economic growth pressures and the uncoordinated, independent initiatives of private entrepreneurs, produced America's commercial strips.

Consider the results. Roads whose rights-of-way might be only 60, 80, or 100 feet wide have become visually broadened to the point of being formless. Parking lots adjoining roads effectively increase the perceived streetscape breadth many times over. Most strip buildings stand in isolation, surrounded by cars, with no relation to each other or to the road on which they front. Few commercial strips have any shape or coherence.

To avoid the risk of disappearing amidst the clutter of cars and signage, many strip buildings attempt to outshout their neighbors, sometimes cloaking themselves in architectural garb designed to heighten their own visibility and identity. But even this strategy becomes ineffective when all the buildings sharing the strip do likewise.

Why are the buildings along suburban commercial streets so often pushed back behind vast parking lots? Why not reverse this pattern, allowing buildings to form a more traditional street and sidewalk edge with parking behind? Why not have more attractive landscaping between road and buildings, or perhaps more clustering of neighboring buildings? Why must the front yards of so many developments be full of cars?

Part of the answer stems from our continuing romance with the automobile. Both developers and merchants normally assume that potential customers, driving along in their cars, will be most attracted by and likeliest to stop at a commercial establishment with plenty of visible parking area right up front. If they can not see all those parked cars, customers might conclude that the establishment in question does not have adequate parking, the kiss of death for suburban retailing.

Further, some planners, embracing purely functional design rationales, place parking compounds as close as possible to the roadways feeding them. This tactic establishes an undeniably economical, sequential traffic progression, moving from the relatively high-speed road to the low-speed parking area, followed by the very low-speed (and often risky) walk from parking space to building (a distance presumably minimized).

Unfortunately, this logic sacrifices the streetscape, along with sidewalks and any kind of shared pedestrian experience. Lost is the potential for serious window shopping, almost impossible to do from a moving automobile hundreds of feet away from store windows viewable across rows and rows of parked cars.

This land-use pattern depends on signs to replace window shopping. Only the signs and the occasional building-as-logo (McDonald's comes to mind) disclose the nature of specific stores and merchandise. But you have to be a fast reader. Sometimes there are so many signs to scan that you can easily miss the one you are looking for. In fact, searching for and reading commercial strip signs poses a serious driving hazard. And have you ever tried to find a numerical street address along a commercial strip?

With all of the ingress and egress drives, curb cuts, intersections, stop signs, and traffic signals, most commercial strips have turned into traffic nightmares, especially on

Saturdays and during intense shopping seasons. This is hardly surprising given that you may have to move your car from one parking lot to another several times as you proceed down your shopping list. Imagine the number of automobile movements this antipedestrian environment generates.

Rockville Pike, the extension of Wisconsin Avenue north of D.C., is a perfect, superscale example of the American commercial strip road. For all of its incredible variety and quantity of retail services—from lumber yards to car dealerships to fast-food outlets to discount stores to fashionable shopping malls—it is essentially a nonplace, a nonstreet.

Its visual, bituminous width sometimes approaches 1,000 feet. The number of signs, both freestanding and attached to buildings, is mind-boggling. If you go past your intended destination (assuming you can find it), getting back to it can be perilous.

Yet Rockville Pike has almost anything and everything you could ever want to buy if you do not mind the ugliness, and if you have the patience and fortitude to run the traffic gauntlet. It is for this reason that area citizens persist in venturing bravely onto the pike for periodic shopping expeditions. They know that eventually they will find a parking space, one they will not have to pay for.

May 3, 1986

High-tech Highways

Driving to Dulles International Airport, I always look studiously at the slick buildings and rolling landscape along the highway, inevitably wondering how many new projects have sprung up since the previous journey.

For several years, the corridor between Tyson's Corner at the Capital Beltway and Dulles Airport has been among the hottest real estate growth areas in the region. If you asked a commercial real estate broker where the action was, he or she would invariably point to Northern Virginia, west of Washington.

Similarly, Interstate 270, stretching northwestward in Maryland from Bethesda to Frederick, was the "hot" corridor of the 1970s. It is still relatively hot, but increasing traffic congestion and overburdened public facilities are dampening somewhat the economic flames that characterized the previous decade.

The Dulles and I-270 corridors typify a species of suburban development first given life by national road-building policies adopted in the 1950s. The federal government, along with the states, mounted an unprecedented, multibillion dollar interstate highway program. Its ambitious goal was the creation of a nationwide network of limited access, high-speed highways and urban beltways that would carry traffic nonstop between and around, rather than through, major U.S. cities.

Not only would such highways accommodate interstate and intercity traffic (seen 30 years ago as vital to effective civil defense, as well as to commerce), they also would serve commuters traveling between suburban home and urban workplace.

Of course, it did not take long for planners, developers, local governments, and corporate executives to realize that urban workplaces could be moved to the suburbs. These new highways promised seemingly unlimited amounts of acreage, desirable road frontage, and convenient access for employees who could live in newly developing, not-too-distant subdivisions.

Like commercial strips, highway corridor land, with its use and potential value established by zoning, could be subdivided into parcels and developed independently by individual owners.

But development along limited access highways took a form different from commercial strips. Zoning often prescribed that parcels be relatively large in size—usually several acres—to accommodate large-scale structures and on-site parking, while still preserving substantial amounts of open "green" space. A parallel network of roads, accessible from highway interchanges, had to be built to serve the highway frontage and its hinterland.

At the same time, many jurisdictions decided to exclude so-called heavy industry—transformation of natural raw materials, chemical processing, combustion, or other operations yielding noxious environmental wastes—from these corridors. In-

53

stead, they wanted their beltways and certain radial highways to be flanked by "clean" industry—research and development institutions, "light" manufacturing, warehousing and distribution centers, and corporate headquarters.

Companies were expected to build handsome buildings while employing lots of local residents. Modern corporate architecture presumably would blend with pastoral landscapes and tastefully display company names and logos, thereby advertising themselves to thousands of motorists passing by each day.

Thus, the pattern of development was clearly etched. Today, throughout the United States, thousands of miles of suburban highway exhibit similar characteristics, looking much like the road to Dulles Airport.

Along these highways, most buildings stand in isolation, sometimes fronting and parallel to the highway, sometimes placed askew to it at apparently arbitrary angles. Others

appear to have turned their backs to the road. A few buildings have two fronts. One may be designed and scaled for the highway, in effect the formal and most public front. But there also may be a front for the service road and parking lot, from which people actually approach and enter, opposite the highway.

Buildings may sit close to the highway right-of-way, but more frequently they are set back, sometimes several hundred feet. This tactic actually can increase the amount of time that the building remains within a passing driver's field of vision, providing a better opportunity to form a lasting impression and possibly to read the name of the company. It also reduces the ambient highway traffic noise for occupants of the building.

Building size and massing vary widely, from low and sprawling flat-roofed boxes to highrise towers. Materials range from the utilitarian and unpretentious—corrugated metal or painted concrete block—to the elegant and expensive—granite, marble, cast stone, or reflective glass. Brick and precast concrete probably are the most commonly applied veneers.

Although architectural styles and motifs can be diverse, most buildings nevertheless appear to be composed of rectilinear solids

sheathed with ribbon-windowed, panelized curtain walls of varying proportions and colors. Occasionally, special inflections occur at corners, parapets, and entrances.

The motorist experiencing these episodic, linear industrial parks at 55 miles per hour might ask what they all add up to. Not too much, I would suggest.

Undoubtedly, high-tech highways make economic sense locally by augmenting employment opportunities and tax revenues. But from a design point of view, they rarely exceed the sum of their parts. Being so separated from one another, most buildings, no matter how artfully designed, merely become three-dimensional billboards, usually surrounded by nothing but parking lots.

Workers in most of these buildings are wholly dependent on the automobile for going anywhere or doing anything special during lunchtime. The absence of retail services within walking distance means getting in a car and driving elsewhere—probably a shopping center—to find a restaurant or a drugstore.

Clearly, zoning and transportation policies have not led to ideal settlement patterns, lovable architecture, or uncongested traffic. But in a free enterprise system driven by incremental market forces, could it be otherwise? Only if the "system" were to adopt more aggressive policies regarding land use, site planning, and design.

Not surprisingly, development along most limited access highways is subject to very few meaningful design standards. Typically, there is no consensus about setbacks, relationships between buildings, building massing, or the mixing of uses. Few precedents exist for the aggregating of parcels or the clustering of separately owned buildings so that together they might add up to something visually grander and more unified than their parts, and possibly capable of supporting affiliated commercial services.

One wonders if there is not some way for each separately developed structure to participate in a larger order or formal framework that could exist at the scale of the highway itself. For example, prudent land-use policy and design standards could lead to increased building density and height around or near adequately sized interchanges, or between interchanges. Some measure of visual connectivity could be achieved through a shared set of criteria applying to building orientation, setbacks, signage, colors, landscaping, and parking.

Of course, such policies easily fly in the face of free enterprise. And they might even be offensive to many architects who prefer complete autonomy in designing their piece of the landscape and the building occupying it.

Yet a reasonable dose of collective design standards might choke creativity and corporate self-expression much less than expected. The overall esthetic payoff could greatly exceed the relatively painless cost of contributing to a better roadscape.

May 10, 1986

3.

Celebrating Commerce
Festive Buildings

Festival Marketplaces ... Waterfronts Preferred

I n a neglected piece of urban land, preferably near water, combine the forms and rituals of a circus, a baseball game, a shopping center, a beachside boardwalk, and a county fair.

What do you get? A festival marketplace—very likely one developed by an enterprise started or inspired by James Rouse, who created Columbia, Maryland, as well as Baltimore's Harborplace. Rouse is credited with inventing the concept of the "festival marketplace," the term commonly used to characterize this brand of city revitalization.

Such places have been built in Boston, New York, Norfolk, Toledo, and Flint, Michigan. More are being planned, and many small or medium-sized cities probably would love to have a project like those already constructed and widely touted.

The festival marketplace concept has evolved into a kind of formula that depends on several key variables, of which some are economic, some political, and some esthetic.

Location. Clearly, location is paramount. The ideal site is one adjacent to a river, bay, or lake, perhaps a derelict waterfront or port area near the heart of a city. Already developed or gentrified neighborhoods would be inappropriate because of elevated land values and existing physical constraints. Nevertheless, easy transportation access—by foot, car, bus, or subway—is indispensable. A site on the fringe of downtown, or in the suburbs, would never work.

Usually linked to a city's original founding and history, most urban waterfronts recall past times and traditions while offering unique vistas and a sense of place and identity difficult to achieve "inland." Above all, people are naturally drawn to water and maritime activity.

City Participation. In most instances, the feasibility of festival marketplace projects is contingent on substantial municipal commitment and involvement. Not only must cities and citizens desire such developments, but they also must help pay for them through private/public partnerships.

Civic support can include the condemnation and furnishing of land at little or no cost (often it is leased), mortgage financing at below market interest rates (through issuance of industrial revenue bonds), infrastructure improvements (streets, parking facilities, utilities), state or federal subsidies (such as the U.S. Department of Housing and Urban Development's Urban Development Action Grants), and tax relief.

The city, in turn, gets something back. It frequently shares in development profits, receives interest on monies lent, and increases its tax base and revenues. However, the greatest benefit for the city may be indirect—festival marketplaces can catalyze additional development that might otherwise never occur. In the long run, tax revenues, employment, housing opportunities, and commercial activity may rise many times over because of investment spurred by the marketplace project alone.

Occupancy and Activities. Ever since Rouse resurrected Boston's Quincy Market in 1976, the programmatic recipe for success has been well understood. A festival marketplace must contain a variety of tightly spaced, specialized eating places, shops, and vendors—with emphasis on "specialty." Big chain store tenants are shunned, while small-scale merchants are wooed and cultivated, often with much hand-holding by the lessor.

Although one or two large restaurants may move in, many smaller food operators—selling everything from apple strudel to zabaglione—are the mainstay both for stimulating and satisfying the public's limitless appetites. Most of the food sellers occupy stands or kiosks with shared seating in public aisles or courtyards. This strategy, with culinary sights and smells permeating the atmosphere, guarantees that marketplace visitors will always be hungry. Few people escape the building without buying at least a chocolate chip cookie.

Likewise, merchandisers' boutiques, stalls, and pushcarts offer diverse arrays of novelties and wares, some of which are actually useful. One finds hats, posters, balloons, T-shirts, kites, books, jewelry, leather goods, and artsy-craftsy items too numerous to mention. Obviously, you do not go to a festival marketplace for a television or a washing machine.

Critical mass must be achieved in a festival marketplace, a high density of both sellers and buyers. Otherwise, the chain reaction engendered by people working, looking, moving, eating, and spending will not be sustained.

One other ingredient essential to the mix is street theater. Visitors themselves create scenes worth watching, but beyond people-watching, you can see magicians, tumblers, clowns, jugglers, mimes, and musicians. They add a lively, spontaneous dimension to the festival arena, especially for children.

Architectural Attributes. What should a festival marketplace look like? At Boston's Quincy Market, next to historic Faneuil Hall, architect Benjamin Thompson was able to sidestep this question because the project entailed rehabilitation of an existing landmark building that formerly had been a marketplace. But at Baltimore's Inner Harbor, the slate was clean, as it was in Norfolk, Toledo, and other cities.

Consequently, a family of new buildings has been designed, mostly by architect Thompson. His festival marketplace building types are basically linear pavilions reminiscent of Victorian-era cast-iron and glass pavilions suffused with light and well

suited to growing ficus plants. From certain viewpoints, marketplace structures, with their sloped metal roofs faceted by ridges and valleys, suggest an image of circus tents.

Although organized linearly, marketplace buildings are not necessarily straight—they bump and bend. They may have short wings, pavilion extensions topped with gables, or gazebolike massing at their ends and corners. Upper-level terraces can be carved into or project from the main structure to allow sitting, eating, viewing, and strolling.

Typically two levels high, pavilions are framed with steel trusses and beams. The steel framing is usually uncovered and appears visually to have little weight or mass. Glass curtain walls, permitting views both into and out of pavilions, reinforce the sense of lightness, transparency, and accessibility, even with brightly colored awnings extended.

Inside, much of the building's other systems also may be exposed—ducts, pipes, electrical conduits, and lighting fixtures can festoon the basic structure. With banners, flags, signs, plants, furniture, and people, it all adds up to an esthetic cacophony that somehow hangs together.

A distinct vocabulary of materials and colors seems to prevail. Structural metal may be painted in shades of white, beige, or gray, but when chroma is desired, the favorite colors seem to be Victorian green or Rustoleum red. Decorative trim is likely to be brass and oak. Ten years ago, big splashes of primary colors dominated signage and decor. Now pastels are in fashion, along with lots and lots of stripes.

The exterior landscape is no less important than the interior. Expansive, paved terraces (usually brick and granite) surround pavilions and lead to the water's edge. Topography sometimes generates amphitheater contouring. Planters, benches, fountains, and light standards complete the picture.

Most would agree that festival marketplaces have proved to be a good idea. Nevertheless, one wonders about their staying power. Planning, design, and merchandising formulas, repeated often enough, eventually can become stale. In 50 years, history could repeat itself as people look at an abandoned marketplace pavilion on a waterfront somewhere and dream of new uses and higher density.

September 20, 1986

The Clones
of Harborplace

Festival marketplaces," those lively waterfront developments revitalizing several previously forsaken American downtowns, are like many other contemporary phenomena—updated versions of ancient and enduring urban traditions.

Historically, many cities came into being because of a natural human inclination to engage in trade at a single, animated, identifiable place. The Greek agora, the North African souk, or the Middle Eastern bazaar exemplify traditional marketplace environments where diverse commerce could occur in an atmosphere of competition, free choice, and festivity.

Prior to our automotive century, such marketplaces were located naturally in the hearts of cities, readily accessible by road or water. Open and inviting to the public, they had to be conducive to the display of wares and, on occasion, allow for the gathering of large groups of citizens.

Today, even more than before, these characteristics remain essential to the success of the festival marketplace concept.

But they are not all that is needed. Even the hottest idea in the hottest location may require special kinds of design and merchandising, along with economic and civic support not easily obtainable. And once a development is designed, financed, and built, there is still the market test—will people come to visit *and* spend enough money to make it all worthwhile?

To appreciate what can happen when seemingly obvious criteria are not satisfied, one only has to consider well-known contemporary failures, attempts to create centers of attraction that never attracted. Detroit's population-repelling, fortresslike Renaissance Center (complete with metaphoric moat) and Washington, D.C.'s, misconceived, badly located, ill-fated Visitor's Center (at Union Station) come to mind.

James Rouse and his Enterprise Development Company, creators of latter-day festival marketplaces, seem to have come up with the right formula. In the 10 years since Rouse's first project was completed—Boston's Quincy Market (report-

edly enticing 10 million visitors yearly, as many as Disneyland)—a family of festival marketplaces has started to grow.

Baltimore's Harborplace, the famous centerpiece of the city's Inner Harbor redevelopment, has far exceeded expectations. Conceived in controversy, endorsed by a voter referendum, and constructed finally at the end of the 1970s, it has become the festival marketplace architectural prototype, despite opening several years after Quincy Market.

Harborplace could not lose. Occupying one of the city's prime downtown sites only a few dozen yards from the water, it attracts Baltimore natives as well as tourists from out of town. The bustling, intimate harbor, its northwest corner framed by Harborplace's twin, green-roofed marketplace pavilions, is filled with scores of boats at anchor, in marina slips, or in transit.

As backdrop for the boats, pavilions, and plazas, and within easy walking distance, are the mirror-finished Hyatt hotel, parking garages, towering office buildings, Maryland's Science Center, the National Aquarium, the Power Plant amusement center, parks and playgrounds, and a variety of high-density housing.

In addition to the normal festivities generated daily by the confluence of all these facilities and activities, summertime weekends attract ethnic festivals to the Inner Harbor. For Harborplace's merchants and food sellers, this translates into even more potential customers and receipts.

Harborplace has achieved annual sales in excess of $400 per square foot, three times the revenue generated by many retail shopping centers. Of course, rents are double or triple those at conventional centers, a reflection of the higher development costs associated with numerous architectural amenities and nonrentable public space designed into the buildings and landscape.

In 1983, another festival marketplace, Norfolk's 80,000-square-foot Waterside, was completed by Rouse on the edge of the Elizabeth River. Rouse was quoted to have described the site once as a "ratty waterfront and not much of a downtown." It, too, was an instant success. A few months after Waterside opened, Norfolk's mayor credited it with dramatically increasing tourism, convention business, and new development in the surrounding area. Real estate assessments and tax revenues shot up, and people began to think again about living downtown.

Soon Norfolk was making plans for a World Trade Center, several office buildings, new condominium apartments, renovated hotels, a hotel-marina-housing complex, and the Cousteau Ocean Center, as well as for future expansion of Waterside. It is claimed that more than $100 million in new construction has been catalyzed by the $14 million spent for Waterside. And Elizabeth River frontage and the downtown area are being transformed in the process.

Waterside was created through public/private collaboration. City officials and business interests were aware of the risks but convinced of the potential, as was Rouse. Therefore, to make it happen, Norfolk pro-

vided all of the financing (at 11.5 percent interest). It also invested another $27 million in surrounding park and infrastructure improvements. But it gets half of Waterside's profits, which, when added to tax revenues from related development, will more than return Norfolk's investment.

Portside is a 60,000-square-foot, $15 million Rouse marketplace in Toledo. Like Waterside and Harborplace, it too sits on a waterfront, the banks of the Maumee River, in a city whose downtown had been likened to "Dresden in 1945."

Two years ago, *Business Week* magazine stated that "Portside is expected to draw 5 million visitors, generate $18 million in sales, and create 700 jobs" during its first year. Indeed, Norfolk's Waterside had drawn 6 million visitors and had sales exceeding $300 per square foot in its first year.

Also, like Norfolk, Toledo's civic officials and business leaders led the effort for revitalization. Owens-Illinois and the Toledo Trust Company first built two new office buildings on the waterfront, flanking Portside. As Portside was being built, another office tower and a 250-room luxury hotel went up. Today, Toledo has a convention and performing arts center nearby, along with more new hotels, housing, and offices.

To finance Toledo's waterfront development, including Portside, $81 million was raised from a variety of sources: $19 million through revenue bonds; $14 million from Urban Development Action Grants; a $13.5 million first mortgage from the local building trades' pension fund; $9 million in loans from Toledo Trust; a $1 million gift from a church; and investments from other local companies and private citizens.

Again, the city of Toledo, which spent $7 million on public improvements, will receive 50 percent of Portside's profits. Over the long run, however, the biggest payoffs are expected to be a revived downtown and renewed civic pride.

More festival places will appear, adding to the list. Others, like Manhattan's South Street Seaport, are already part of the thriving collection. And some downtown festival centers are not on waterfront sites at all—6th Street Marketplace in Richmond, the Pavilion at D.C.'s Old Post Office, or Philadelphia's Gallery at Market East.

No matter where they are or what incidental problems they may precipitate, all of these projects demonstrate that fruitful urban development is not just a matter for the private sector alone, or for government alone. It requires shared vision and mutual effort. And it takes heaps of planning and patience, not to mention money. Too often, only short-term, short-sighted actions and thinking prevail.

Modern festival marketplaces may not endure in their present form, and their architectural imagery may become repetitive and jaded. Nevertheless, the collaborative process by which they are developed always will serve as a laudable model for building new city pieces out of old ones.

September 27, 1986

Inside the Atrium

Since the 1960s, the nation's capital has become increasingly "atriumized." It seems like every other new office building downtown, along with many in the suburbs, contains a grand interior space with a glass roof and several ficus trees.

Hotels, corporate or institutional headquarters, shopping centers, and multi-use projects are also primary beneficiaries of the "atriumizing" trend in real estate development and design. They join many predecessor civic and cultural buildings designed when atria were thought to be appropriate and economically feasible only for prestigious, monumental edifices.

As a building design concept, the atrium is nothing new. Its prototypes are ancient and geographically diverse. Egyptian, Greek, Roman, Islamic, and Renaissance architects all made use of this design strategy.

Atrium, a Latin word, brings to mind the villas of Pompeii or the religious and secular buildings of Paris, Rome, or Florence with their colonnaded and cobbled courtyards.

Light, ventilation, and privacy were major factors in the making of atria in traditional houses found in many cultures, especially in warm, dry climates. Such traditional courtyards provided necessary, additional façades where windows and doors could be placed, but through which people on the street could not observe household activities. The courtyard was a social gathering space as well as a passage space, a storage space, and a space for collecting rainwater and growing plants.

New or old, an atrium building is one organized around an intentionally shaped, centralizing, enclosed space that may or may not be roofed. When not open to the sky, an atrium space may have habitable building stories both above and below it. And it does not necessarily occupy the geometrical center of a building. Rather, its centrality is perceptual.

The decision to create an atrium building occurs very early in the design and development process. For an atrium's form and purpose are inextricably linked to a building's basic intent, its massing and the ordering of surrounding spaces, zoning regulations, building codes, and economic feasibility. Today's architects and developers employ the atrium building type for many of the same reasons that motivated their predecessors centuries ago, persuading the public of its timeless amenity.

An atrium constitutes, above all, a grand, memorable focal space or room. It can unify, both visually and functionally, a building's interior, especially in large structures composed of large as well as small rooms. An atrium, being a centralized reference space, helps occupants and visitors maintain their orientation and sense of location when moving through a building.

Atria can serve as primary places of arrival, even when reached after a number of steps taken from entrances on street façades. Like exterior entry courtyards, they

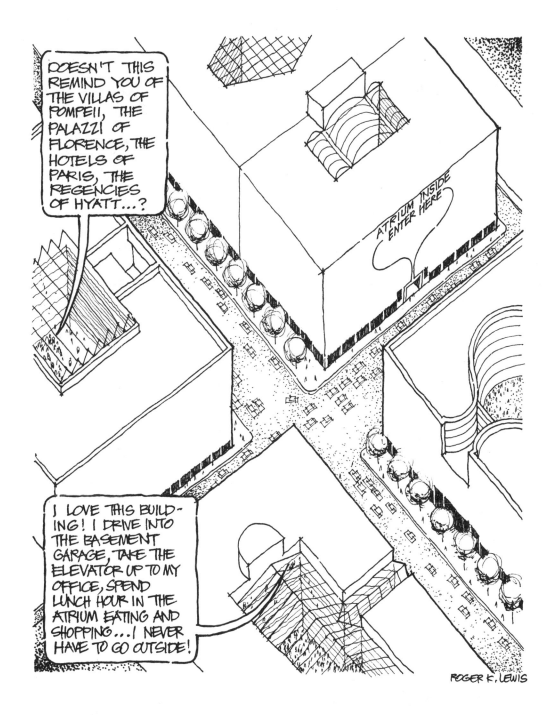

allow people to slow down, stop, look around, and pick up additional visual cues about where to proceed next. Sometimes, one's ultimate destination within a building may be visible from the atrium.

An atrium can also serve as a giant foyer, acting as a central circulation space feeding subsidiary spaces. It can be lined by passageways or corridors at many levels while grand (or modest) staircases, escalators, and elevators ascend and descend. Consolidating both horizontal and vertical circulation within and around a single atrium space facilitates movement and reinforces the atrium's symbolic and practical significance.

Atria with glazed roofs or without roofs bring natural daylight into the middles of buildings. As buildings grow in size and thickness, these broad windows to the sky become especially important for the envi-ronmental comfort of those who must spend considerable amounts of time working inside—and who otherwise might not get a room with a view or outside window.

Some atria can admit and control solar radiation in winter to reduce heating as well as lighting costs. However, improperly designed atria can have negative energy effects. Gain of unwanted heat through a glass roof in the summer demands substantially increased cooling and ventilation capacity, and loss of heat in the winter requires additional heating capacity.

Atria both past and present can be veritable gardens, interior landscapes furnished with trees, shrubs, vines, ground covers, trellises, fountains, and terraces. They may be designed more to be seen than to be occupied or moved through. In some cases, such indoor landscapes may be more attractive than the landscape or streetscape found outside the building.

Since an atrium greatly increases the number and cumulative length of a building's façades, shops and restaurants can occupy not only ground level spaces facing streets and sidewalks but also spaces fronting on the atrium space.

In urban settings, an atrium may be well connected at sidewalk level to surrounding street spaces, and even provide through-block circulation from street to street or corner to corner. With free and easy movement of pedestrians between interior and exterior realms marked by clearly visible and accessible entrances, atrium-facing merchants may do as well as their sidewalk-related counterparts.

On the other hand, some atria have proved difficult for commercial retail tenants. In most instances, they suffer from lack of exposure to traffic because the atria they inhabit do not enjoy immediate linkages to the outside world. Without such linkages, even the most beautifully designed atrium space may not draw in sufficient numbers of potential customers.

In some buildings, the atrium may be located within the building mass so as to emerge partially and show itself on the façade. Inward-facing atrium façades often echo exterior façades, sharing the same decorative motifs, the same materials, the same proportioning, and the same fenestration.

But sometimes the stylistic character changes from outside to inside, perhaps radically. The exterior façades of atrium-containing buildings frequently offer no clue at all about what is to come. Such buildings, like coconuts, reveal nothing of their surprising contents until you get inside.

Having definite length, width, and height, and bounded by the enveloping building mass, an atrium exhibits unique geometrical and proportional characteristics, just like any other architectural space. Atria can be high, long, wide, or thin. They can be cubic, oblong, triangular, round, hexagonal, octagonal, or irregular. The feelings and sensations one experiences within an atrium space are determined by these visual characteristics, as well as by an atrium's overall volume, appointments, light quality, and modes of activity.

Historically, it is worth noting that until the 1960s and 1970s, many jurisdictions outlawed multistoried atrium buildings. They were considered serious fire hazards because of the chimney effect that could quickly spread flames and combustion gases from lower to upper floors via the atrium. But more sophisticated fire and smoke suppression technology, especially increased requirements for sprinkler systems throughout high-occupancy structures, has resulted in building codes that permit multistoried atria when properly equipped.

Atrium buildings raise several questions. What are the economic consequences of developing atrium buildings? Do commercially successful atrium spaces siphon off street activity to the latter's detriment? Why are some atria animated and vibrant while others appear lifeless and austere? Indeed, could there be too many inwardly focused atrium buildings in a city like Washington, D.C., much of whose existing streetscape fabric is so rich?

August 24, 1985

The Atrium
as Theater

The atrium, an ancient architectural idea, often seems remarkably theatrical and futuristic in its modern manifestations. How many science-fiction films have you seen with scenes shot in spaces resembling the interiors of a Hyatt Regency hotel or the National Gallery of Art's East Building?

What makes these spaces so fantasylike, tantalizing to be in, and suggestive of other centuries or other worlds?

Size is one factor. Atria may be tall and wide enough to contain easily a multistory building or an interplanetary spaceship. Or they may be long enough to accommodate an ocean liner. In such spaces, your senses seek a scale of measurement and dimensional reference while your imagination speculates.

Atrium construction technology further contributes to this potentially mind-expanding experience. Atrium roofs and exterior walls often are fabricated with elaborate, three-dimensional, exposed frameworks of tubular steel spanning great distances.

These transparent structures—space frames, trusses, girders, and beams—typically have complex connections visible from below that serve as high-tech ornament. Sheathed with glass, such structural forms create dramatic silhouettes against bright backgrounds of diffuse light.

Seeing multiple floor levels from atrium top to bottom may further enhance speculation. Might it be a cross section of some piece of a future, Orwellian city where inhabitants, like the environment, are carefully controlled and tempered?

Indeed, the fantasy-inducing potential of such atria can lead to theatrical behavior. Washington's Intelsat building is a series of cosmic-looking, ingeniously linked office "pods" and atrium spaces crisscrossed by overhead pedestrian bridges. It is reported that an employee, obviously unable to resist Intelsat's galactic suggestiveness, dressed up as "Star Wars" Darth Vader and paraded through Intelsat's atria.

But there is more to atrium allure than futuristic technology or fantasy. An atrium can become a kind of festive, real-world theater, a place where people can come to see and be seen, to act, to pose, and to consume. Shopping center designers and developers have long capitalized on this

phenomenon, recognizing that people are attracted by festivity as well as by the pragmatic conveniences of parking, varied and concentrated shopping, and weather protection.

Festive theatricality is well represented by Washington's Pavilion in the Old Post Office Building, which also houses the National Endowments for the Arts and Humanities in its upper floor levels. Completed in 1899, this massive Romanesque Revival structure, designed by W. J. Edbrooke, was saved from demolition in the 1970s through the efforts of many thoughtful Washingtonians.

Restored by General Services Administration with architectural assistance from Arthur Cotton Moore Associates, it contains a 10-story-high roofed atrium approximately 190 feet long and 100 feet wide. Like many of its contemporary successors, its roof is framed with exposed steel trusses. Another set of trusses, supporting only themselves, spans the atrium just above

the main floor levels occupied by the Pavilion. They create an implicit, structurally outlined tent canopy, as if a circus might occur below.

As a result, there are really two zones, one below the other, within the single atrium space. The Pavilion, developed by the Evans Company and designed by Benjamin Thompson & Associates, occupies the lower zone's three levels. It contains cafés, restaurants, shops, and a stage and seating/assembly area.

Entering the Old Post Office Building's atrium the first time is a great surprise. You arrive at the sides or corners, not on the atrium's axis. Your view and movement are arrested momentarily by the incredible scene, and one of your first responses is to look up to measure the awesome space conceived by Edbrooke. But soon you look down again.

You quickly become oriented, realizing that the main level connects directly to the lower level via a broad stair located astride the building's principal axis. Most important, the north half of the main atrium floor is carved away so that there is a visual merging of the two levels.

A balcony level sits atop the roofs of the main level's retail shops at the south end. This third, restaurant level occupies less than one-fourth of the atrium area. Thus, from many positions in the atrium, you see simultaneously the bottom (stage) level, plus the balcony and main levels stepping down to it from south to north. It is a space whose organization and order are quickly deciphered and understood, aided by the interior landmarks of tower and grand stairway.

The Pavilion bristles with hundreds of light fixtures glowing yellow and white, colorful banners, signs, potted plants, brass hardware, and café furniture. Umbrellas and rotating ceiling fans scribe circles overhead. Blond oak and Victorian green trim wrap horizontally around wall surfaces, while gray and salmon-colored ceramic tiles establish patterns on the floor.

Above the Pavilion proper with its truss canopy is the upper zone of the Old Post Office atrium space. Buff and cream-colored, its soaring interior façades are formed by pilastered piers surmounted by small and large semicircular arches. Wide corridor galleries are open to the atrium between piers, and a series of vertical white banners hangs in a single plane directly below the ridge of the roof.

Yet the higher reaches of the atrium's upper zone almost disappear by contrast. This part of the space seems quiet and subdued, a separate environment clearly related more to the offices than to the Pavilion. In fact, to see its glazed roof structure from below, you must tilt your head back quite far. Otherwise, you can spend hours in the Pavilion and never really see the top of the atrium without consciously looking up.

The Old Post Office's new life now seems predestined. How could it not work—a giant room in a unique building in a great location, its bottom filled with eating and shopping attractions, its perimeter accommodating federal offices. For that matter, the latter could just as easily be hotel rooms, since the success of the bottom depends very little on what occupies the upper levels.

There seems to be a perfect fit between its immense form and the collective, celebratory nature of the carnival-like activities that occupy it day and night, seven days a week. If the same commercial uses were located in the bottom floors of a conventional building, could such a place ever be comparable either economically or experientially?

Nearby National Place, designed by architects Frank Schlesinger and Mitchell/Giurgola, contains a three-level atrium within the northeast quadrant of the block at 13th and F Streets N.W. The Shops at National Place, a Rouse Company undertaking, surround the atrium and line the diagonal, interior pedestrian street leading to the Marriott Hotel and Pennsylvania Avenue on the south side of the block.

Like the Pavilion, National Place's combination of stores and restaurants, its accessibility, and its festive decor attract visitors in droves. But unlike the Pavilion, the Shops' atrium is imbedded within an office building that actually rises above it. Natural light enters through a continuous, sloping clerestory on the atrium's south side and not through its roof.

The Shops and the Pavilion are the downtown counterparts of suburban shopping malls. They add much to the life of the city. But how many atria can the city ultimately absorb? Will everyone soon be shopping inside atria rather than along sidewalks and streets?

Even festive atria survive and thrive only so long as commercial tenants attract enough customers to buy their merchandise. Festivity and fantasy alone will not pay the rent.

September 28, 1985

4.

Home Sweet Home
The Indispensable Dwelling Place

There's No Place Like Home

Be it ever so humble, there's no place like . . . home sweet home." Such aphorisms attest to the special nature of real estate that people inhabit and call home.

But the meaning of *home* and its synonyms can vary. *Home* sounds domestic, friendly, intimate. It describes an idea as well as a place. *House* clearly refers to a place, yet it seems more architectural, describing an object, a built artifact. *Housing*, being collective and generic, brings to mind unit types, densities, economics, statistics, government policy, and mortgages.

No matter who you are, what you do, or where you live, your own personal dwelling has a significance unmatched by your workplace or by civic places that constitute the public focal points of cities and suburbs.

However modest or temporary, whether owned or leased, your home is undeniably your "castle," a quasi-sacred, inviolable space that uniquely shelters your household. It satisfies profound needs for space, privacy, utility, security, and comfort. To guests or the public, it can display your tastes, your economic and social status, your lifestyle preferences, your activities, and your fantasies.

The neighborhood, district, or building complex in which you live may be equally revealing of lifestyles and status. As collections of dwelling units, they are social and cultural communities created and maintained by the people who occupy them. A neighborhood's amenities, its history, and its physical character are, by association, public extensions of each private dwelling and dweller within. Thus, consideration of any dwelling, whether apartment, townhouse, or mansion, necessarily must include the dwelling's context.

For many, a home and its neighborhood symbolize permanence, stability, continuity; they form a tangible and enduring link to both past and future. Even in today's mobile society, places you once inhabited never completely lose that special quality of remembrance, of having been yours for some part of your life.

All of this suggests that those who design and build houses and housing, or who set housing policy, face great challenges and responsibilities. Fundamental, powerful human drives and aspirations must be addressed in creating innovative and inspiring dwelling environments. At the same time, equally powerful limits are imposed by economic realities, technology, public services, site, climate, and cultural traditions particular to a region, a city, a neighborhood, and a people.

With every adult citizen desirous of a place to live, a "market" exists on a mass scale. But it's a highly fragmented, locally variable market. Historically, fulfilling this market's needs has always created opportunities for entrepreneurial home builders, craftsmen, materials manufacturers, engineers, and architects who actually produce the dwelling product. In recent times, it also has generated opportunities for real estate brokers, attorneys, bankers, and investors who expedite (one always hopes) and finance often sophisticated transactions associated with selling, leasing, or financing dwellings.

And sovereign nations and states, through their governments and government officials, have long viewed the dwelling unit as a commodity susceptible to regulation. Such regulation may be focused on the actual supply of dwelling units, their cost, how they are financed and produced, what they look like, how big and how well built they are, or to whom they are made available. Thus, we hear much about national housing policy and the housing industry, but very little about national policy regarding health spas, shopping centers, hotels, or office buildings.

To many architects, the practice of residential design, for which this complex issue of private and public concerns may be only a backdrop, occurs in two categories. Category one, multiple *housing*, involves the design of residential aggregations—subdivisions, urban or suburban complexes, and individual apartment buildings. Housing clients are either nonprofit sponsors (governmental or institutional) or profit-motivated developers.

In the second category is the single-family *custom house* (either a principal or vacation residence) designed for a private client seeking to fulfill personal goals, rather than business or economic ones. A project in this category may be a totally new house or the remodeling of an existing one.

When architect and client collaborate to create the client's own home, the dreams of both designer and occupant emerge and interact. With luck, their dreams can be synthesized. If the architect is talented, the contractor is competent, and the client's intentions and resources are well matched, a "dream home" can result. The owner acquires his or her mythic, though usually functional, personal territory, while the architect adds to the list of "works by . . . ," presumably suitable for photographing.

Custom houses represent a minuscule portion of the housing market but greatly influence the style market. In fact, architecture journals tend to publish more custom houses than housing. Accordingly, many architects prefer to engage in design experimentation doing an elegant home for a client, especially with a generous budget, than to struggle with the problems that accompany the majority of multifamily or speculatively built tract housing projects.

When designing market housing, the architect is deprived of client/user idiosyncracies that so often help shape a custom house, not to mention the design flexibility frequently afforded by a private client's economic resources. Instead, the architect must design a generalized, receptive environment for occupants whom he or she may never meet, but who nevertheless have no fewer dreams or idiosyncracies than the affluent. Their market characteristics—ranges of income, ages, family sizes, tastes, and lifestyles—will be assumed, but their feelings about eight-foot ceilings will probably be disregarded.

Market housing must be affordable, both for the developer and the targeted consumer. It must respond to legislated zoning relating to density, height, bulk, yards, open space, sidewalks, streets, and parking. Unlike the single home, denser multi-unit housing must be more resistant to fire and more sensitively designed for light, ventilation, and privacy. Most important, the designer of housing, as opposed to a house, must stitch together dwellings, buildings, and exterior spaces to make some greater whole that celebrates both unity and diversity, community and privacy.

If you examine dwelling environments in many cultures built over many centuries, you begin to realize how clever and ingenious people have been, with or without architects, in fashioning appropriate houses and housing settlements. Likewise in America, particular housing patterns and types of dwellings have evolved in response to diverse circumstances and desires, producing a rich housing history that helps explain American culture—how we live and what we consider important.

December 14, 1985

A Place to Live, to Dream

During the 19th century, if you wanted to know something about the design of houses, you might have consulted a "pattern book" such as *Palliser's Model Homes for the People*, published in 1876.

Pattern books literally offered drawings and details reflecting then-fashionable styles of domestic architecture. Guides to taste, they were also specific enough to guide an owner and builder in the construction of a new dwelling.

For the consumer, today's pattern book equivalent is represented by the many magazines published monthly showing the latest fashions and trends in home design. Most emphasize interior decoration and furnishing, and only occasionally is documentation—plans, sections, elevations, details—sufficient to replicate accurately an entire house. For home builders, pattern books for constructing single-family homes continue to be published, though rarely are they found in drugstore magazine racks.

But dwelling "patterns" can refer to more than stylistic models or templates in books. In architecture schools, students learn about patterns of composition, massing, geometry, space, light, structure, surface, and use. They are taught that, rather than simply reproducing sets of patterns already prescribed and published, they should instead explore more fundamental patterns that transcend stylistic affectation.

The basic dwelling and its patterns of form and use are often the first kind of architectural exploration students encounter, partly because the act of "dwelling" is a universally shared and comprehensible experience. However, it does not take long for students to discover that dwelling patterns and history are incredibly complex and diverse, that the options for design are far richer than first imagined.

A dozen years ago, architects Charles Moore, Gerald Allen, and Donlyn Lyndon wrote *The Place of Houses*, a book that aspired to being an accessible, theoretically based alternative to the traditional pattern book. Written for consumers, not just designers, it uses history to illustrate timeless concepts about dwelling patterns—how dwellings relate to landscapes, to streetscapes, and to each other, how they are shaped and assembled, how they are used, and what they can mean to their inhabitants.

The authors talk about houses being comprised of three "orders": the order of rooms, the order of machines, and the order of dreams.

Rooms, they say, are "empty stages . . . fixed in space by boundaries . . . animated by light, organized by focus, liberated by outlook." Assembled horizontally and vertically, rooms form a larger order of linked spaces relating to each other and to the outside world. This room order can have its own hierarchy of size and function, usually with major rooms surrounded by minor rooms. Occasionally, minor rooms may be "encompassed" by a major space that wraps around them, such as an encircling porch.

The order of machines refers metaphorically to those elements of a house, other than rooms and the structure enclosing them, that provide comfort, security, and convenience. Some are in fact machine-like—heating and cooling systems, plumb-

ing, electrical networks, appliances—but other "machines," like stairs, closets, fireplaces, and furniture, are relatively unmechanical. To make and occupy a house, rooms and machines must be thoughtfully woven together.

Then comes the order of dreams. The authors theorize that a house inevitably is and should be "like" something else. It should suggest or recall, consciously or subconsciously, images or ideas from other times, places, or domains. A dwelling as a whole, plus its constituent elements and contents, can have metaphoric significance. Only by creating your own "order of dreams," state the authors, can you truly possess, personalize, and give spirit to the otherwise impersonal orders of rooms and machines.

Moore, Allen, and Lyndon ask "what places have lurked in the recesses of your mind . . . secret gardens or labyrinthine mazes, arches of triumph or alpine waterfalls, latticed porches or patios cooled by the splatter of fountains?" Are they "penthouses spacious enough for Fred Astaire and Ginger Rogers to grace . . . or staircases grand enough for Scarlett O'Hara to descend?" Some such place "transmuted and miniaturized . . . is the home for your imagination."

The Place of Houses also talks about how dwellings are fitted to the land. A farmhouse sitting on a slight rise amidst open fields or a vacation house perched dramatically atop a cliff "claim" the land. Houses nestled in woods or knitted snugly to the shoulder of a hill "merge" with the land. Houses with courtyards "surround" land. A house or housing that directly faces streets, plazas, or desirable views "enfront" these special places, which in turn requires enfronting façades.

The process of dwelling design involves mapping patterns of activity and use, proximity, movement, entry and arrival, view, light, and ventilation, among others. This then leads to design "inflections," the making of patterns of rooms, walls, roofs, windows, doors, porches, and ornament that ultimately constitute the three orders.

Moore, Allen, and Lyndon also list items, so often taken for granted, that people collect and bring to their personal dwelling environment—furniture, housewares, clothing, pets, plants. Most important and precious are certain collectibles, whether heirlooms, paintings, or baseball cards, that reflect their owners' unique values, family histories, fantasies, passions, or experiences. The authors argue that incorporating what is "yours" into your dwelling's "orders" is indispensable to creating a humane place to live, a home instead of a unit of housing.

The analytical model postulated by *The Place of Houses* seems to transcend debates about taste or style per se. Indeed, it seems applicable to many different cultures, regions, historical periods, economic levels, technologies, and housing densities.

Indian tepees or adobe pueblos, African huts or Asian yurts, Pompeiian or Palladian villas, European castles or Connecticut Avenue condominiums—all could be comparably analyzed and understood as dwellings according to this model.

The model's validity stems from its insistence on a humanistic, rather than formalistic or stylistic, description of a house. It recognizes common human needs for shelter and comfort, for privacy and security, and for intimacy. It identifies common patterns of human activity—sleeping, cooking, eating, bathing, socializing, working, playing, storing, displaying—that any dwelling, whether modest or grand, must accommodate and enhance. And it advocates an architecture that evokes images outside of itself, beyond function and budget—the order of dreams that humanizes the orders of rooms and machines.

December 21, 1985

Subdivision
or Neighborhood?

Many people probably search for a home with three dominant criteria in mind: size, cost, and location.

To most consumers, questions of housing "architecture," style, density, and urban design usually take a back seat to concerns about closets, kitchens, bathrooms, security, utilities, taxes, mortgages, and maintenance. Housing developers, understanding the interests of their market, naturally tend to build and merchandise housing to address these consumer concerns.

On the other hand, architects and planners tend to think about housing quite differently than do consumers. Designers categorize housing by "type," which refers not to the amenity package offered with a dwelling, but, rather, to its basic physical characteristics—its form and the way dwellings are aggregated and placed within urban or rural settings.

Housing density (number of dwellings per unit of land area, usually acres) affects land value, traffic, and the need for roads and public services—schools, police and fire protection, utilities. Even microclimate (patterns of shading, wind, air quality) is affected. Density also has an impact on commerce, influencing market potential for community retail services.

Housing type, density, and method of dwelling aggregation in turn determine a neighborhood's physical character. Yet specific housing types and densities do not correlate with specific social or economic characteristics. At any density, a dwelling occupant may be rich or poor.

To regulate the physical character of cities and suburbs, legislated zoning codes use dwelling type and density designations to categorize residential zones. Codes narrowly define unit types—single-family detached houses, townhouses, walk-up or highrise apartments—and stipulate maximum densities varying from one dwelling unit per acre (or less) to hundreds of units per acre. However, codes rarely prescribe unit sizes, architectural style, price levels, sociological criteria, or urban design objectives.

The freestanding house typifies the lowest range of density and the most restrictive land use. Many people take for granted that the single-family detached (SFD) house is the ideal home, the desirable norm for those who can afford it. Other types of housing, especially multifamily housing, seem to be no more than necessary, acceptable deviations from the norm.

This long-standing cultural bias is rooted in the belief that prosperity, security, freedom, and personal fulfillment are inexorably linked to ownership, control, and occupancy of land, the "manor," and its "manor house." Land traditionally was the only true and permanent form of wealth. Historically, such dominion also had practical advantages; land could be used for agrarian, commercial, recreational, and, with enough gardeners, esthetic purposes.

Few house lots are literally manors. Lot sizes vary widely, from a few thousand square feet to half an acre to several acres in rural areas. A mobile home lot can be as small as 2,000 square feet, a lot size commonly found in dense urban settlements in Europe, Asia, and Latin America.

Many street-conscious American SFD houses of the 18th, 19th, and early 20th centuries sat on small lots with little or no street setback except for a porch or entry stoop. Their owners may have been conscious of economies afforded by density. Not only did each house consume less land, but the quantity of infrastructure required for each house—roadway, curb and gutter, sidewalk, and utilities—was less. Despite proximity to neighbors and passersby, privacy could be achieved through the simplest of architectural devices—shutters, curtains, closed windows, and fences.

Small SFD lot sizes do not result in spacious front, rear, and side yards. However, densely arranged detached houses can be located on small lots with great architectural payoffs. Judiciously placed fences or walls can help make very comfortable, intimate private gardens or yards. The houses themselves, spaced closely together along a street or around a court, can create equally intimate and charming streetscapes.

But intimate charm goes just so far. The automobile, an apparently unlimited supply of land, and the symbolic strength of owning house and "grounds" reinforced the 20th-century American trend toward subdivisions with mini-estates lining relatively wide streets. Indeed, this pattern characterized many traditional American towns and their picturesque main streets, which became the desirable model.

Thus, instead of lots containing a few thousand square feet, with widths from 30 to 50 feet and depths from 80 to 120 feet, suburbia opted for much larger lots with widths of 80 feet or more and depths of 150 to 200 feet. While smaller lots might yield densities of 8 to 12 units per acre, conventional subdivision lotting typically yielded only 2 to 4 units per acre.

Houses retreated farther from the street, producing spacious front lawns. Streets widened, sometimes to the point of losing their domestic scale. Only after many decades might saplings planted along the right-of-way mature into street-defining trees with columnlike trunks supporting branch and leaf canopies. Nature, not architecture, would vitalize the street space.

In the 1960s and 1970s, planners and architects encouraged developers to build and government authorities to sanction the clustering of SFD houses. This land-use strategy generally maintains overall tract density at levels prescribed by zoning, but allows clusters of smaller lots integrated with common open land. In some cases, cluster houses can abut their own lot lines on one or two sides to increase yard sizes on opposite sides.

Clustering increases net density, respects topography and other natural features, reduces lot improvement costs, and, of great importance to designers, enhances possibilities for creating a tighter, more intimate residential fabric and streetscape within each housing cluster.

However, many SFD homes are still built on conventionally subdivided, bulldozed lots with marginally useful side yards, long utility branches and mains, and meandering streets. Little, if any, of the original site features—topography, vegetation, and trees—remains. Despite architects' romantic attachment to the imagery and densities of Edgartown, Savannah, or Kalorama, and despite the potential economies inherent in developing land more intensely, the forces of consumer taste and automobile accommodation remain powerful.

Equally important, most homeowners really desire neighbors who share their values and status. Designers may idealize the intermixing of land uses, densities, and socioeconomic classes, but the average consumer probably prefers a detached house in a community of similar houses occupied by similar people. Aspiring to any other model would require an American residential revolution.

January 4, 1986

House Typologies

Visualize "house," and your first mental image is likely to be a two-story, gable-ended shape much like the houses in the game of Monopoly.

Or your architectural memory might focus on special houses like the White House, the Octagon house (really a hexagon), or a château in France's Loire Valley. If you grew up in Texas or California, you may think of one-story ramblers with overhanging roofs shading picture windows and sliding glass doors.

The single-family detached (SFD) house, standing free on its own piece of land, has always offered its owner, designer, or builder the greatest flexibility in determining its size, shape, and style. Consequently, types of SFD houses seem limitless, ranging from manufactured homes to modest bungalows and Cape Cods, from center-hall colonials to spacious villas and palaces.

Yet all houses, small or large, ancient or contemporary, generally contain two primary spatial zones: public rooms or areas where people arrive, circulate, gather, socialize or dine; and private spaces—bedrooms and bathrooms—where people sleep, bathe, and perform other activities of a more personal nature. Service spaces for food preparation, storage, and "machines" can sometimes form a third zone, although they often are integrated with the other two.

These zones can be organized vertically, usually with private spaces upstairs and public spaces downstairs. Collections of rooms assembled in this way may derive visual and functional unity from a central stair along with foyers and hallways linking individual rooms to the "nonroom," central stair space. Grand foyers and staircases are sometimes the most dramatic and memorable architectural events in such houses.

Another fundamental room-ordering system, also quite ancient, places rooms around an atrium or central courtyard that provides light, air, and space for circulation and other activities. Pompeiian villas and Italian Renaissance palazzi are well-known historical prototypes for such houses.

In atrium houses, the zone of public rooms may be on the ground floor, surrounding the atrium, with private rooms above in upper stories. Or public and private rooms can be separated horizontally by the atrium, with public rooms on the street side and private rooms on other sides. Sometimes, the atrium becomes an entry courtyard facing the street or a private garden court away from the street.

Houses can have "wings" containing one room or a zone of rooms that penetrate or embrace the landscape. With their "footprints" patterned like Ls, Us, Ts, or Is, houses can stretch, step, and bend to fit the topography and geometry of their sites. Wings allow houses to expand, although mating new wings to old bodies can be a formidable design challenge.

In the 16th century, the great Italian architect Andrea Palladio developed an extensive repertoire of house typologies em-

bodying wings, courtyards, and pavilions based on Roman prototypes. His designs, organized symmetrically about a centralizing room, court, porch, or pavilion, have influenced the composition of stately houses ever since.

Three-part houses (central pavilion with two side wings) and five-part houses (central and end pavilions connected by two hyphenlike wings) typify many English and American houses of the Colonial period. In today's neo-Palladian houses, such wings and pavilions probably accommodate automobiles, television and stereo systems, or hot tubs.

A familiar and favorite strategy for shaping an SFD residence is to organize it on one level. Primitive house types—tepees, African huts, Indian hogans, log cabins, igloos—are one-story structures because of limited construction techniques, cultural tradition, and convenience. Availability of land is also a factor; putting domestic activities on one level obviously requires more territory but less structural prowess than putting them on two or more levels.

Most one-story houses likewise separate zones of relative privacy and communality. Part of the house normally consists of a living room, dining room, and kitchen, while the other part is dedicated to bedrooms, baths, narrow hallways, and closets. Unless there's a basement or usable attic, no stair is required.

Early in this century, Americans discovered the bungalow, a house type imported from India. Akin in scale to the Cape Cod cottage (a derivative of English cottage architecture), the bungalow became popular because it was compact, economical, and easy to construct. Although unpretentious in both size and decoration, the bungalow typically had a front veranda that imparted graciousness and a hint of formality to an otherwise simple, one-story box with an attic.

Stretch a bungalow or Cape Cod cottage and you get a rambler or ranch style house. These became de rigueur in the American Sunbelt where land was plentiful, lots were big, and the climate was hospitable most of the year. Conserving heat in winter by stacking public and private floors between a basement and attic, inside a relatively compact envelope, seemed unnecessary.

The Prairie houses of Frank Lloyd Wright furthered the popularity of these lowrise American house types. Stressing earth-hugging horizontality with cantilevering roofs floating over walls of windows, Wright's houses often were organized geometrically around a primary vertical object—most notably the fireplace and chimney—rather than around a singular space or room. In contrast to houses whose figural centers were stair halls or courtyards, Wright-inspired homes contain interlocked spaces that radiate outwardly from the solid, central hearth.

After the 1920s, International Style houses—designed by architects such as Richard Neutra, Walter Gropius, Marcel Breuer, and Mies van der Rohe—caught the public's attention with their open, "free" plans. Wright had pioneered the use of fluid, horizontal space focused centrifugally on the landscape as an alternative to inwardly focused, rigidly defined rooms. But later Modernists went even further, sometimes eliminating any vestige of a spatial or sculptural "center." Rooms and activities merged into a space "continuum" that in turn merged visually with the outdoors through glassy walls.

Many houses built in America during the last half-century clearly show the effects of these modern design ideas. Living and dining rooms became one space. The family room was invented, often flowing into the kitchen, which in turn might flow into the dining area. Instead of front porches of consequence, side and back porches grew larger. Backyard patios and decks further extended the public living zone via sliding glass doors.

Following World War II, the suburban split-level house arrived. These hybrid houses indeed are split vertically into two wings offset from each other by a half-story. An entry foyer and scissor stair lead up and down half levels to public or private zones. This configuration, well suited to sloping lots, easily produces cathedral ceilings and walk-out basements.

Despite modern spatial gestures found in new generations of house types, builders rarely abandoned completely the historical imagery of previous centuries. Vestigial classical columns and porticoes, cornices, and decorative trim are still tacked on to otherwise contemporary house forms to increase their market acceptance. Even manufactured housing, perhaps assembled partly by robots, can be given traditional styling.

Look closely at SFD houses you inhabit or visit. No matter how they are decorated, their antecedents, typologically speaking, may not be what you thought they were.

January 11, 1986

Housing the Elderly

Are you a yuppie, a swinging single, an empty nester, a suburbanite with a spouse, children, pets, and mortgage? Maybe you are a retiree struggling to make ends meet with a meager pension, Social Security benefits, and Medicare.

Whatever category you fall into, there is a housing type somewhere just for you. Indeed, over the past two decades, developers and architects have become increasingly sophisticated at identifying special segments of the population with special housing needs. Essential characteristics of these targeted markets include age, marital and family status, income, education, profession or employment, and social status.

Developers have always built a variety of housing in American cities and suburbs, but they used to assume a more homogeneous, adaptable market population. The primary design variables, reflected mostly in price or rental levels, were unit size, qualities of detailing and finish, and density—from single-family to rowhouse to walk-up to highrise.

In recent years, expanding anthropological, sociological, economic, and demographic scholarship has illuminated our culture and its population more revealingly. To describe people as rich or poor, young or old, single or married, is no longer sufficient to characterize behavior or to predict environmental needs. Today's informed citizens expect their dwellings to "fit" better, to suit their personal idiosyncrasies, to be less universally adaptable.

From a housing point of view, few population subgroups have been scrutinized more than the elderly, who represent not only a significant percentage of our total population but also a percentage that is increasing rapidly from decade to decade. This trend is likely to continue as medical science improves life expectancy.

The elderly both control and consume a large share of our national wealth—"gray power" is a meaningful aphorism economically and politically. Most important, no matter who you are now and how you might be demographically classified today, you eventually will be one of the nation's elderly. It is a market here to stay.

Yet housing for the elderly has become a serious problem for contemporary society because people no longer dwell together as extended families with several generations constituting one household under one roof. On the contrary, modern mobility—social, economic, and geographic—has facilitated family fragmentation. Younger generations often feel little or no obligation to accept responsibility for their parents, who they assume will take care of themselves. Failing that, there's always the government or some charitable organization.

Of the tens of millions of persons in America classified as elderly, some are affluent. But many find themselves at or near the poverty level. Some are healthy and robust, but many are not. Some live with spouses or other companions, but millions live alone. Most have worked hard all of their lives and feel that, at the least, they should be able to rent or purchase shelter that is safe, secure, and comfortable.

Government, nonprofit institutions, and private developers devoted considerable attention and resources to building housing for the elderly in the decades preceding the 1980s. The process and problems of aging were the focus of intense sociological and behavioral research during this period. Both study and experience produced new architectural and urban design thinking.

What makes elderly housing special, and how does it relate to the rest of the community? Should there even be *elderly housing*, a term that, to some, connotes segregation, the imposition of a kind of architectural and urban quarantine?

Location. The elderly are often less mobile. Many no longer drive, and some who do should not. Therefore, otherwise self-sufficient elderly prefer living in areas convenient to public transportation and to shopping, especially for routine services, commodities, and food. The ideal home would be within walking distance of such facilities. Also, proper nutrition is sometimes a problem as regular shopping and cooking, especially for one, become difficult. Proximity to affordable restaurants thus may be an important locational criterion.

Security. As people age and faculties diminish, physical self-confidence also diminishes. Reflexes slow, strength and endurance decrease, and sensory acuteness drops. With this comes a natural desire to avoid physically threatening situations. As a result, the elderly prefer to live in environments in which they feel more secure, both from intruders and from the risks of bodily injury.

Commodity. Conditions that cause the elderly to worry about personal security also point to other limitations not as important to younger generations. Diminished manual dexterity, often related to arthritis, can make it extremely difficult to operate conventional, everyday devices—water faucet handles, stove valves, door and window hardware. Going up and down steps or stairs may be onerous or even unhealthy for some.

Most people shrink in height and lose agility with age. Thus, the heights of kitchen counters, cabinets, furniture, and bathroom fixtures, standardized for the whole population, may not be appropriate for the aging. How often have you looked in a mirror over a bathroom lavatory, seeing only what is above your eyebrows? How many times have you felt you were taking your life in your hands climbing in or out of an ordinary bathtub?

Ambient Comfort. Little research is required to learn that, as you age, you become more sensitive to temperature, humidity, and air quality. Older people understandably want more control of the atmosphere they live in and are less able to tolerate, both physiologically and emotionally, deviations from their preferred comfort levels. While the senses of smell and taste may diminish, the ability to detect drafts seems to sharpen.

Possessions and Territory. With aging, people become increasingly attached to certain "things"—pieces of furniture, mementos, books, works of art, clothing, ordinary household items—with which they part reluctantly. The attachment may be based on necessity, but much of it stems from personal remembrance, sentiment, and nostalgia. Such artifacts transcend materiality; they can manifest and symbolize a life. Therefore, to many aging citizens, having a proper place for these things is of utmost importance. Even if such a place is too small to house the resident with all of his or her keepsakes, such a uniquely furnished domestic territory is nevertheless precious and sacred.

Community and Privacy. What about the desirability of residentially "concentrating" elderly persons? For many reasons—sharing of past lifetime experiences, lifestyle similarities, mutuality of needs, discomfort with or disdain for contemporary culture, desire not to burden or be burdened— many of the elderly prefer the company of their peers. They dread dependence as much as they abhor solitude. Therefore, elderly housing works best when it creates a

sense of shared identity and protected territory within, but not isolated from, the urban fabric. It must offer both community and privacy, the opportunity to choose to associate with friends and relatives, or to be alone.

Unfortunately, creating elderly housing is not an inexpensive undertaking. Until recently, most housing for the aging built in the United States benefited from federal or state subsidies. As such assistance disappears, younger generations once again may find it necessary to extend their families, along with their houses, to shelter their elders.

February 22, 1986

5.

Increasing Density
Dwellings Connected

From Rowhouse
to Townhouse

When I grew up in Houston in the 1950s, few people had ever heard of a "townhouse." You lived either in detached single-family houses or in apartment buildings. "Rowhouses" were considered an inferior species of residence found only in older, presumably blighted sections of eastern cities like Philadelphia, New York, Baltimore, or Boston.

Perceptions changed when inventive merchandisers started calling rowhouses townhouses. Although rowhouses derived historically from high-density urban precedents in Europe and Colonial America, they seemed perfectly suited, once renamed, to locations outside of central cities. Thus, today's "townhouses" are often not in town at all.

Developers, architects, and land planners have long realized that "attached" housing means increased densities and economies by comparison with traditional subdivision development. Yet attached housing, unlike many types of apartments, still can provide most of the basic amenities associated with subdivision homes. In fact, attached housing offers significant esthetic opportunities for building and streetscape design, opportunities difficult to exploit with detached homes.

Attaching houses to each other creates larger residential building masses that can aspire to a collective grandeur and presence exceeding the sum of individual parts. Yet dwellings still can have their own identity, expressed through appropriate roof, façade, and entrance gestures, within the overall composition of the continuous housing form. This can occur whether there are two, ten, or even dozens of houses in a single row.

Unfortunately, many contemporary townhouse developments consist of buildings that are nothing more than incoherently assembled rows of units. Dwellings between "party walls" (shared walls and foundations between units) shift back and forth at will while bumping up or down as topography dictates. Colors, materials, fenestration, ornamentation, and roof shapes may vary randomly from unit to unit.

But well-designed rows or blocks of attached housing, by virtue of their size, extendability, and disciplined façades, can contain, define, and shape exterior spaces—linear streets, courtyards, gardens, village greens, or urban plazas.

In cities where block and street patterns are clearly established, contiguous rowhousing fronting streets and lining blocks reinforces such patterns. And it is these patterns, projected into three dimensions, that can provide a recognizable sense of identity and place, a public urban image that transcends the individual house or property owner. Thus, attached housing is potentially more public spirited in its visual contribution to city space and place making.

Remarkably high densities can be attained with attached housing, even when it departs from traditional row geometry. Ten to 12 units per acre, along with related parking, drives, and roads, is typical of townhouse

zoning in many jurisdictions. But much higher densities—15 to 20 units per acre—are possible as dwelling "footprints," lot size, yards, and streets are made smaller. High on-site parking ratios (sometimes as much as 1.5 or 2 cars per unit), more than any other factor, push effective housing densities downward.

Accompanying increased density is obviously improved efficiency in site infrastructure—paving for streets and sidewalks, utility mains, landscaping. The more dwellings on a street or parcel, the less the infrastructure cost per unit, all other factors being equal. And it could be argued that, with proper design, individual dwelling unit security is higher because of both actual and potential collective surveillance, a kind of "safety in numbers" psychology.

To many designers and homeowners, reducing the size of traditional front yards is a desirable objective. More lot area can be dedicated to private use—usually at the rear—for terraces, gardens, and play areas away from public streets, and firmly under the control of the occupant. Common or public spaces in front then can be used collectively and maintained by a municipality or homeowners' association, while homeowners themselves are spared from weeding and mowing front lawns on fair-weather weekend days.

Unquestionably, each square foot in an attached house costs less than a square foot in a detached home. Party walls result in less exterior wall surface, in turn reducing the amount of insulation, windows, and exterior cladding required for each dwelling unit. The relative compactness and reduced exterior surface area of townhouses lead to reduced energy consumption and lower utility bills as compared to detached housing.

Construction of attached housing can be systematized, possibly yielding additional savings in construction labor, materials, and overhead. With construction savings, plus savings in lot and lot improvement costs based on increased density and infrastructure efficiency, the total development cost of an attached housing unit, for a given amount of floor space, is substantially less than that of conventional detached housing.

But attached housing has disadvantages. Party walls are one potential source of trouble. If they are not massive and airtight, sound will leak through them. Even with solid, heavy masonry party walls, impact noises and other structure-borne sounds may be transmitted audibly from one dwelling to another. There is nothing quite like having your neighbor's stereo speakers backed up to the wall against which you have placed your bed.

Unit-to-unit privacy also may be compromised simply because of window proximity in exterior walls. If adjacent windows of neighboring units are only a few feet apart, and if both are open during fair weather, eavesdropping becomes unavoidable. Your neighbor's cookout or patio party, its sounds and smells, may invade your domain. Likewise, you may be able to observe, perhaps involuntarily, everything going on in neighboring yards or courts overlooked by your upper-story windows.

Sometimes, attached housing is configured so that windows in one unit directly face windows of another unit only a short distance away. This, too, can be distracting to residents concerned about both visual and acoustical privacy. There are dimensions of separation that most people perceive as too small—less than about 20 feet—while window-to-window distances of 30 feet or more seem more comfortable, more protective.

It is generally harder to build additions to attached housing as household population, activities, or affluence increase. When feasible, additions usually can be constructed only at the back, away from the street. With limited lot area, or setback constraints prescribed by zoning, such extensions may be undesirable or impossible. Further, front or back additions deepen the dwelling unit, perhaps cutting off existing rooms from light, air, and view. For this reason, architects often design townhouse additions to be relatively "transparent."

In recent years, as attached housing has gained wider and wider market acceptance, builders and designers have looked for new ways to combine dwelling units. Innovative housing types have evolved—duplexes piggybacked over flats, fourplexes and sixplexes, corner-turning townhouses. Much of the effort has focused on the product—the building and the unit within.

Unfortunately, sometimes not enough effort is focused on site planning, on the shaping of public spaces—streets, squares, courts—edged and defined by these buildings. Too often, rows of attached housing seem scattered about, serving only to separate one parking lot from another. Instead, townhouses, whether in rows or otherwise, should add up to form "townscapes."

March 15, 1986

Garden Apartments and How They Grow

Metropolitan Washington, like most American cities and suburbs, contains tens of thousands of garden apartments. Garden apartment projects ring the Capital Beltway, cluster around shopping centers, and line arterial roads and highways. Sometimes they coexist with other types of housing—highrises, townhouses, and even single-family homes.

Many are composed of disorderly arrays of buildings sitting in landscapes dominated by drives, parking lots, cars, and trash dumpsters. In some complexes, getting oriented and finding an address or specific apartment are practically impossible, especially at night.

Undifferentiated grass lawns, perhaps in need of weeding, stretch between and around buildings. In older projects, deciduous and evergreen trees may have grown to substantial size, along with shrubs planted many years previously. But rarely do you see a literal garden, formal or informal, in English, French, or Italian traditions. In fact, garden apartments, the most typical form of lowrise, middle-density housing in America, probably should be called walk-up apartments instead.

The association of apartments with gardens began in the 19th century when planners first contemplated transplanting relatively dense housing types from inner city to suburb. Until then, most of the country environment outside of cities was reserved for pastoral cottages and villas owned by the affluent. That the petite bourgeoisie or laboring classes might choose, let alone be able to afford, nonagrarian country living then seemed socially and economically inconceivable.

Nevertheless, designers like Ebenezer Howard and Frederick Law Olmsted were able to contemplate more integrative, utopian strategies for settling and shaping land. Cities, they and others believed, could and should be gardenlike for all inhabitants.

They foresaw verdant metropolises with both densely occupied structures and open space, yet without congestion. Proper physical and mental health would be ensured by adequate light, ventilation, and sunshine. Beautifully designed and maintained gardens, public and private, would stimulate the senses while providing areas for passive and active recreation. Future cities would become giant parks, belts and gardens of green linked together by picturesque, meandering roads and lanes, with building masses used to frame and punctuate the landscape.

Thus was born the idea of the apartment block as "object-in-the-garden." Suburban apartment buildings started appearing at the turn of the century in both Europe and America. But it was not long before there was less and less garden.

It was, of course, the automobile that invaded Eden. One only has to consider area and density figures to realize how and why the automobile took over.

Start with an acre of land, approximately 43,000 square feet. Garden apartment densities can range from 20 to 40 dwelling units per acre, with 25 to 35 units per acre

being fairly common (about two to three times the density achievable with townhouses). Assume a single apartment building three stories high and containing 36 units, 12 of which are at ground level. If the average apartment size is 800 square feet, then the building will cover approximately 10,000 square feet of land, almost one-fourth of the acre.

A double-loaded parking lot (cars on two sides of a driving aisle), including aisles and access drives, consumes about 350 square feet per car. If one parking space is provided for each of the 36 apartments, then a 36-car parking lot and access drive will consume approximately 13,000 square feet of land.

If 1.5 parking spaces per unit are required, about 19,000 square feet will be paved. Providing 2 parking spaces per apartment produces 25,000 square feet of paving, covering nearly 60 percent of the given acre. In the latter case, with the

building covering 10,000 square feet and the parking taking up 25,000 square feet, only about 8,000 square feet—less than 20 percent of the original acre—remain as open space.

It is not unusual, especially in suburban locations poorly served by public transportation, for jurisdictions (through zoning) and developers to insist on parking ratios of 1.5 to 2 cars per dwelling unit to accommodate both residents and visitors. In these circumstances, it is easy to see why some garden apartments would be better labeled "cars 'n' apartments."

Nevertheless, garden apartments have undeniable economic advantages, whether designed for sale or rental. On a square footage basis, they are the least expensive type of housing to build, cheaper than high- or midrise apartments, cheaper than townhouses or detached homes.

Visualize a prototypical garden apartment building segment, one section of units sharing a single entry and stairway. The most efficient version usually contains 12 units, organized in three stories with four apartments per floor. In the center, the common

stairway leads directly from the outside to each floor. Sometimes, the stairway is fully enclosed, but often it is open to the weather, though it may be roofed.

In plan, two units per floor sit back-to-back on one side of the entry stair, mirrored by two units back-to-back on the other side of the stair. Each pair of units shares a party wall. Half the apartments have windows facing the "front," while the other half inevitably face the "back." Except for units at the ends of buildings, most apartments have only one exterior window wall.

Walls between adjoining 12-unit segments also become party walls, along which changes in topography, or back-and-forth shifts, can be made. Thus, the hypothetical 36-unit building sitting on its acre might consist of three 12-unit segments, three stories high, with three separate stairway entries. With identical apartments stacked vertically, with kitchens and bathrooms aligned and backed up to each other, this is an extremely simple building type to design and construct—over and over again.

The garden apartment's efficiencies are many. Segments can be standardized, repeated, and joined together to make buildings of varying size. A segment's roof and foundation serve 12 units, but their area is equivalent to only 4 units. Interior party walls and floors are shared. A single stair provides access to 12 apartments. Elevators, a major construction expense, are not required as they would be in higher apartment buildings.

Most significant from a cost point of view, building codes in many jurisdictions allow garden apartments to be constructed using conventional wood framing, just like townhouses or detached homes. Exterior walls and party walls may have to be fire resistive; but sometimes even these are framed in wood. Such construction is usually less expensive than masonry, steel, or concrete.

Garden apartments come in all sizes, price ranges, and styles. "Amenity packages," both within apartment units and communally, vary widely. After several postwar decades of predominantly lackluster apartment building, design consciousness seems to be rising. Despite the unavoidable presence of on-site parking, more creative thinking by developers, architects, zoning commissions, and consumers may yet transform the garden apartment into the vision seen a century ago.

March 22, 1986

The Apartment . . .
Unit or Suite

An apartment, according to the dictionary, is a "suite of rooms" in an apartment building. But not all apartment units seem like "suites."

Apartments, whether inhabited by the rich or the poor, come in endless varieties, ranging in size from tiny, one-room efficiencies to villalike, multilevel penthouses. Most common are one-, two-, and three-bedroom "flats" that are easily stacked and packed in apartment buildings.

A certain spatial sameness pervades many apartment unit types, whether located in suburban garden apartment complexes or downtown highrises.

Most units contain a kitchenette or kitchen, plus one or two bathrooms and, with few exceptions, an insufficiency of closets and storage. Living and dining areas often are combined into one space, frequently with only the living area adjacent to windows.

The dining area may be little more than an interior alcove, doglegged off the living room and adjacent to the kitchen. Except for the living room and bedrooms, everything else—kitchen, baths, closets—abuts the interior, windowless wall separating the unit from the public corridor.

In units with two or more bedrooms, there is almost always a master bedroom, so-called because it has more area, more closet space, perhaps a dressing area, and maybe its own master bath.

Efficiency apartments, containing from 250 to 400 square feet, can be the most economically inefficient unit type. This occurs because the costliest components of any apartment are its kitchen, bathrooms, plumbing, and heating and airconditioning equipment. Just building bedroom square footage is relatively inexpensive, adding surprisingly little to the total unit cost beyond the basic core components and systems costs.

Yet rental rates tend to escalate dramatically with each additional bedroom, much faster than cost increases arising from bedroom construction. For example, building a 400-square-foot efficiency apartment, with

kitchen and bathroom equipment comparable to larger units, can cost nearly as much as building an 800-square-foot, two-bedroom apartment. But the latter may rent or sell for more than twice the former, making it the more profitable unit for the landlord or developer.

Graciousness in an apartment depends more on the size, dimension, and proportion of rooms than on room count. Who has not been in an apartment where spaces felt excruciatingly tight, narrow, or claustrophobic?

The entry vestibule, if there is one, may have a coat closet just big enough for "a" coat. If two or more people arrive or depart simultaneously, such vestibules can become gridlocked.

Many apartment kitchens seem designed to accommodate one very thin person. Opening the door of any of several appliances—dishwasher, refrigerator, oven—or pulling out a drawer may render the entire

kitchen momentarily unusable. Often the apartment building's mechanical ventilation system, which supposedly exhausts air from kitchens, seems to work in reverse, drawing in alien odors produced elsewhere.

Interior corridors, normally about three feet wide, lead to bedrooms and may function well if perfectly straight and dimensioned properly by the contractor. But let there be a bend or two in the corridor, or shrink its width a couple of inches, and your shoulders will rub constantly against its walls, knocking pictures out of alignment, while your shoes scuff the baseboard paint. Of course, the biggest thrill with such passageways occurs when moving furniture.

And how many unfurnishable rooms have you been in? How often have you seen a living room in which traffic patterns, doorways, windows, and perhaps a fireplace left you nowhere to arrange furniture sociably or hang artwork? There are countless apartment bedrooms where closet, door, and window locations prevent reasonable placement of anything but a narrow bed, or where the only place for a large bed is up against a window.

But apartment units do not have to be like submarines. Architects and developers can create delightful interior spaces that are shapely, comfortable, and commodious simply by making the available space pay higher dividends. Combining or overlapping spaces—living, dining, and kitchen areas —is probably the tactic most frequently used to make small rooms look and feel bigger. But careful planning and dimensioning, especially in entries, halls, and kitchens where inches are critical, can make a big difference.

Because space in most apartments is at a premium, the location of doorways, closets, and windows is crucial. Their placement affects not only practicality but also spatial perception. Windows, by their size and position, can make rooms seem smaller or larger, or they can reinforce a room's geometry. Generous views and access to the outside, via a balcony or terrace, can extend interior space into the landscape, perhaps making modest rooms grander.

With larger windows, natural light will penetrate farther into an apartment's depth. In fact, the relationship of rooms to windows and room proportioning is what limits the overall depth (the distance from window wall to public corridor wall) of most apartments. This depth varies from 25 to 35 feet, typically the sum of the dimensions of one room, the unit's private hallway, and one bathroom.

Many apartments have balconies. Some balconies are like small outdoor rooms, airy open places to sit, socialize, barbecue, or grow plants. But with low ceiling heights, opaque railings, and solid walls flanking either side, balcony spaces, though private, can be compressive, dank, and somber, ideal for growing mushrooms. The light quality within living spaces behind such balconies likewise can be gloomy.

Numerous balconies are too vestigial, so small as to be virtually useless. Often, balcony railings seem shaky, conveying the impression that, should you be foolish enough to lean against them, both you and the railing would disappear. Like any space, a balcony's design qualities—size, proportion, accessibility, openness, detail—will determine whether people or snow tires sit on it.

Apartments are typically sandwiched between floors that limit ceiling heights to eight feet, among the more constraining architectural factors. This greatly restricts the potential for volumetrically shaping spaces in three dimensions. Thus, most apartment designers do little more than arrange partitions to create reasonable room layouts and efficient circulation.

However, with slight increases in the floor-to-ceiling dimension, design possibilities increase dramatically. Architects can play with contrasting ceiling heights. Coffers, domes, or vaults can be introduced over special places and spaces. Decorative elements on walls—coves, bases, cornices—can be more sculptural. Even floor levels can vary.

Sometimes, architects design duplex apartments to occupy two floor levels interconnected by a private, interior stair. Like a townhouse, one level can contain bedrooms while the other contains living, dining, and kitchen areas. Most important, two-story spaces can be developed. Buildings with duplex apartments may have alternating floors without any public corridors or elevator stops (called "skip-stop" buildings).

Doing more than the conventional, going beyond the minimal, is likely to cost more and therefore lead to higher rents or selling prices. Nevertheless, much apartment construction is done routinely with little effort given to making the best possible living units using available resources. Even small, simple gestures, measurable only in inches or perceivable only as detail, can go a long way toward transforming an apartment "unit" into an apartment "home."

April 12, 1986

Homogenizing Elderly Housing ... HUD's Standards

In creating housing during past decades, architects and developers often had to comply with Minimum Property Standards promulgated by the U.S. Department of Housing and Urban Development (HUD). But frequently, "minimum" standards became "maximum" standards.

For any housing receiving federal assistance or insurance, HUD dictated minimum areas for dwellings, depending on type and occupancy, and minimum sizes and dimensions for occupiable living spaces within dwellings. They stipulated requirements for bedrooms, living and dining rooms, kitchens and bathrooms, closets and other storage space. Rooms had to accommodate appropriate furniture, and some dwellings had to provide access throughout for persons confined to wheelchairs.

HUD's Minimum Property Standards also set forth site-planning criteria along with criteria related to environmental comfort, safety, and construction. Naturally, they did not require things considered to be luxuries, such as dishwashers or airconditioning. And, of course, they in no way addressed esthetic or stylistic considerations.

Subsidized elderly housing, like all low-income rental housing, is always constrained by strict construction budgets. In fact, congressional statutes may establish specific dollar ceilings on the total cost per unit of such housing. Thus, it is no surprise that "minimum" property standards were transformed into "maximum" standards, or that architects often found themselves having to justify, either to their client or to governmental authorities, why their elderly housing designs exceeded "minimum" standards.

One result of this attempt to apply uniform national standards, coupled with stringent cost limitations, has been the proliferation of types of elderly housing that exhibit common architectural characteristics. Certain developments have a look somehow telling you that you are seeing federally assisted low-income housing—the "project" look.

Begin with the dwelling unit itself. The majority are one-bedroom apartments with 8-foot ceilings; they contain one bathroom, a small kitchen, and a combined living/dining space. Thousands of them, regardless of location, are planned in the same way. You enter into a small entry foyer with a tiny coat closet, then move into the kitchen/living/dining area forming one half of the unit with the bedroom/bath area forming the other half.

Kitchens and baths almost always are located next to interior corridor walls. The bedroom has a window, and the living/dining area usually has a bigger window, perhaps even a sliding glass door leading to a balcony or patio. This pattern of repetitive fenestration stretching horizontally and vertically across building façades is one of the clues visually typifying multifamily housing, elderly or otherwise, especially when most or all of the apartment units are identical.

HUD-inspired one-bedroom apartments normally contain about 500 to 600 square feet. They can be assembled along both sides of a corridor and stacked one upon another to make buildings of almost any height. For buildings of more than two stories, access is provided by elevators and required firestairs. In short, most such buildings and the units within them are efficient, cost-effective, yet architecturally quite banal.

Millions of elderly citizens occupy thousands of midrise and highrise, double-loaded corridor apartment buildings in American cities and suburbs. With few exceptions, these slablike, flat-roofed buildings are faced with monochromatic brick, and some may have recessed or projecting balconies (optional, budget permitting) incorporated into their façades.

On the ground floor is a "day room" or lounge where residents can socialize or just sit to read, meditate, observe, or fall asleep. There is a communal laundry, and perhaps a separate room for television. Outside, some kind of terrace and garden can provide a place for tenants to go when the weather is favorable, perhaps even to tend their own flowers or vegetables. Rarely is on-site parking provided for more than a fraction of the project's occupants.

Most elderly housing is designed so that there is little or no stair climbing. Security control and surveillance regulating entry into buildings may be included. In some projects, congregate dining may occur, often with meals prepared elsewhere and transported to the project's communal dining space. This is especially critical when proper nutrition becomes problematic for tenants. In effect, an elderly housing project can be like a giant "boarding house."

In contrast to this more urban housing model is a type of elderly housing found in less dense suburbs, small towns, or rural counties. These projects are low in scale, rarely exceeding two stories and often only one story in height. They may employ the same apartment layout as their city cousins, but more design flexibility—related to unit geometry, not size—is often possible on such sites.

Dwelling units are commonly aggregated into small buildings that contain only a few apartments, and these prototype buildings then can be clustered on their site to form a kind of village or campus environment. In many cases, each apartment may have its own entrance directly from outdoors. Sometimes, two or more apartments share a common entry or stair, as in garden apartments. Communal facilities may be housed in a separate building centrally located on the site.

Again, the systematic repetition of the prototype apartments and prototype buildings gives a visual clue to the nature of such projects. But the institutional image of this type of development can be alleviated through creative site planning and architectural treatment of clustered buildings. For example, small-scale prototype buildings, even while containing relatively standardized apartment units, can be designed to look like large, traditional homes with porches or bay windows.

Low-density elderly housing can employ a wide variety of exterior materials in addition to brick. Vertical or horizontal wood siding, plywood, wood shingles, or stucco can be used. Aluminum and vinyl sidings, with their attendant savings in cost and maintenance, are sometimes applied, as are fibrous composition panels manufactured to resemble some other material.

Of course, not all housing intended for the elderly is low-income housing filled with apartments shaped by HUD's Minimum Property Standards. Many conventional apartment buildings, large or small, highrise or lowrise, are geared primarily to elderly tenants without necessarily looking like elderly housing. Retirement communities all over the United States are filled with housing types, along with diverse recreational facilities, that could accommodate any kind of resident. Many older structures—houses, schools, commercial buildings—have been rehabilitated and remodeled to create new housing for the elderly behind previously existing façades.

Fortunately, HUD recently decided that its Minimum Property Standards approach to housing design was too inflexible. It finally concluded that there was sufficient oversight by state and local building authorities, by the housing market and competitive building industry, and by design professionals to eliminate much or all of the federal regulations that police design.

Unfortunately for many, it also decided that most housing subsidies would be eliminated. Consequently, just as design latitude increased, the opportunities to explore it decreased.

March 1, 1986

Atypical Housing . . . Images From Afar

During and after the 1967 World's Fair in Montreal, architect Moshe Safdie's Habitat generated tremendous excitement. People were impressed by Habitat's dramatic and complex form, more so than by its innovative but costly method of prefabricated concrete construction.

Habitat was intended to suggest new directions for the design of multifamily housing, directions that promised more than conventional housing types—garden apartments, high- or midrise slabs, row-housing—could deliver.

But Habitat was not without its precedents. It evoked images of vernacular settlements on hillsides in Greece, Italy, or North Africa. Many of these settlements are collages of densely packed, cubic forms, homogeneous in scale, material, color, and detail. Picturesque pedestrian passageways, narrow streets, plazas, and courtyards

seem to be carved out of the assemblage. Viewed as a whole, an entire town can appear to be a single, richly textured building wedded intimately to the land.

Of course, something often is missing—the automobile. Cars may be excluded from entire sections of such towns. At Habitat, Safdie piled up cubes to create a kind of manufactured hillside; under the "hill" were voids for parking cars.

Well into the 1970s, architects continued admiring these innovative, romanticized housing models with their modular, visual complexity and relatively high density. Derivative apartment projects were built in cities such as London and Paris. Even here in Washington, D.C., Georgetown University built a dormitory, designed by John Carl Warnecke, that looks like a brick-faced, hillside habitat stepping down toward and overlooking the Potomac River.

The romantic, Mediterranean associations of Safdie's Habitat, along with its technological and economic implications, were eventually questioned. Not only did such housing seem impractical as a way of building but it also offered an architectural vision stylistically unrelated to most urban or suburban contexts.

Long before Habitat, architects had invented housing configurations departing from the tried and true. In Renaissance and baroque cities of Europe, designers rejected the accidental picturesqueness of medieval cityscapes and vernacular, collage building. Instead they sought to introduce rational, spatial order into city streets and plazas. Nonmonumental buildings, especially housing, would constitute the infill required to shape and line public spaces.

This strategy resulted in villas and "condominiums" being configured on the exterior by the urban circumstances of their sites, while their interiors assumed their own internal, spatial ordering. Often exterior massing and façades told little about interior room arrangements and shapes. One could not look at a building and automatically deduce that it was an apartment building or the palazzo of an aristocrat.

Architects occasionally took familiar housing unit types and created new building types. One of the most notable examples is

Cumberland Terrace, the terrace housing of John Nash, built in London in the early 1800s. Like his Renaissance and baroque predecessors, Nash recognized the importance of using buildings to shape urban spaces. Thus, he did not hesitate to assemble dozens of townhouse units into much larger buildings hundreds of yards in length.

Edging the east side of a London park and fronting on a grand street, Cumberland Terrace is 750 feet long. Classically detailed and finished with stucco, Nash's terrace housing has great presence. Yet each house within the row has its own identity, commencing with a small entry garden bordered by a low, unobtrusive cast-iron fence. An approach walk from the public sidewalk leads through the garden to an elevated, elegant entry porch and front door. Carriage houses, the garages of yesteryear, are found at the rear, with access from an alley roadway.

Historically, mixed-use development that includes housing also has produced special building types. Traditional European and Asian city streets often are lined by shops with apartments above, perhaps owned or occupied by the shopkeepers below. Periodically between shops are doorways, sometimes with little or no identification or visual celebration, leading to stairs that climb to the residential floors.

Sometimes the second floor, directly over the shop, is used as office space, producing a more hospitable stratification of uses. With potentially noisy, less salubrious, intensely public retail activity at ground level, semipublic, more subdued office activity at intermediate levels serves as a transition to private and, it is hoped, tranquil residential occupancy on the third floor.

This traditional housing-over-shops model has been stretched considerably in recent times. Today, where zoning permits, developers have erected sizable projects with many floors of apartments, either flats or duplexes, over floors of leasable office space, in turn perched over one or more levels of retail shopping, eateries, and entertainment establishments. Like many urban buildings of premodern Europe, some contemporary projects may not reveal immediately where and how uses occur, or what the uses are.

Recently, developers and architects have recycled older buildings such as surplus schools, defunct factories, and outmoded warehouses to create housing. Leaving the old shell intact, designers can insert a variety of apartment unit types within the structure, sometimes exploiting high ceilings or carving out interior courtyards and multilevel atrium spaces. With the growing interest in historic preservation, plus the desirability of maintaining the existing urban fabric, the number of such transformations is likely to increase.

Another kind of atypical housing blend occurs when projects interweave conventional housing types unconventionally. Harvard University's Peabody Terrace, graduate student housing on the Charles River in Cambridge, was designed by José Luis Sert in the 1960s. Sert's scheme, though hardly contextual with its exposed concrete frame and infill panels of red, green, brown, and white (Cambridge is mostly red brick and wood clapboard), seemed at the time to break new esthetic ground. It juxta-posed and visually integrated apartment building masses that ranged from low and horizontal to high and towerlike. Thin, tall structures seemed to grow innately out of low and midrise structures surrounding grass-covered or paved courtyards. It was urban yet suburban all at once.

Tiber Island, part of Washington, D.C.'s, Southwest Urban Renewal effort of the 1960s, was designed by Keyes, Leth-bridge, & Condon in a somewhat analo-gous way. Although more traditional in its use of building types, it too employed a common design vocabulary throughout to unify and enclose a variety of exterior spaces flanked by dwellings, from town-houses to highrise flats, all on one site. Like a Mediterranean village, Tiber Island can appear to be a single building of many layers and levels when seen from a distance.

Possibilities for new multifamily housing types increase in the absence of restrictive zoning. Indeed, typical single-use zoning may discourage architectural innovation. Segregating land uses by housing type seems questionable given today's diverse lifestyles, mobility, technological amenities, and design options. In fact, why zone by type at all? Parameters of density, not building type, should prevail.

A reader's letter recently posed an inter-esting question: Why not develop housing as part of, perhaps on top of, shopping centers? Why not explore new ways to weave more housing, and new types of housing, into downtown districts that become lifeless after working hours? Why not use more underutilized land or struc-tures for housing, even if located in nonresidential zones?

All that is needed are some changes in at-titudes, some enlightened public policies, and a few amended laws.

April 19, 1986

6.

The City's Architecture
Evolving Styles

Style . . . In the Beholder's Eyes

Style is a wonderful word. According to the dictionary, it can mean: manner or type of expression ("which style?"); distinction, excellence, or originality in the manner of expression ("what style!"); or fashionability (how "stylish!").

When we talk of an "architectural style," we are usually concerned with the first definition above. However, every historic architectural style has become recognized only after first becoming both distinct and fashionable.

Before considering specific architectural styles, categorization of generic architectural elements of style—the constituent pieces of buildings—is in order, since architects use most of them to shape buildings and urban spaces regardless of style type.

Think about and look at buildings in the city or in your neighborhood. If you squint slightly while looking, you will lose some of the specific, stylistic detail, but you will still see most of the basic compositional components.

The overall massing or volumetric form may be evident, whether a single volume or an aggregation of volumes. Related to the massing is the form of the roof, if visible, and its profile or silhouette against the background of sky, landscape, or other building masses.

You perceive wall surfaces and patterns of openings within them, usually windows or doors; these are among the most important elements susceptible to manipulation for stylistic purposes. *Fenestration* (architects' word for window and door patterns in façades) greatly affects comprehension of building mass, scale, and type, plus what we experience when inside.

Standing closer to a building, you realize that the individual window openings and the windows themselves contribute significantly to character and style. Designers must consider window types, sizes, proportions, frame and sash details, groupings or subdivisions of glass areas, along with the position of the window plane in relation to the wall face (flush? recessed? projecting?) both inside and outside.

Entrance elements—walkways, stairs, porches or porticoes, canopies, and principal entry doors—are integral parts of building massing and wall compositions, although their expression can vary greatly. Some are subtle, others ceremonial.

Columns (architects rarely call them posts or pillars) and collections of columns can stand free, form rows or colonnades, support roofs or pieces of buildings, mark edges and corners of spaces in the absence of walls, or become part of walls by emerging only slightly as pilasters.

Elements that span space horizontally—lintels, beams, trusses, slabs, arches, vaults, domes—are found sitting atop walls or columns. Some, like lintels, beams, and arches, are generally perceived as two-dimensional, planar elements over openings in walls or between columns. But slabs, vaults, and domes are clearly spatial and three-dimensional, as are some trusses. When rows of columns or piers (in effect, very abbreviated walls) are joined and spanned by horizontal elements, they become arcades, loggias, trellises, or galleries.

Building materials, plus color, are still another set of elements through which architects have developed stylistic expression. Inevitably, every component of the built environment has a color and is made of materials whose visual texture may or may not be revealed and exploited for stylistic effect.

Entering a building, you may see that architectural style is not just an exterior phenomenon. Most of what is outside can also appear inside and be used in the same way. The walls of rooms can be treated just like building façades. And clearly the organization of a building's interior, especially its floor plan, affects the organization of its exterior. Thus, the floor plan and the spaces within a building are elements subject to manipulation, capable of telegraphing stylistic intentions.

Finally come the purely decorative elements, the ornament, the stuff that is optional from a functional and technical point of view. Some decorative elements have historic origins based on construction necessity and were not always matters of choice. Even as their constructional necessity diminished, their purely decorative role became conventionalized, and architects continued to use or interpret them independent of any technical considerations.

For the most part, decorative motifs are applied at points in buildings where the elements already cited here either change direction or meet other elements—at joints both large and small in scale. A building meeting the ground at its bottom and the sky at its top is perhaps the biggest of these joints. Corners where walls meet, whether inside or outside, are often subject to ornamental elaboration. Openings in walls for doors and windows—sills, jambs, and heads—are one of the architect's favorite set of joints for embellishment. Joints of opportunity occur when columns meet floors (the column base) and spanning elements at their top (the column capital).

Where overhanging roofs, balconies, or bay windows intersect walls, decoration may also appear. Sometimes, architects decorate unbroken surfaces by use of inscribed or applied patterns that do not reflect joints between elements. Or they may use construction materials that come in small units—wood, brick, tile, stone—to establish decorative surface patterns.

We see friezes, moldings, belt-courses, and fasciae girdling building volumes or rooms from top, through middle, to bottom. Moldings and frames encircle openings, often changing from lintel to jamb to sill. Decorative trim may appear where two different elements come together in the same plane, at right angles, or at any other angle for that matter, frequently to conceal rough edges or gaps between dissimilar materials. Brackets of all shapes and sizes may mediate between horizontal and vertical elements while perhaps serving a structural purpose.

Of course, architects sometimes choose as their decorative strategy the minimizing of applied ornament. They rely instead only on the required constructional elements, essential assembly details, and finishes to provide a kind of natural, presumably honest and unpretentious system of self-ornamentation.

If now you were to stop squinting and examine this shopping list of architectural ingredients, you would realize that people rarely analyze buildings this way. Rather, an overall impression or image is conveyed, often very quickly, which you intuitively understand to be a style, even if you do not know its exact name or historical period or the labels for all its parts.

This is not accidental. Most good architecture utilizes dominant themes enhanced and reinforced by subthemes, secondary analogies, and counterpoints. Minor design events that can be viewed separately contribute simultaneously to major events, in turn adding up to one all-encompassing impression of the whole. There is a consistent visual language and vocabulary of expression chosen willfully but thoughtfully by the architect.

Like symphonies with their key signatures, movements, tempos, melodic motifs, and orchestration, buildings must be composed and assembled piece by piece over time, yet always with the imprint and memory of a unifying conception, a "big idea." Unlike symphonies, however, buildings are rarely experienced in isolation; their composition must acknowledge the physical context in which they stand, be it urban or suburban.

Architects tend to be innovative, searching for new esthetic ideas, new forms of graphic expression, new visual symphonies. If they invent a new way of making buildings, a new scenario for the whole and its kit of parts—if other architects seek to emulate or refine it—and if patrons and the public accept it, then a style is born. Even then, it must still exhibit those generic architectural elements familiar to us all.

December 8, 1984

Continually Recycling Classicism

In recent times, architectural "style" has seemed to resemble the weather. Wait a bit, and it changes whether you like it or not.

What is new and interesting today may seem stale and boring tomorrow. Esthetic values change periodically as stylistic gestures emerge, find advocates, gain public acceptance, become clichés, and are finally condemned and rejected by proponents of the next stylistic revolution.

Until the end of the 18th century, American architectural styles were fairly unpretentious. Only occasionally did buildings display touches of applied decoration that might lift them out of the realm of vernacular, regional architecture. And when that occurred, Americans went figuratively to Europe.

Eighteenth-century Europe was unquestionably the cultural mecca of Western civilization. Although many colonists were convinced that America would be the land of unprecedented political and economic opportunity, Europe remained the undisputed source of precedent and inspiration for art, music, literature, and architecture.

So while Americans were busy exploring and exploiting the New World, Europeans of the 1700s were rediscovering the ancient worlds of Greece and Rome, just as they had done during the Renaissance of the 15th and 16th centuries. Given the exuberance and occasional excesses of late 17th-century baroque and 18th-century Rococo architecture, classically inspired purging and purification seemed inevitable. To rational minds in the new scientific age, Greek and Roman classicism was more orderly, logical, systematic, and therefore symbolically appropriate. Resurrected again were academic styles that contrasted sharply with those of the romantic, ethereal, post–Renaissance era.

What are the familiar hallmarks of this historical classicism, first developed over two millennia ago and continually rediscovered? The austere Doric order of Greek and Roman temple façades contains the basic elements. A triangular pediment, ending the roof, sits atop a large, horizontal lintel, the entablature. In turn, the entablature is supported by several columns sitting on a base and forming a portico, or porch.

Looking more closely, one discovers other layers of composition where surfaces and joints gain definition. The columns are fluted, tapering gradually toward a capital—a simple, round molding and a flat, square slab. The entablature is divided horizontally by moldings to create a cornice with a frieze (alternating *triglyphs* and *metopes*) and architrave below. Precise, modular dimensional relationships govern sizes of columns, spaces between columns, and entablature components.

Other classical orders were more elaborate as Roman designers gave columns individual bases and fancier capitals (the scroll-like Ionic and leafy Corinthian being the most familiar). Entablatures and pediments became more ornate and occasionally fragmented. These elements could be imprinted onto virtually any surface or around any kind of opening. Equally important, Romans used circular arches and domes. The Greeks had employed only wood beams, trusses, and stone lintels to span space.

The naive, picturesque beauty of English or American vernacular could never compete with architectural symbols and formulas derived from civilizations that historians and philosophers persisted in idealizing and idolizing. The writings of the Roman architect Vitruvius, who set forth clearly and uniquely the virtues and principles of Roman architectural composition, inspired in turn the great 16th-century Italian architect Andrea Palladio to update and reinterpret those principles. In so doing, Palladio invented his own, widely influencing European building styles, particularly in England.

The precise compositional prescriptions enunciated by Vitruvius, and then by Palladio 15 centuries later, offered apparently undeniable, absolute standards for proportioning, dimensioning, and decorating buildings of all types, not just temples. In fact, architectural theorists of the Enlightenment, impressed with the "natural" mathematical relationships found in music, were convinced that the eye, like the ear, responded favorably only to "classic" visual forms composed in harmonious, mathematically correct ways analogous to music.

To Americans like Thomas Jefferson, who was familiar with such theories and had visited Europe, the adapted classicism of Vitruvius and Palladio was just what the new republic needed. England's yoke was gladly thrown off, but not its classical architectural heritage.

This heritage both predated and survived the American Revolution. You still see Georgian and Federal styles of the late 1700s and early 1800s. They are represented by buildings of simple overall mass with understated but unmistakably classical details, as if still clinging to the unpretentiousness of early American building while striving for European refinement.

Typical are two- or three-story houses faced with brick or wood, a door and transom window in the center, and shuttered windows placed symmetrically on each side. Dormers may project through the gable-ended roof (remember the pediment). Most buildings of this style have fireplaces and chimneys adjacent to the gable at each end.

The classical decoration might entail small broken or unbroken pediments over the entrance door and each of the dormer windows; pilasters or columns at each side of the door; a cornice and frieze with many tiny, teethlike brackets (*dentils*) under the slightly projecting roof eave; and simple belt-courses or moldings encircling the building at its base, usually over basement windows. Transom windows over doors and the tops of dormer windows can be semicircular, rectangular, or triangular.

Naturally, variations were endless, though often subtle. Entrance doors could exchange positions with an adjacent window, either right or left, in houses with three windows across. This created asymmetry within a larger symmetrical composition. The more affluent the owner, the more elaborate the decoration and entrance might become. Porches with classical pediments, entablatures, and columns—minitemples—could project from the building. Wings might be added to each side of the house to form centralized three-part or five-part buildings in accordance with Palladian strategy.

But as the 19th century began, when the Classic Revival was well under way in Europe, American architects—William Thornton, Charles Bulfinch, Benjamin Latrobe, James Hoban, Robert Mills—decided that the relative calm of Georgian architecture would not be adequate to express American, democratic aspirations; these could be embodied only in the explicit, revivable architecture of Greece and Rome.

The U.S. Capitol Building, despite its many transfigurations by feuding designers, reflects clearly the continuing thread of classicism woven into Washington's monumental public buildings. Thomas Jefferson's design for the University of Virginia, modeled so elegantly on Rome's Pantheon, temple façades, and arcades, and further seasoned by the lessons of Palladio, bears unequivocal witness to the spirit of Jeffersonian classicism, the American transplanting of ancient, idealized models.

Indeed, for the first half of the 18th century, the sanctioned style was Classic Revival in one guise or another. You see it in Washington, D.C.'s, Doric-style St. John's Church on 16th Street and the Custis-Lee Mansion at Arlington Cemetery, in the Ionic-style Treasury Building next to the White House, and in the Old Patent Office (today's American Art/Portrait Gallery Building) with the Parthenon as its portico.

Of course, it did not last. At midcentury, it was time for a Romantic Revival. Music, art, and literature were already going "romantic." Pure architectural classicism, along with subdued Georgian and Federal styles, was to be put in the closet for a while, but it would return. One only had to wait for the cycle of novelty and boredom to repeat itself.

December 15, 1984

From Roman
to Romantic

American architecture is the art of covering one thing with another thing to imitate a third thing, which if genuine would not be desirable."

This Leopold Eidlitz quote accompanies the photograph of the Smithsonian's Arts and Industries Building (1880, designed by Cluss & Schulze), which is described by the American Institute of Architects' guide to architecture in Washington as "a fairy-tale castle in polychrome brick." It seems to fit much of the Victorian 19th century.

The intellectual, systematic classicism of the early 19th century had become tiresome to many stylists looking for something different to pursue. In the 1830s and 1840s, anyone keeping a finger on Europe's architectural pulse could feel new rhythms. When London's Houses of Parliament were rebuilt after a fire in 1834, the style chosen was Gothic.

The Industrial Revolution had begun. New technologies were changing not only how people worked, traveled, and communicated but also perceptions about the world and society's ability to control it. People on both sides of the Atlantic believed that freedom and justice were no longer abstract philosophical concepts; the new American experiment might succeed.

In architecture, liberty meant abandoning arbitrarily rigid rules or formulas connoting dictatorship and absolute rule. Designers of buildings wanted to be free from the stylistic strictures of ancient Greece and Rome.

Surprisingly, their search led back to the Middle Ages. Gothic was in. Its symbolic soaring and thrusting upwards, its conscious interplay of mass, structure, and detail, its mixing of symmetries and asymmetries fascinated midcentury architects.

Instead of temples, historicists turned their attention to a variety of building types—cottages, châteaus, castles, and cathedrals. Instead of Rome and Athens, architects drew inspiration from Venice and the pre-Renaissance towns of Italy, France, central Europe, and England.

It may seem paradoxical that the new age of industry and machines should generate interest in asystematic, often mystical buildings typical of medieval times. But it made sense to the romantics of the 19th century, for whom Gothic architecture symbolized freedom, truth, nature, and adventure, while formalistic classical architecture seemed unspirited, sterile, static, dispassionate, even oppressive.

In 1848, English art critic and social reformer John Ruskin penned *The Seven Lamps of Architecture* to explain the virtues of designing natural, humane, appropriately symbolic environments. His declaration of principles, influential both in Europe and America, advocated among other things: honesty of expression in materials and decoration (painting plaster to look like stone was dishonest!); the nobility and beauty of nature (form follows nature—straight lines are unnatural!); and stylistic eclecticism that is "frank" and "audacious." He especially admired the richly decorated Italian Gothic style exemplified by the Doge's Palace in Venice or Giotto's campanile in Florence.

The European Arts and Crafts Movement, with its emphasis on picturesque, figural, nature-based decoration and informal (as opposed to formal) composition, had gained momentum and was propagated widely in the era of great international exhibitions that began in London in 1851.

Mark Twain expresses an American view of the romantic zeitgeist in *The Innocents Abroad*, his account of the first commercial trans-Atlantic steamship excursion to Europe in 1867. He recalls visiting the great Gothic cathedral at Milan:

"At last, a forest of graceful needles, shimmering in the amber sunlight, rose slowly above the pygmy housetops, as one sometimes sees, in the far horizon, a gilded and pinnacled mass of cloud lift itself above the waste of waves, at sea . . . so grand, so solemn, so vast! And yet so delicate, so airy, so graceful! A very world of solid weight . . . in the soft moonlight only a fairy delusion of frostwork that might vanish with a breath! . . . an anthem sung in stone, a poem wrought in marble!"

Fourteen chapters later appears his terse comment on the Acropolis in Athens: "I remember but little about the Parthenon."

So, while Queen Victoria reigned (1837 to 1901) over the British empire, American architects again followed England's lead, and sometimes France's. In Washington, D.C., Victorian buildings kept filling in the baroque plan conceived by L'Enfant.

What are the architectural characteristics of this half-century of "romantic" building? In contrast to earlier classical structures, Victorian architecture was much freer in its use and distortion of classical motifs and often directly allusive to Gothic motifs.

Generally, roof pitches became steeper, angling sharply toward the sky, unlike more earthbound classical pediments. Square, round, or octagonal towers, turrets, and projecting bays topped by cones or pyramids mark many of the buildings of this period.

Red brick was frequently the favored material, exploited by 19th-century architects like never before. Since a brick can be set to overhang slightly the one below it (a technique known as *corbeling*), it was easy to develop substantial, three-dimensional

relief in brick wall surfaces. Thus, many Victorian buildings have elaborate cornices, brackets, dentils, friezes, window and door moldings, and belt-courses modeled entirely of individual bricks in lieu of stone or wood.

Top stories or attics were expressed through variations on the mansard roof, named after the 17th-century French architect who revived its use. Steeply sloped roof surfaces accomplished several purposes: diminishing the apparent height of buildings by shortening façade wall height; celebrating more dramatically the presence of another potentially decorative, textural material, the roofing; improving the quality and utility of attic spaces; and affording new opportunities for ornamentation at roof ridges, corners, eaves, dormers, and chimneys.

Sometimes, Victorian roofscapes became veritable fantasies of form. Beginning perhaps with a simple mansard roof, architects could add projecting subroofs over large and small dormer window assemblies with sharp pediments or curvaceous arches, or pull numerous chimneys and parapets through the roof.

With the interest in verticality, plus the technical ability to use ever larger panes of glass, architects stretched windows upward. Small, six-over-six, multipaned windows typically considered Federal gave way to taller, visually more slender two-over-two and even one-over-one compositions between vertical *mullions* (thin columns separating adjacent panes of glass or windows). Windows often had glass transoms under semicircular, partially circular, or, in purer Gothic language, pointed, arches. Rectangular windows might have slightly curved or straight carved stone lintels flanked by brackets to create a drapery image.

Victorian decoration is unforgettable: wrought-iron finials atop roof ridges or spires, sharply profiled against the sky; quasi-naturalistic wood or metal filigree around the tops of porches and columns, in windows, and along parapets and railings.

But the austerity and rationality of Rome were to make a comeback. The watershed, neoclassical 1893 Columbian Exposition in Chicago catalyzed a new generation of architects, many of them trained at Paris's Ecole des Beaux-Arts. The architectural principles of classical antiquity were being revived for the second time in the New World, one century after Jefferson and almost 60 years after Queen Victoria ascended the throne of England.

January 5, 1985

Enough of the Victorian!

n his biography of Theodore Roosevelt, Edmund Morris mentions parenthetically that one of the president's first acts was to ask Congress "to purge the Executive Mansion of Victorian bric-a-brac and restore it to its original 'stately simplicity.' "

This effort began in 1902, a few years after the classically monumental Columbian Exposition. Victorian was out. Roman and Renaissance historicism were back in as Washington, D.C., again readied itself for another stylistic cycle.

Well before 1900, a variety of non-Gothic precursors had appeared. In Washington, the Old Pension Building (1883) at 5th and G Streets N.W., was among the most notable. Designed by General Montgomery Meigs, it was an all brick approximation of the Palazzo Farnese, a well-studied Italian Renaissance building. While lacking giant column orders and temple fronts, the palazzo model offered fairly pure classical details, mainly window pediments and friezes, plus very ordered and symmetrical façades.

Other Victorian-era architects had already returned tangentially to Rome via the transitional Romanesque, which must have appeared to be an appropriate stylistic bridge between romantic Gothic fashion and revivalist academic classicism. *Romanesque*, descriptive of European architecture from the 10th through 12th centuries, used thick, massive, brick or stone walls, plus circular vaults and arches to span space.

In the able hands of H. H. Richardson and other architects, the Romanesque Revival of the 1880s and 1890s briefly thrived. However, because Romanesque Revival buildings embodied many of the compositional mannerisms of Victorian-era architecture, they were destined to be eclipsed by the second American Classic Revival.

American architects, having journeyed to Europe to study at the famed Ecole des Beaux-Arts in Paris, imported principles of building composition that dismissed the romanticism of the 19th century. Architecture students again embraced the ancient models: Greek and Roman temples, Roman baths, villas, triumphal arches, arcades, colonnades, and the column orders that comprised the classical languages of Vitruvius and Palladio.

The Ecole used that language, with its grammar of symmetry, centrality, and hierarchy, to create freestanding, monumentally scaled, imposing buildings. Their systematic "formality" contrasted sharply with the picturesque, unbalanced, often casual "informality" of Victorian edifices.

Marble, granite, or limestone—not brick—were the preferred materials for making walls. Arches and vaults had to be circular, not pointed. Slender towers, turrets, cones, and pyramids were taboo. A rational system of proportions and dimensioning was again required, along with disciplined application of Roman architectural orders.

In plan, a Beaux-Arts design had a grand space or room in the middle with secondary and minor spaces filling in around the perimeter or in radiating wings. Local, subordinate asymmetries to accommodate functional necessities were okay, but the overall layout had to be clearly "balanced." Also, rooms or other spaces—

courts, hallways, vestibules—had to be "figural," that is, in the shape of a regular, recognizable, usually symmetrical figure (square, rectangular, round, oval, octagonal).

The desirability of such space-making tactics justified thickening walls beyond any structural or fabrication necessity in order to achieve the requisite figure. Walls could fatten and inflect to the point where, in addition to separating major rooms, they could contain small intrawall spaces for storage, niches, alcoves, or other service functions, as if the whole plan were carved out of an originally solid monolith of stone.

Equally fascinating was the willingness of Beaux-Arts architects to insist on and apply this strategy to any kind of building, despite location, size, purpose, or available building technology. They believed that architectural classicism embodied univer-sal, timeless, irrevocable principles that were nevertheless flexible enough to be used anywhere, anytime. In fact, success in Beaux-Arts design depended on how ingeniously an architect could manipulate the conventional elements of classical composition to arrive at an original yet undeniably derivative design, still following the accepted, immutable "rules."

During the first 40 years of the 20th century, a lineage of classically eclectic, monumental buildings, alluding directly to architectural antiques of the Roman Empire, appeared and superseded the legacy of the Victorian period.

The McMillan Commission began classicizing and aggrandizing Washington's Mall after 1902. In 1908, Daniel Burnham designed Union Station, Carriere & Hastings designed the Old House Office Building, and McKim, Mead & White designed the Army War College at the confluence of the Potomac and Anacostia rivers.

Architect John Russell Pope spent four decades leaving his indelible mark on Washington with buildings modeled unabashedly on ancient precedents: 1910, Temple of the Scottish Rite (the Tomb of Mausolus at Halicarnassus); 1930, DAR (Daughters of the American Revolution) Constitution Hall and the National City Christian Church at Thomas Circle; 1935, the National Archives; 1941, the National Gallery of Art; 1943, the Jefferson Memorial.

Other noteworthy classics include: the 1910 Pan American Union (Organization of American States) Building by Albert Kelsey and Paul Cret on the west side of the Ellipse; the Corcoran Gallery up the street, designed by Ernest Flagg; Henry Bacon's Lincoln Memorial, 1922; the Supreme Court, designed by Cass Gilbert in 1935; and, of course, the buildings of the Federal Triangle, built between 1928 and 1936, and designed by several different architects following consistent, mutually accepted guidelines as to height, mass, style, and materials.

While we tend to remember these landmark public buildings, many other derivative buildings were developed privately for commercial and residential purposes. Bank buildings represent a favorite application of Beaux-Arts classicism.

The exuberance of 19th-century romanticism did not lapse entirely. Some architects continued to create buildings whose stylistic flavor was more Victorian than classical. Developers built rowhouses similar to their predecessors, although Gothic decorative motifs yielded to classical ones.

Meanwhile, in both Europe and America, some architects and their patrons were rejecting historicism, revivalism, and the Beaux-Arts tradition. They were looking for new, unprecedented ways to design architecture transcending style. But their efforts were little felt in the nation's capital.

Washington's classical character had been too firmly established, and its zoning and height restrictions precluded skyscrapers and the demonstrative technological styles they were engendering. Cities like Chicago and New York would become the foremost repositories of modern architecture. With a few notable exceptions in the 1930s, D.C. was to adhere to its comfortable tradition of the traditional in architecture until after World War II. Even then, there would be discomfort with things modern.

January 12, 1985

Like It or Not, Here Comes Modernism

For nearly a century and a half after L'Enfant envisioned Washington's plan, the city's architecture was styled using visual languages derived directly from Greek, Roman, and medieval precedents. But during this same period, despite the prevailing classical and romantic currents of fashion, designers elsewhere were pursuing new, historically unprecedented directions.

For the first great international exposition in London in 1851, engineer Joseph Paxton designed the Crystal Palace in Hyde Park. This gigantic, factorymade, cast-iron and glass structure foretold a new age of building unencumbered by the necessity for heavy, load-bearing masonry walls. The Palace's Victorian decoration was visually subordinate to the translucence and transparency of its lofty vaulted roof and membrane-thin walls of glass, its soaring skeletal framework, and the exhibits it contained—arts and crafts on the one hand, tools and machines on the others.

Gustave Eiffel built his tower in Paris for the 1889 French centennial, again demonstrating new design potential and fabrication techniques that bore little stylistic or technical relationship to antiquity. The Eiffel Tower and Crystal Palace were rationally engineered, yet romantically inspired architectural feats whose first appeal was dramatic and sensual, like a Gothic cathedral, not subtle and intellectual, like a Palladian villa.

One hundred years ago in New York City, the Brooklyn Bridge was being suspended by cables across the East River. Even while the pointed arched openings in its masonry support towers paid homage to Gothic revivalism, it foretold the future of lightness and steel and systems management. New mechanical building tools and machines were being perfected, Otis's elevator among them.

During the decades immediately before and after 1900, both European and American thinkers—philosophers, social critics, scientists, as well as artists and architects—were convinced that utopia was at hand. The 20th century was the ultimate future. Unprecedented technological, social, economic, and political achievements would ensure the attainment of liberty, justice, prosperity, and happiness for all the world's peoples.

Questioning tradition and ever ready to embrace such utopian trends, some architects condemned stylistic revivalism and the tedious reuse of ancient motifs. They believed them to be costly and meaningless, outmoded symbols irrelevant to the values and experiences of the new culture. It was again time for change.

In the American Midwest, architect Louis Sullivan, foremost representative of the late 19th-century Chicago School, was designing buildings clearly signaling the advent of modern architectural thought. Both his Wainwright Building in St. Louis (1891) and his Carson, Pirie, Scott department store in Chicago (1904) rose many stories and were supported entirely by prefabricated metal skeletons. Exterior walls were only an infilling and covering curtain separating inside from outside. They supported nothing but their own weight.

137

Windows became much larger, admitting more light as they stretched almost from floor to floor and column to column. The imprint of the skeletal frame on the façade became a dominant expressive characteristic. The resulting interior spaces, interrupted only by grids of relatively slender columns, were multidirectional and infinitely subdividable by optional partitions. Internal vertical shafts contained stairs and elevators. Here was a new style and a new kind of real estate, liberated from the conventions of stone technology and masonry wall imagery.

But Sullivan and others were worried. Commenting on the 1893 Columbian Exhibition with its stage-set, "mercantile classicism" of plaster, Sullivan predicted that "the damage wrought to this country by the Chicago World's Fair will last half a century."

Washington, D.C., certainly proved him correct about the Fair's influence. In 1894, architect/developer Thomas Franklin Schneider built The Cairo hotel on Q Street. Among the first highrise, steel-frame apartment buildings in the country, its 160 feet of height offended neighborhood and city residents. It prompted D.C.'s unique and vital height-limiting zoning ordinance, but it also reinforced the city's propensity for classicism.

After the turn of the century, Sullivan's disciple Frank Lloyd Wright likewise staked out the Midwest with buildings having little or no European precedent. Seeking a nonderivative, antirevivalist, honestly native American architecture, Wright condemned "the styles" and evolved his own highly personalized design philosophy and formal language. While the Chicago School advocated technological and functional appropriateness ("form follows function!") with its significant implications for future urban real estate, Wright primarily explored the nature of single buildings wedded to the landscape.

His "organic" architectural legacies—freely flowing space, visual integration of inside with outside, emphatic expression of horizontal planes, abstract geometrical decorative patterns, and buildings shaped by the circumstantial pressures of site and climate—strongly influenced contemporary architects. However, few were willing or able to emulate his style literally.

At Princeton University in 1930, Wright discussed his contempt for the classic cornice, so beloved in D.C. Citing the roof collapse at the neoclassical Wisconsin State Capitol as symbolic, he characterized the cornice as the image of a "dead culture," useless by comparison with a genuinely protective overhanging roof. To him, a cornice was an "embalmed" marble vestige of an originally wooden Greek temple having no place in an architecture for 20th-century democracy. Few Washingtonians shared his viewpoint.

Meanwhile, Wright's European counterparts developed alternative manifestoes. The Bauhaus movement in Germany, led by Walter Gropius, combined 1920s' interests in building craft, engineering and economic efficiency, social and political reform, and constructivist art to create a new International Style of architecture. Like zealous classicists, Bauhaus adherents espoused utopian ideals of public welfare, truth, objectivity, and logic.

This meant a totally new architecture for the future: honest use of modern materials, especially steel, concrete, and glass; open, flexible plans; elimination of nonfunctional decoration; and systematization and standardization of construction. Architectural beauty, said proponents of the Bauhaus, would result naturally and inevitably from a rational process of analysis, composition, and building, but without appliqué and allusion. They were convinced that a universal, culturally neutral mode of architectural expression (hence the label *International*) would supersede individualistic, historicist manifestations of style, taste, and tradition.

Moreover, new 20th-century architectural challenges awaited, since the Great War was over. Instead of churches, villas, and civic monuments, architects would be designing industrialized housing for the middle classes, soaring curtain-walled office buildings, assembly-line factories, mercantile centers, airports, hospitals, and even entire cities. These projects would be complex and socially interventionist. The architectural styles of the past seemed especially inappropriate and pretentious for such revolutionary and optimistic times. The individual and the collective could at last coexist.

Aware of all of these movements, many American architects still adhered tenaciously to the Beaux-Arts tradition, particularly in Washington. How ironic that monumental classicism, proclaimed as the appropriate symbolic architectural style by Stalin, Hitler, and Mussolini for each of their respective realms, was also adopted by capitalistic democracies as the style most befitting public edifices and banks.

Nevertheless, during and after the Depression era of the 1930s, passion for tradition and historicism would be cooled by the arrival of Art Deco and Art Moderne. A few architects and clients finally would be influenced by the rationalist, stripped classicism of prewar Italy, the International Styles imported from Germany and its neighbors, and the compositional innovations of a Swiss-born French architect, Le Corbusier.

January 19, 1986

Streamlining
the Machines

America's prosperity of the Roaring Twenties vanished after the 1929 stock market crash. The era of the Great Depression was marked by massive unemployment at home and the solidification of fascism in Europe. To address the nation's economic woes, Franklin D. Roosevelt offered the New Deal to a struggling constituency disinterested in Europe's problems.

But some American architects, builders, and consumers were not disinterested in Europe's architectural ideas. Architectural and social manifestoes of the 1920s must have seemed made for New Deal consciousness. Thus, despite well-established Beaux-Arts momentum, new design ideas were being imported from Germany, France, and Italy, as well as from Chicago and New York.

The International design movement idealized machines and machine images. Le Corbusier, a Swiss-born French architect who shared such notions with his contemporaries, was infatuated by 20th-century technical artifacts, especially airplanes and ships. He talked about their functional forms derived inevitably from performance necessities rather than from stylistic whim. Like Germany's Walter Gropius, Erich Mendelsohn, and Mies van der Rohe, he admired clean and purified lines, so well suited to motion and speed. He lauded efficient, appropriate use of materials and multisystem engineering.

Along with his Bauhaus counterparts, he rejected the literal application of historic motifs to buildings. Instead, he advocated the invention of new motifs expressive of the machine age. Buildings were mechanized tools to serve society. Design was a matter of social, economic, and technological ethics.

How did Le Corbusier's ideas—plus those of Louis Sullivan, Frank Lloyd Wright, the Internationalists, and other contemporary architects and artists—affect the direction of architecture during the Roosevelt years?

One direction was taken by designers who embraced the Art Deco and Art Moderne styles, unquestionably International in spirit and appearance. Art Deco had begun in earnest with the 1925 Paris "Exposition Internationale des Arts Décoratifs et Industriels Modernes." Derived in part from turn-of-the-century Art Nouveau, it pushed jazz era and age-of-speed themes.

Designs included angular, abstract geometrical motifs, forms with rounded edges, and streamlined packaging. Industrial designers—Raymond Loewy, Norman Bel Geddes, and others—adopted streamlining as the appropriate image for the 1930s, and even Frank Lloyd Wright, borrowing from Japanese Shinto philosophy, had preached in 1930 the need to "be clean," to use "clean lines . . . for clean purposes."

Streamlining made practical sense for machines that had to move through air or water, but it became purely symbolic when applied to home appliances, furniture, and buildings. Think of the toasters, chairs, lamps, ashtrays, and diners of that era. Recall scenes from movies of the 1930s and

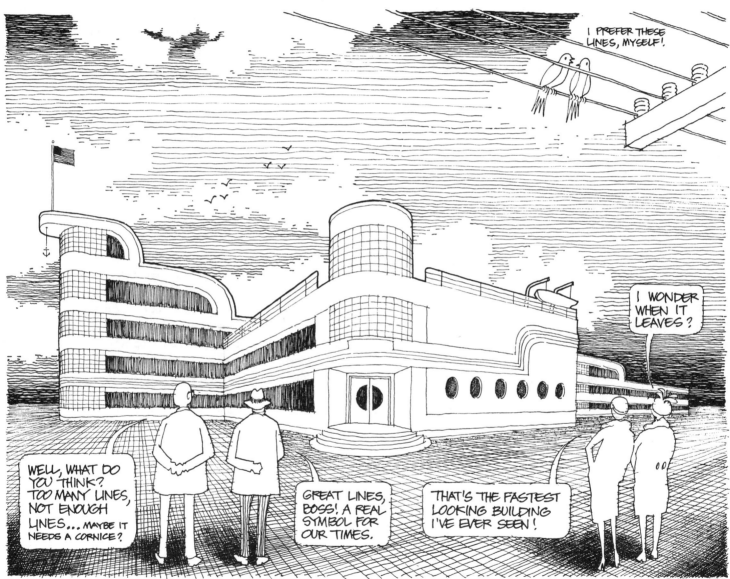

early 1940s in which sets were dominated by sweeping horizontal lines, rounded corners, horizontal metal railings, glass block, neon tubes, flat roofs, and doors with half-moon windows in them.

Throughout the Depression, streamlining must have suggested a utopian future, an escape from the present, a promise of things to come. What better place for Art Deco imagery than movie palaces? In every American city, architects designed theaters whose exteriors and interiors celebrated such escape with streamlines and Moderne ornament.

Washington, D.C., had its Penn Theatre on Capitol Hill, the Uptown on Connecticut Avenue, and the Silver Theatre in Silver Spring. The Silver was built in 1938 as part of the Silver Spring shopping center, one of the first such centers in the area and a prototypical example of Art Deco styling applied to commercial real estate.

In 1936, Clarence Stein and Hale Walker designed Greenbelt, Maryland. They used brick and painted concrete block to impart lean and clean style to this cooperative New Deal community, amalgamating Art Deco and Internationalist thinking.

Another stylistic direction, not totally unrelated to Art Deco, involved a kind of stripped classicism, sometimes referred to as between-the-wars rationalism. It characterized many of the monumental civic buildings constructed in fascist Italy as well as in democratic America. Such buildings were composed like Beaux-Arts edifices in plan and overall massing, including entrance columns and porticoes, but they lacked the traditional layers of embellishing detail and ornament.

In 1930, Paul Cret designed Washington's Folger Shakespeare Library, a building that author E. J. Applewhite describes as "an Art Moderne version of the stripped classical style." Cret attempted to reconcile traditional Beaux-Arts composition with modernism's disdain for ornament, which is limited on the Folger's exterior to Art Deco aluminum grillwork and subtle relief in the stonework.

Former classicist Cret, while perhaps resisting and yet responding to the influences of Le Corbusier, the Bauhaus, and Art Deco, went on to design the 1937 Federal Reserve Building at Constitution Avenue and 20th Street N.W., in the "starved" classical style. With Navy architect Frederick Southwick, he later designed the towering Bethesda Naval Hospital based on a conceptual sketch actually made by President Roosevelt.

All of these structures are undeniably rational with their diagrammatic, orderly plans and elevations. Their fundamental geometries are symmetrical and balanced. All are faced with smooth stone and display principles of classical composition—clear organization of façades into base, middle, and attic top is one typical characteristic. But their vertical wall and column surfaces are essentially clean, planar, and without elaborate ornament. Some labeled them "government modern."

Of course, private sector construction was curtailed substantially between 1930 and World War II's end in 1945. However, during this 15-year period of turmoil, the forceful proponents of modern design, although frequently unemployed, had been consolidating. Many European designers immigrated to the United States where their Modernist rationale would at last gain enthusiastic, mainstream support from those who invest in and build real estate as well as from those who design it.

Architects and clients who admired the efficiency, logic, and potential cost-effectiveness of clean, streamlined, unadorned architecture would build more after the war than was built in the previous 15 decades.

January 26, 1985

Midcentury Modernism

At the northeast corner of the intersection of Connecticut and Rhode Island Avenues stands the Longfellow Building, considered Washington's first truly "modern" office building. To emphasize its importance as an interrupter of the city's classical tradition, the American Institute of Architects' guide to Washington architecture quotes Alice from Lewis Carroll's *Through the Looking Glass*: " 'It's very rude of him,' she said, 'To come and spoil the fun!' "

This fun-spoiling building, with cantilevered balconies stretching across its Connecticut Avenue façade and its service core contained in a separate vertical shaft, indeed marked the beginning of architectural Modernism's dominance over the style of downtown Washington real estate.

The Longfellow Building was designed by William Lescaze in 1940, nine years after he and architect George Howe designed the Pennsylvania Savings Fund Society tower in Philadelphia, considered the first International Style skyscraper in America.

Swiss-born Lescaze was one of several European architects who ushered in Modernism from across the Atlantic. Before World War II, political pressure had forced the closing of the Bauhaus school, and many of its faculty—Walter Gropius, Mies van der Rohe, and Marcel Breuer, among others—came to the United States.

The American architectural avant-garde, tastemakers, and academics viewed these men as apostles bearing design theories that would leave behind revivalism and historicism. Long before they departed Germany, the Internationalists were sanctified by Henry-Russell Hitchcock and a youthful Philip Johnson in their 1932 Museum of Modern Art book, *The International Style*, which made a lasting impression on many young architects.

Gropius and Breuer went to Harvard to teach, while Mies van der Rohe went to Chicago and the Illinois Institute of Technology. Beaux-Arts methods, values, and faculty were purged. Bauhaus pedagogy and International Style design quickly spread to other schools and soon became the accepted, unquestioned orthodoxy destined to dominate American architectural education, and American architecture, for the next 25 years. And downtown Washington, despite its classicist past, would not resist Modernism's arrival; classicist "fun" was suspended.

Driving along the streets and avenues of D.C.'s monumental and commercial areas, one sees countless office buildings that represent architectural Modernism's effect on the capital's postwar, central-city growth. Although façades vary, there is nevertheless a certain sameness because of consistent height and frequently repetitive colonnaded bottoms.

Behind these façades are the flat slabs, column grids, ductwork, and service cores—elevators, firestairs, toilets, utility rooms, and vertical shafts—that are practically interchangeable from one building to another. They provide the flexible, efficient space that Louis Sullivan, Gropius, and Mies all said was needed for human occupancy and use in the 20th century. And they express the cost-effectiveness and marketability demanded by real estate developers.

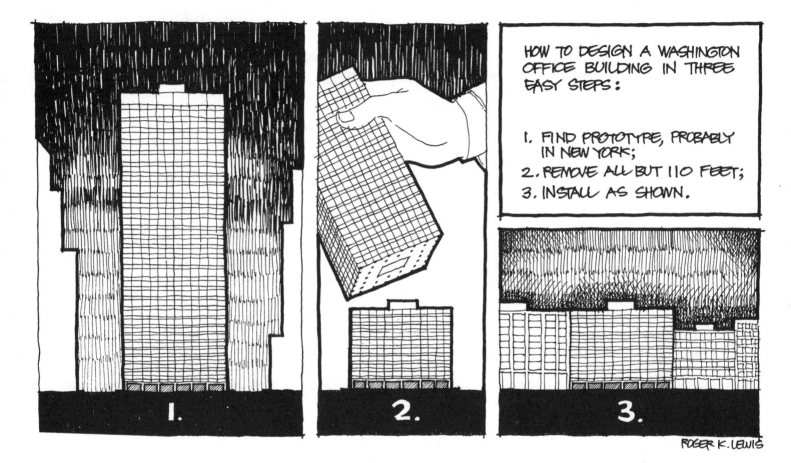

Therefore, façade manipulation, particularly where so many privately owned buildings were constructed on infill lots (as opposed to being freestanding), became the only way to achieve any form of expressive differentiation. But was expressive differentiation desirable? The earlier manifestoes had suggested otherwise. Modern architects had limited tactical choices when manipulating façades if they were to remain faithful to their credos of "less is more" and "form follows function."

A modern building's exterior was expected to reveal in some rational way little more than its skeletal organization, its floor lines, and its dimensional modularity and standardization. Moreover, it was wrapped with a "curtain wall" of relatively minimal thickness hung on the structural frame.

Lots of large, fixed glass windows were mandatory for light and view—energy was cheap and abundant then. Vertical mullions between each window marked the intersection of the partition layout grid—typically based on four-, five-, or six-foot modules—with the exterior surface, the point where interior partitions could abut the window wall.

In turn, some kind of façade element had to occupy the space between the window sills on one floor and the heads of windows on the floor below. Thus, the façades of office buildings seemed well suited to the horizontal, continuous ribbon window strategy that arose in the 1920s and 1930s. Alternating bands of transparent glass and opaque spandrels—these could be brick, precast concrete, stone, metal, or opaque glass—became a favored mode of expression.

This could be further modified and, presumably, enhanced by adding vertical elements to the curtain wall. Thin mullions between windows could be enlarged and stretched vertically up the façade, overlaying both the window and spandrel planes.

Or the architect could telegraph the presence of structural columns behind the curtain wall by widening or thickening only those mullions aligned with the column grid. Such mullions then looked like columns. They too could be extended vertically up the entire façade, much like a raised pilaster on a classical façade, but without the ornamentation.

Still another façade strategy entailed fabricating the curtain wall in large standardized panels, either of metal or precast concrete, spanning from floor to floor. These panels could be one or more window modules in width.

As methodical and limiting as these strategies may sound, substantial variety and decorative effect could nevertheless be achieved. Architects varied the size and proportion of windows, window mullions, window frame details, and curtain wall joint details. Materials could vary greatly in texture, from smooth and slick to rough and reliefed. Modernist dogma dictated that buildings should be monochromatic (plus the glass), but accent colors on integral components were acceptable.

Designers could manipulate the character of the ground floor and the way buildings met the sidewalk by pushing back the plane of storefronts while increasing ground floor height. This left the structural columns in place to form an arcade adjacent to the sidewalk. Window displays, signage, planting, accent lighting, and some entrance "statement" ideally completed the picture.

Before being transformed and implanted in Washington, much-publicized modern office building prototypes had been done elsewhere by well-known architects for well-known clients. Among the most famous are New York's Lever House, designed in 1950 by Gordon Bunshaft of Skidmore, Owings & Merrill, and the Seagram Building by Mies van der Rohe and Philip Johnson, completed in 1958. Both are on Park Avenue. Perhaps more than any others, these two buildings and their architects influenced commercial and corporate architecture throughout the world for almost two decades. Literally hundreds of facsimiles and adaptations exist. In D.C., it is easy to find office buildings that look like sawed-off or stunted versions of these or other similar projects.

The zoning height limit made Washington's versions of these structures often appear to be the bottom third or fourth of an itinerant New York skyscraper. Along H, K, and L Streets between 15th and 21st, you can see plenty of mutations. Slightly taller ones may be seen scattered around the metropolitan area.

Interestingly, the architectural debates of the 1950s and 1960s were not between classical and modern stylists. Instead, they were between architects who, while unquestionably modern, rejected the purist, utopian precepts of orthodox Internationalism in favor of their own personal, stylistic mannerisms. They believed that Modernism was not a style. There were alternatives to the steel, concrete, brick, and glass boxes so vigorously embraced by the architectural profession and much of its clientele.

February 2, 1985

Beautifying the Box

You would probably claim to know a modern building when you see one. Yet there are unquestionably many different modern "styles." What then makes a modern building "modern" if there is no stylistic uniformity? What are Modernism's diversities?

During the last decade or so, critics of modern architecture have tended to treat Modernism in design as if it were a singular style. And the particular style most often cited to illustrate the failure of modern design is that inspired by the work and polemics of Mies van der Rohe, the ultimate modern, "corporate box" architect.

What latter-day critics and presumably much of the public found lacking in many modern buildings were traditional architectural conventions, motifs, and symbols. Having stripped away classical ornament, modern designers allegedly neglected to invent acceptable substitutes for these historic, culturally based elements. Tom Wolfe's *From Bauhaus to Our House* asserts that modern architects condemned such elements as "bourgeois."

But further looking reveals that such simplistic, polarizing, black/white contrasts are misleading. The purity and potential sterility of orthodox Bauhaus and International Style design were not blindly embraced by all post–World War II architects, despite their having studied under the European masters.

Other branches of Modernism sprouted as many architects abandoned the exclusive strictures of the Bauhaus in search of new iconography. Tom Wolfe labeled some of these renegades "apostates," and they included such unlikely bedfellows as Eero Saarinen, Edward Durell Stone, Louis Kahn, I. M. Pei, and even old Bauhauser Marcel Breuer.

One alternative to the minimalist, slick buildings cleanly enveloped in glass, metal, or smooth masonry were buildings that "broke the box." They derived their primary expressive imagery from manipulation of building mass, volumetric complexity, and surface texture or relief. Their architects took many design cues from Le Corbusier's extraordinary work in which he harmoniously combined seemingly abstract, three-dimensional geometric composition with two-dimensional, almost classical proportioning and systematization.

Whole buildings, as well as building façades, offered dynamic sculptural opportunities for the play of solid against void, of light against shade. The chosen material for structure and finishes was often concrete. Notable advocates, among them Yale's Paul Rudolph and Harvard's José Luis Sert, believed that modern buildings should be shaped to show on the exterior specific internal functions, spaces, and service networks.

During this same era, another kind of Modernism evolved, exemplified by Washington's Kennedy Center, completed in 1969. Designed by Edward Durell Stone, it is clearly a modern building smoothly packaged. But this slightly decorated, mas-

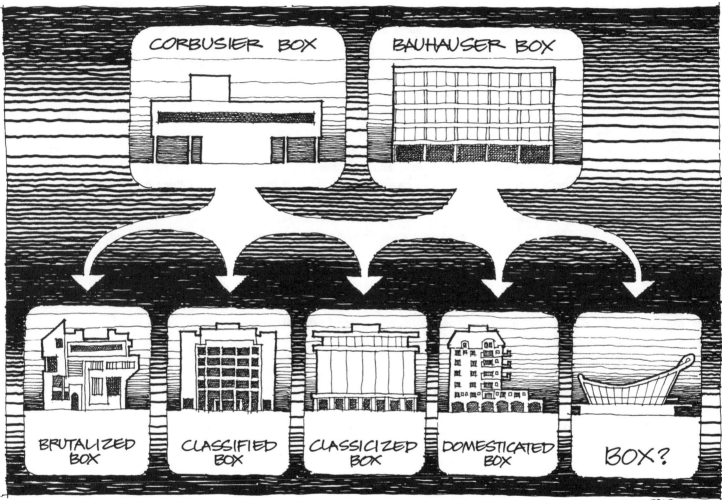

CORBUSIER BOX   BAUHAUSER BOX

BRUTALIZED BOX   CLASSIFIED BOX   CLASSICIZED BOX   DOMESTICATED BOX   BOX?

ROGER K. LEWIS

sive white marble box ringed by slender gold columns alludes in its vaguely classical way to a Greek temple or perhaps the Lincoln Memorial.

Next-door is the enigmatic Watergate complex, designed by Italian architect Luigi Moretti in 1965. Its neo-baroque forms, stop-and-start balconies, and appended details disguise somewhat its massiveness and ribboned horizontality. Someone said that "the Watergate Apartments are a wedding cake and the Kennedy Center is the box it came in."

In 1964, Stone's new building for the National Geographic Society was completed. It had a lidlike top, a colonnaded base, and a skin of mullions and vertical strip windows running from base to lid.

The Museum of American History (formerly Museum of History and Technology) opened in 1964, the first new Mall building since Pope's 1941 National Gallery of Art. The successor firm to McKim, Mead & White designed this blockbuster sheathed in pink Tennessee marble, aspiring to relate its ornament-free mass to the Federal Triangle across Constitution Avenue. The Air and Space Museum, designed in the early 1970s by Hellmuth, Obata & Kassabaum, exhibits similar gestures.

While white boxes and concrete crates were being built, still another brand of Modernism appeared. More humane and pluralistic in detailing, material, and color, these buildings typically made use of brick as well as concrete, metal, glass, wood, and other materials. They generally displayed more scale-giving elements on their façades—railings, balconies, screens, and trim.

Then there was Eero Saarinen, a stylistic chameleon capable of out-Miesing Mies, as he did in his high-tech General Motors Technical Center, while indulging in metaphoric romanticism with his birdlike TWA terminal at Kennedy Airport, and his unprecedented, winglike Dulles International Airport. Conceived in the 1950s, Dulles remains one of the capital area's most memorable and admired structures. But what style or branch of modernism does it represent?

In its own way, Dulles upholds an ageless tradition of exploiting the structure of a building for expressive purposes, like the Capitol's dome or the National Cathedral's pointed arches and flying buttresses. But it clearly depends on modern technology and a language of detail invented, not borrowed, by its architect. Somehow, Saarinen's symbolic design still seems right for its purpose and its Virginia landscape.

As the 1970s began, the pluralism of modern design expanded even further. Mies's influence was weakening. Le Corbusier's was still strong, but architects were listening to other masters: Louis Kahn and his Philadelphia entourage, Charles Moore and his bicoastal (California and Connecticut) entourage, plus nonpractitioner Colin Rowe, an English architectural theorist at Cornell who was influencing a new generation of designers.

In 1966, a relatively unknown architect, Robert Venturi, had written a new, "gentle" manifesto, *Complexity and Contradiction in Architecture*. Its messages would greatly affect the stylistic course of Modernism in the 1970s and 1980s.

February 9, 1985

The Advent of Post-Modernism

If you were to conduct a survey of stores selling furniture or light fixtures, you would probably find that most of their inventory is stylistically "traditional," not "contemporary."

American suburbanites overwhelmingly prefer "traditional" rather than "modern" homes. Subdivisions are full of houses styled Colonial, Federalist, Queen Anne, Cape Cod, or Tudor. The majority of houses built around D.C. have porches, pediments, pilasters, columns with capitals, cornices, and trim—both exterior and interior—whose decorative origins are classical, not modern.

Lawyers, doctors, accountants, trade associations, corporations, and government officials often furnish their office interiors with furniture and decoration recalling or replicating styles of the 18th and 19th centuries, despite the stylistic aspirations of the buildings they occupy.

To many people, modern architectural motifs may seem appropriate for commercial and institutional buildings, but these same individuals persist in adhering to traditional motifs when shaping their personal environments.

Why do so many reject Modernism? Did modern architects fail to interpret properly both history and public taste when searching for new architectural languages? Were American home builders, furniture producers, and antique dealers ahead of architects in understanding the relationship between style, culture, and consumption?

Recall Washington's history. Born in the 18th century, it soon acquired its own distinct architectural heritage of classicism and historic revivalism exemplified by its monuments and buildings, both public and private. In no other American city is this heritage so strong or so readily perceived. This is true today, even though few classically styled buildings were built in D.C. between 1945 and 1975.

Modern buildings in the nation's capital, no matter how well designed, always seemed out of place to some Washingtonians. What proved comfortable in Chicago, New York, Philadelphia, or Los Angeles just did not seem to fit here comfortably.

Yet in the 1960s, "good" architects did not "do" historicist buildings. Such projects were left for those considered hacks or panderers to low-brow tastes. Many architects still practiced according to the exclusivist manifestoes and principles of orthodox Modernism—less is more, form follows function. It was only a matter of time before mainstream sensitivities and taste would embrace the sophisticated values of modern architecture—or so we all believed.

Well, not all. Robert Venturi wrote *Complexity and Contradiction in Architecture* in 1966. His "gentle" manifesto proclaimed that "a valid order accommodates the circumstantial contradictions of a complex reality." Hybrid designs that have "messy vi-

The Advent of Post-Modernism

tality" were preferable to pure and simple ones. "Less is a bore," he wrote, arguing that richness of meaning was better than clarity of meaning, that "more is not less."

What did this all mean to architects? Venturi's manifesto challenged many assumptions made by modern architects as to the role of architecture in society. Venturi suggested that architecture is a medium, not a machine. Buildings could be both symbolic and literal conveyors of messages and memories; this might be ultimately more important than their functional performance or formal rationality and simplicity.

He advocated being inclusive rather than exclusive. He praised ambiguity, plurality, and multiplicity in style and meaning, whether for a building or a city. It was no sin to use ordinary elements—the "honky-tonk," the profane—to make designed environments. Venturi rejected notions of utopian perfectability, asserting that "Main Street, USA" was not only reality but was also esthetically desirable.

Suddenly the old rules were called into question. It sounded like any design at all, even if ugly, might be appropriate if its decoration provided sufficient doses of nostalgic relevance and meaning. These historical and cultural references would be read like a book or experienced like the Las Vegas strip. No compelling, abstract, utopian order was needed.

Similar or derivative themes were sounded by other architectural theoreticians and practitioners. They advocated a "collage" approach to design coupled with the direct use of architectural history, both American and European. In the past resided the primary sources for creating buildings rich in symbolism and allusion, artifacts of memory as well as innovation and prophecy. Abstract, high-tech, or platonic geometries of the Modern Movement, denuded of ornament, were judged incapable of providing any of this.

To strict Modernists who felt themselves liberated from the irrational manners of historicism, revivalism, and eclecticism, this seemed heretical. Were there really no timeless, universal, immutable principles? Was the choice of design styles and motifs merely a matter of personal taste and variable circumstances?

Some architects believed that this new heresy, soon to be labeled Post-Modernism, was merely a polemical reaction to the failure of many modern buildings to charm the public, to solve society's problems, or to achieve other lofty goals enunciated by the original apostles who brought the word from Europe. Some thought it was simply the next phase in the diversification of modernism and were less worried about its polemics.

Since the mid-1970s, many new buildings, most of them privately developed, would wear Post-Modernism's imprecise label, or a piece of it. These fundamentally modern structures have façades that distinguish them in one or several ways from their more orthodox modern brethren:

- They may be polychromatic, using pastel colors and diverse materials, rather than being predominantly monochromatic and monolithic.

- They may use classical elements, building fragments, and ornamental details—Greek or Roman columns, arches and keystones, cornices, pediments, entablatures, friezes, and trim.

- They may echo or caricature such classical elements or motifs without literally duplicating them (elements may be painted on or made of metal, plastic, or plywood).

- They may collage diverse stylistic elements and motifs to achieve visual complexity while still alluding to some single historical style or building overall.

- They may replicate or recall a specific historic building or style of the past—unabashed revivalism—or they may be zealously contextual, mirroring the compositional and stylistic attributes of neighboring or abutting buildings.

The historic building preservation movement also contributed to the growth of Post-Modernism. The reuse of old buildings or the incorporation of their disembodied façades into new buildings led architects to relearn historical styles as they were increasingly obliged to cope with them in practice.

Given Post-Modernism, is "traditional" Modernism dead? Hardly! But one thing is evident. Stylistic pluralism, eclecticism, and permissiveness are today's ordering principles. Architectural styles, like other fashions, now emerge and change at an unprecedented rate.

February 16, 1985

7.

To Save or Not to Save
Historic Preservation

Preservation . . . Desirable but Difficult

Twenty-five years ago, "historic preservation" was hardly a controversial issue in real estate development.

It was a different time. Inner cities needed revitalizing as roads and highways grew longer and wider in the service of expanding suburbia. Renovation and restoration were actions taken only when it made economic and functional sense for older buildings to be saved and modernized.

Otherwise the removal of aging buildings, or for that matter aging neighborhoods, precipitated relatively little debate about old giving way to new. Indeed, the cultural presumption of the era, and for much of this century, was that newer meant better.

Societal sensitivities began changing in the 1960s, however, as people started to question this presumption. Many noticed that often what was new proved esthetically less satisfying than what had been declared obsolete and discarded. They also realized that, in many cases, irreplaceable cultural assets were disappearing forever.

The historic preservation movement gained momentum in part because of renewed interest in all cultural history. Finding and protecting roots became increasingly important. Connections to the past seemed especially relevant at a time when the future appeared both promising and threatening, technologically fertile yet potentially dehumanizing.

Interest in ancestors and antiques, old movies and orthodox religion, intensified. Overwhelming numbers of historically based novels, biographies, TV docudramas, and films appeared. Revivalism ran rampant, as did critics of Modernism.

The efficacy and prudence of postwar public policies aimed at reshaping cities seemed dubious. Many 1950s and 1960s urban renewal efforts met with limited social and economic success over the long run. Not only did basic urban problems persist, but in the process of experimentation vital parts of cities were compromised or destroyed.

In 1961, Jane Jacobs wrote her landmark book, *The Death and Life of Great American Cities*, in which she strongly condemned then popular notions about city life, urban economics, social welfare, and the physical environment. She advocated preserving rather than clearing away the existing fabric of most city neighborhoods. For her, intervention needed to focus on helping people change status rather than on changing streetscapes and demolishing buildings.

Later in the 1960s, academic and professional architects began looking anew at architectural history. Since World War II and the advent of Bauhaus educational philosophy, architecture schools had treated architectural history as an isolated body of factual knowledge—names, places, and dates to be memorized—rather than as a living legacy to be preserved or emulated.

VALUE SHIFTS

FROM THE
1960's...

TO THE
1980's...

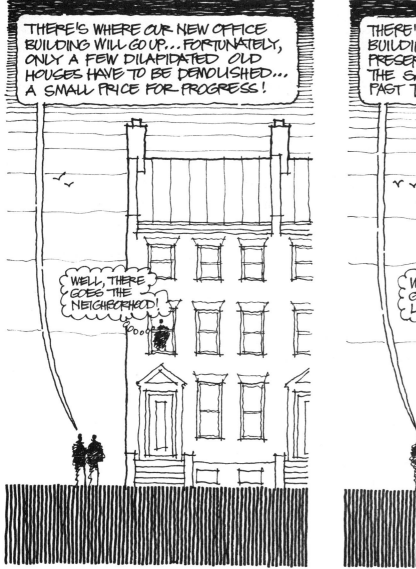

Prevailing avant-garde design values had rejected historicism. It was okay to study history, but not to replicate it. And a corollary of this principle was that most old buildings, unless they could be counted among the great "monuments," were dispensable.

In the last 20 years, contemporary architect/educators, such as Robert Venturi and Charles Moore, have contributed substantially to the profession's rediscovery and reuse of architectural history, beyond the realm of detached scholarship. Just as the public was becoming increasingly sensitized to the past, so too were new generations of architects.

Of course, much of the public had always felt more comfortable living in traditionally styled dwellings. American home builders and manufacturers of furnishings never embraced Modernism enthusiastically. For them, historic preservation meant neo-Colonial houses full of neo-Colonial furniture.

Thus, it is understandable why today more people want to save more old buildings. Architecture is perhaps the most tangible public embodiment of the past. Properly maintained, buildings can endure and be useful for centuries, longer than most other artifacts humans create. They are living museums.

Therefore, why not save most, if not all, old structures and neighborhoods? Why are there still debates about historic preservation? What should be the criteria for declaring buildings and places historic landmarks and saving them for future generations, possibly at great expense?

Addressing these questions first requires acknowledging that both private and public decisions about historic preservation are matters of judgment and point of view, rather than matters of fact. What seems historically precious to one may seem readily disposable or uninteresting to another.

You might perceive a particular neighborhood as a slum marked by poverty, crime, physical deterioration, and social instability. But someone else might perceive it as a temporarily neglected environment symbolizing people, events, and a way of life that should not be forgotten. You might see buildings as obsolete white elephants, but others might see them as venerable remnants of bygone architectural epochs.

There are distinctly different reasons, apart from age, for considering a building something worthy of preservation:

- It may have intrinsic esthetic qualities of design and craftsmanship that are widely recognized—like the Taj Mahal.

- It may exemplify a unique "type" of building, ensemble of buildings, place, or object (without necessarily being the most esthetically compelling example), or be the first of its type. The historic value of such types increases as the number of surviving types diminishes.

- Irrespective of design merits, it may be associated with specific historic events or periods that have special significance to a particular society or societal group. Washington's extinct Rhode's Tavern was such a building.

- Likewise, it may be associated with significant historical figures who designed, built, owned, used, or occupied it—such as Mt. Vernon, George Washington's home on the Potomac River.

- It may have become a literal, physical landmark with symbolic as well as navigational attributes for people who see it or know that it is there—think of Washington's Dupont Circle fountain.

Judgments about historic preservation are really judgments about the meaning of words like *unique, significant, recognized, special, symbolic,* and *esthetic*—and about history itself.

Thus, while acknowledging the value of preservation, we still must decide what not to preserve. For despite our nostalgic impulses, there are still plenty of buildings that have outlived their usefulness without having attained historic status. And we will always need to create new, more technologically sophisticated architecture to accommodate future growth and explore new design possibilities.

Yet even after reaching consensus about what merits saving, actually carrying out historic preservation—economically, legally, politically, technically, and esthetically—remains a formidable and expensive task.

August 8, 1986

Slowing Down
the Wrecking Ball

There was a time when Washington's Willard Hotel, the Old Post Office and Pension buildings, or parts of Alexandria or Georgetown might have been razed to make room for new development.

And as recently as 10 years ago, few real estate developers, mortgage lenders, architects, or contractors would have seriously considered attaching new buildings to old façades.

What has changed? Most important, attitudes and sensitivities have shifted. Architecture of the past, notable either for its esthetic or historic significance, is being identified and admired by an increasingly larger segment of the public. For many, aging architectural relics hold more appeal than the modern edifices typically replacing them.

Diverse interest groups—ordinary citizens and consumers, architects, developers, government officials, and politicians—have

been willing to do more than just recognize such architecture. Individually and collectively, many have committed substantial energy and resources to the preservation, restoration, or adaptive reuse of these structures.

State and national registers of historic districts, neighborhoods, and buildings have been established, creating a systematically documented inventory of America's architectural heritage. While registering does not automatically preserve a building, at least it makes everyone stop and think before moving in the wrecking balls and bulldozers.

Federal, state, and municipal laws have been enacted to encourage or even ensure architectural preservation, sometimes through the provision of income and property tax benefits for owner/investors (benefits no longer being preserved).

Finally, architects and their clients have invented unprecedented, sometimes ingenious design concepts for capitalizing on historic preservation opportunities.

What are the basic strategies for saving old buildings, or fragments of old buildings? How can preservation be carried out while

simultaneously creating late 20th-century environments with state-of-the-art materials and technologies?

First consider historically authentic restoration. Its intent is to restore, rather than to remodel, older buildings or environments so they appear essentially as they did when first designed and constructed.

Historic restoration, like most other approaches to preservation, demands thorough, careful research. Architects and historians must discover and reconstruct physical conditions that may no longer exist. Both historic documentation and field studies yield the necessary clues and evidence.

Restoration experts try to recreate faithfully forms, details, and decoration as they originally were or might have been at a given time and place. Prevalent styles, construction techniques, materials, and colors are examined in an attempt to achieve accurate reproduction. Restoration almost al-

163

ROGER K. LEWIS

ways involves remedial construction—fixing or rebuilding worn, deteriorating, or collapsing components—common to most types of preservation work.

Restoration research and reconstruction efforts are painstaking and tedious. Both architects and builders must possess detectivelike instincts, inexhaustible patience, and a desire for perfection. Diligent craftsmanship, even more than creativity, is indispensable.

Unlike pure restoration, adaptive reuse of antique buildings generally seeks to transform old structures into new ones without significantly changing original, exterior architectural imagery. Adaptive reuse is akin to organ transplantation. Skin and skeleton remain intact, but innards are replaced, giving an old body new life.

Usually a building's "shell"—foundation, superstructure, and façades—are preserved while its interior spaces, partition-ing, and mechanical systems (heating, airconditioning, plumbing, electrical, lighting) are rebuilt to accommodate new uses and exploit new technologies.

The degree of adaptive reuse and renovation depends on the age and condition of the historic artifact. Sometimes old buildings need complete gutting, with only foundations, outer walls, and roof structures remaining. In this case, floors are reconstructed and additional new levels may be added, increasing total usable floor area without affecting the façades or overall bulk of the original building. Preserved façades still may need remedial attention—new windows, masonry repair, moisture proofing, and thermal insulation.

Developers and architects have successfully recycled aging buildings that, a few years ago, would have been routinely demolished. Old schools, factories, and warehouses have been converted into housing, hotels, offices, and shopping marts. Not only have single buildings been transformed, but numbers of disparate, abutting buildings have been amalgamated to bring multi-use projects under unified management.

Preserving and interconnecting contiguous urban buildings for new commercial uses saves both the buildings and the existing city fabric and streetscape. But sometimes, the forces of urban growth and zoning mandate densities well above existing, historic densities. When this occurs, how can old structures on a site be saved as site density is substantially raised?

The new-to-old graft is the answer. Employing this strategy, owners and architects preserve parts of existing structures while adding new construction around, above, or behind them.

More and more prevalent is the façade graft, in which only one or two of an older building's exterior walls are saved. The rest of the building, including its foundation, disappears. This fragmentary preservation strategy requires very careful demolition of the original structure, plus elaborate temporary shoring and bracing of the preserved façades while new construction proceeds behind them.

Occasionally an old façade may be wide and high enough to mask completely the new edifice. But more often it is absorbed into a larger façade composition, either integrated into the new skin or projecting out from it.

Surrounding new façades can visually echo preserved façades through the use of similar materials, colors, textures, and window patterns. However, architects often go the other way, opting for contrast rather than analogy by designing new façades that differ radically from old ones. The visual presence of richly composed, historic façades, offset against more neutral, minimalist façade surfaces, may be enhanced.

All methods of preservation pose recurring questions, cost being among the most persistent. With few exceptions, preservation projects entail considerable time and expense, often more than required when creating new architecture from scratch (even after demolition of older structures). For commercial property, higher development costs obviously mean higher rents and sales prices.

Beyond cost, however, is the question of appropriateness—not only economic, but also historic and esthetic. Indeed, some of the architectural results, particularly these associated with grafting, seem awkwardly contrived. New-to-old blends sometimes appear to make caricatures of both new and old. Moreover, not everything that is old is beautiful.

Should only a building's façade be saved—a very costly undertaking—as if cultural and architectural history were only skin deep? And why should late 20th-century architecture be increasingly unwilling to manifest its own history, likewise preservable at a future time?

It would be nice if we could be more optimistic about modernity and, at the same time, not have to tear down really wonderful old buildings and neighborhoods.

August 16, 1986

What Is Historic?
... A Matter
of Judgment

Imagine that some future American president proposed abandoning the White House in favor of a newer, more modest presidential dwelling closer to the Potomac River. Suppose, further, that the president's proposal included tearing down the White House and selling off its site at a record-high price.

Certainly few Americans would support such an absurd proposal, no matter how economically pragmatic. The historic significance of the White House is universally understood, even by the most naive. Its preservation, notwithstanding the cost or consequences, probably could never be in doubt.

On the other hand, suppose you lived in an aging but architecturally undistinguished house and decided to remodel it drastically or tear it down. You probably could obtain demolition and building permits without too much opposition from neighbors or preservationists.

Your house and the White House obviously are two extremes where preservation choices seem clear. But between them lie most of the buildings and neighborhoods that you see and occupy. Thus, how do you decide which of the in-between environments to save and not to save, knowing that you should neither save nor demolish just because of age?

The Old Executive Office Building, originally built to house the War, Navy, and State Departments next to the White House, today seems to be indisputably worthy of preservation. Yet for many decades after its completion and well into the 20th century, its removal was a popular idea and periodically a foregone conclusion. How could anyone have seriously contemplated demolishing so unique and historic a structure? The response may be obvious now, but it was not to a previous generation.

It may be currently fashionable and often justifiable to deprecate the Modernist, commercial buildings that filled American downtowns and suburbs over the past 25 years. But 50 years from now, who can be certain that our nostalgia would not turn toward architecture now treated with disdain?

The dilemma of deciding what parts of the past to preserve and what to destroy is well illustrated by the controversy surrounding the Park and Shop property on Connecticut Avenue in Washington's Cleveland Park neighborhood. The vacant, one-story L-shaped shopping center with its parking lot in front now sits in disrepair while awaiting official decisions about its designation as a historic landmark.

The Cafritz Company has owned the Park and Shop for over 30 years and wants to sell it for new development requiring demolition of the existing building. The site is zoned for much more intensive commercial use. An entrance to the Cleveland Park Metro station abuts the site's southwest corner, making it a very attractive piece of real estate.

However, to many citizens of Cleveland Park and some preservationists, this is not just another obsolete, anachronistic commercial building. On the contrary, they

claim that the Park and Shop, built in 1930 by Shannon & Luchs, represents the first of its type in Washington, an early example of "a neighborhood shopping center oriented for the automobile in which the supermarket was the anchor facility."

In the application for designation of the property as a historic landmark (which would prevent its immediate demolition), preservation proponents cited its significance "as an integral and substantial part of the Cleveland Park neighborhood shopping district—the best remaining example of a linear neighborhood commercial development in Washington, D.C."

The application further elaborated on the center's history and occupancy, its architect (Arthur B. Heaton, for 13 years supervising architect of the National Cathedral), its architectural style (Colonial Revival) and esthetic appropriateness, its role as a prototype for subsequent strip commercial centers, and its relationship to the Connecticut Avenue corridor, one of Washington's original streetcar lines.

All of this was intended to demonstrate to D.C.'s Historic Preservation Review Board that this property, in toto, is "significant" —culturally and architecturally. The applicants also had to show that "sufficient time has passed since [it] achieved significance or [was] constructed to permit professional evaluation . . . in [its] historical context."

Cafritz, along with others less enchanted by the Park and Shop, saw the matter differently. To them, it was inconceivable that such an undistinguished building wrapping around a parking lot could be considered historically significant, even if the project was among the first of its kind. They wondered if the Park and Shop was at all meaningful to anyone other than immediate neighbors and interested preservationists, the argument being that a "historic landmark" should be significant to a broader segment of the community.

What they saw was, at best, a mediocre precursor of street-compromising architecture that mostly celebrated the needs of the automobile. They saw a building of dubious constructional and stylistic merit, regardless of opinions stated or published in the 1930s and 1980s.

This property constituted a hole in the urban fabric, much in need of mending. And mending it not only would improve the look and usefulness of the site, it also could contribute positively to the Connecticut Avenue streetscape (assuming that new development was well conceived).

In addition to feeling entitled to freedom of choice about use of a property owned for three decades, Cafritz felt that economic and legal entitlements were being unreasonably threatened. How could an owner be forced to maintain ownership and operation of a dilapidated, financially impractical building on a valuable parcel of land, made even more valuable (and appropriate for denser development) by the abutting Metro stop?

Moreover, those questioning preservation likewise questioned Cleveland Park preservationists' motives, suspecting that historic preservation was really being used as a tool to block potentially undesirable real estate development. Indeed, Cleveland Park residents have been frank in expressing concerns about this part of Connecticut Avenue being invaded by buildings similar to those over other Metro stations.

Who is right? Should the Park and Shop be saved or torn down? Ultimately, it is a matter of opinion, not fact.

If you are convinced of the significance of this structure and its importance to Cleveland Park, Connecticut Avenue, the city, and perhaps even the nation, then you must vote for its preservation, even if it means abrogating private property rights or forgoing new services and facilities.

But if you are not convinced that the Park and Shop is a historic landmark, if you doubt its cultural or architectural significance, then you must vote for demolition.

Either choice entails risks. Save it, and a few years hence, people might see it as an eyesore whose continued existence proved ultimately irrelevant to the visual character or quality of life in a Cleveland Park of the future.

Demolish the Park and Shop, and another banal, poorly scaled, charmless edifice might rise in its place, vindicating the anxieties of citizens wary about new development.

Clearly, the Park and Shop is one of those somewhere-in-between buildings, neither anonymous nor monumental. And the Historic Preservation Review Board, despite all of its collective wisdom, must finally gamble as it deliberates about the meaning of the words *significant*, *historic*, and *landmark*.

August 23, 1986

Adding to Venerable Architecture

Washington, D.C.'s, Preservation League used to be known as "Don't Tear It Down," a name precisely summarizing the organization's once narrower credo and mission.

But today's historic preservation agenda is broader. Preservation is no longer a fringe movement. The idea of preservation has permeated contemporary culture, vindicating much of the stridency and struggle of the recent past. Citizens in general, along with architects, planners, politicians, and developers, are more aware of and sensitive to the value of venerable architecture.

Nevertheless, preservation controversy continues on different fronts. Battles are sometimes fought not over whether to save a historic structure, but, rather, over how new architecture should be added to old, over the esthetics of a preserved structure's expansion or remodeling.

Adding new to old is especially perilous when buildings needing enlargement truly enjoy landmark status. Moreover, debate over architectural strategies can be as lively for monuments built 20 or 30 years ago as for those erected in previous centuries.

Recent and notable battles involve some very famous museums. Two are in New York City—the Whitney Museum of American Art and the Guggenheim. Each was designed by a modern architectural master—the Whitney by Marcel Breuer in the early 1960s and the Guggenheim by Frank Lloyd Wright in the late 1950s.

The Whitney, located on Madison Avenue at 75th Street, has always been a controversial building. An inverted, granite-garbed ziggurat abutting the avenue, its abstract, nearly windowless form cantilevers out in steps over a sunken, moatlike sculpture garden between the sidewalk and the building's base. Visitors cross a bridge to enter.

Even in the 1960s, many criticized the Whitney's brutalism, accusing it of being anti-urban, visually aggressive, uninviting, oppressive. Others admired its simple, un-adorned but audacious geometry. Despite conflicting and evolving tastes, however, the Whitney over time became a well-known cultural and architectural landmark in Manhattan. And most agreed that it was a historically significant representative of both Marcel Breuer's work and one branch of 20th-century architectural ideology.

After two decades, the Whitney needed desperately to expand. With avenue property available next door, an addition could be contemplated that would more than double the museum's gallery, administrative, service, and storage space.

Architect Michael Graves, hired to design the Whitney's new addition, had to decide how to take an existing, famous building, one that has its own integrity and ego, and add to it. Furthermore, the new Whitney addition was to be substantially larger than the original.

Graves understood the theoretical options—related to both style and geometry—for marrying new and old:

- Extension by literal replication—creating a duplicate or clone of the original,

- Extension by allusion and abstract reference—using analogous or transformed motifs from the original,

- Extension by contrast—building an addition whose form and style differ intentionally, even radically, from the original,

- Extension by detachment—visually separating new from old while still making internal links for functional purposes,

- Extension by envelopment—creating a new, larger composition engulfing and subordinating the original.

Graves chose a mixture of allusion, abstraction and, above all, envelopment. The old Whitney was to become one element among many in a much larger, block-long collage of parts. The addition, with new masses abutting and sitting on top of the original structure, would clearly overpower and subsume Breuer's work. The latter's façade and cantilevered profile would still be in evidence, but only as supporting actors in a new architectural play.

Many New Yorkers, and no small number of architects, were outraged by Graves's and the Whitney's proposal. Although pleased that the original was not to be torn down, some critics saw its prospective transformation as perhaps an even worse fate than demolition. To them, Graves's design was a disrespectful affront to Breuer and his building, equivalent to defacing a work of art. They were not opposed to an enlarged Whitney, but rather to Graves's strategy for aggrandizement.

At about the same time, on Fifth Avenue, the Guggenheim trustees were facing an equally thorny challenge. In their bid to expand, they hired New York architects Gwathmey-Siegel to come up with a design for an addition to an even more famous building by perhaps the world's most famous architect.

Like the Whitney, the Guggenheim occupies a corner site, but the only land available is in back of the museum, adjacent to the cross-town street. And the circular, layered geometry of Wright's Guggenheim, unlike the rectilinear Whitney, defies emulation or envelopment; it is a complete and closed organism. Thus the architects chose to extend by detachment and contrast.

They proposed a thin, flat service tower along the interior property line. Well behind and above the Guggenheim's north wing, the tower would support a taut-skin, cantilevered box containing office, storage, and conservation functions on several floors. Presumably, this would preserve the integrity of the original by avoiding contact with it, except for a low-profile connection at the rear of the north wing.

People were still shocked. "Guggenheim Neighbors" was organized and brought in lawyers and architects to oppose the project. Joining them were innumerable critics, few of whom hedged in stating their feelings.

Wrote Kay Larson in *New York Magazine*: "The proposed addition to the Guggenheim forms the tank of a toilet, and Wright's spiral is the bowl."

New York Times architecture critic Paul Goldberger commented: "Whatever its merits, the addition is hardly a discreet work of architecture. It may be tight, well-composed and disciplined, but it is still a huge mass looming over one of the greatest buildings of modern times."

And *Progressive Architecture* opined:

"The fundamental issue is not whether this addition is right or wrong, compatible or crushing, but whether there should be an addition at all, let alone one of this size, in this location."

A similar battle has engulfed the Louvre in Paris, where I. M. Pei has designed an immense addition to this venerable museum. But his solution puts all the new space underground, below the great courtyard, thereby leaving the existing buildings completely untouched. However, to create and signal the museum's new public entry below the plaza level, he designed a giant, 100-foot-high glass pyramid to sit in the middle of the courtyard.

Notwithstanding his rationale for the scheme—the pyramid is a contrasting, platonic form, ancient in origin, simple, transparent—many Parisians, along with critics far and wide, object strongly to this supposedly minimal intrusion. They see it as being out of character with the Louvre's classicism, too high-tech, too big, too disruptive to the Louvre's courtyard.

In the final analysis, few would argue that these museums are not entitled to expand in the interest of serving the public more effectively. Yet no matter how talented their architects or how ingenious the designs, modifying these landmark buildings is inevitably a compromise. And how you feel about such compromises ultimately depends less on facts and intentions than on taste and priorities.

November 15, 1986

Cloning Historic Buildings

The U.S. Department of the Interior, through the National Park Service, reviews proposals for rehabilitations of, or extensions to, historic buildings whose owners seek tax credits available under current law. Naturally, the secretary of the interior has promulgated "Standards for Rehabilitation," design guidelines for owners and architects that preclude changing the "character" of venerable architecture.

However, one of the standards suggests an alternative approach:

"Contemporary design for alterations and additions to existing properties shall not be discouraged when such alterations and additions do not destroy significant historic, architectural, or cultural material, and such design is compatible with the size, scale, color, material, and character of the property, neighborhood, or environment."

This "contemporary design" policy statement, obviously open to broad interpretation, seems to propose that new design and construction be of its time—esthetically, technologically, economically—yet sympathetic with the original to which it is grafted. Does this mean that replication, or cloning, of historic buildings is undesirable?

In fact, some preservationists and preservation administrators are much more emphatic than the regulation, insisting that new additions to historic buildings be clearly distinguishable from the original. Their theory is that imperfect imitation is not sincere flattery. They see replication in any form as unauthentic and superficial, a lampooning of truly historic architecture.

How then does one accommodate new design next to old? How can the apparent conflict between achieving compatibility and differentiation be resolved?

Unfortunately, neither the secretary's standards nor any other published reference offer definitive answers. Responses to such questions depend on subjective judgments, on personal perception, and experience. This applies to owners, architects, neighbors, passersby, government officials, and even historians.

Moreover, time and place affect judgments. What seems appropriate today might seem inappropriate 10 years from now as design trends evolve. A design that appears to "fit" Washington, D.C., might not seem fitting in Chicago, Sante Fe, or other places with different regional architectural traditions.

Adding new to old in Washington is especially challenging, despite codified rules governing street widths, setbacks, and building height and bulk. The difficulties involve design specifics—where to place additions in relation to existing buildings, how to make visual connections, what motifs and materials to use.

ROGER K. LEWIS

Expansion is also tricky in the case of relatively pure neoclassical or revivalist buildings that already seem complete, balanced, and symmetrical. Imagine trying to enlarge the Old Executive Office Building, the Lincoln or Jefferson Memorials, or the Library of Congress (where this problem was circumvented by building an entirely independent addition, the Madison Building).

Perhaps this is why popular images of the White House are typically ground-level, axial views of the central block and porticoes, always framed by trees (as in Gary Trudeau's "Doonesbury" drawings). Seen from the air with its awkwardly extended east and west wings, the White House complex as a whole seems much less elegant.

This is also why the National Gallery of Art wisely chose to expand by building a new, completely detached and differently styled East Building across 4th Street, several hundred feet away from John Russell Pope's 1941 Beaux-Arts edifice. Linked underground, each of the two buildings maintains its own integrity while, at a proper distance, they respect one another.

Likewise, the Smithsonian decided to expand its facilities for exhibition and parking on the Mall's south side by building underground rather than adding new wings to its picturesque yet compositionally complete Victorian buildings. Not only did this preserve the structures, it also preserved and enhanced the garden court facing Independence Avenue.

Recall past debates accompanying attempts to expand the Capitol Building. Design equilibrium and preservation seem finally to have been achieved. Despite continual interior revisions and exterior refurbishing, there now is little danger that some new hulk or wing will be added to this undeniably complete architectural monument.

Then there is the Willard Hotel, closed in 1968 and now reopened as the Willard Intercontinental. The original Willard was designed in a neoclassical French Empire style—with a bit of Italy thrown in—at the beginning of this century by architect Henry Hardenbergh.

The Willard's place, as a place, in the political and social history of Washington is legendary. However, as architecture per se, its significance was thought marginal until its preservation was actively sought and then assured through both private and public efforts since its closing.

Today's Willard complex is the result of a lengthy process entailing a design competition, a turnover of developers and architects, and much work by the Pennsylvania Avenue Development Corporation. A privately owned and operated commercial enterprise, the hotel's survival and ongoing economic feasibility depended on both restoration and expansion—mostly for office space—of the original building.

Unlike many famous Washington edifices, the Willard was an open-ended (or open-sided, to be accurate), street-wall building. The 1901 hotel stretched from Pennsylvania Avenue, fronted by its principal, almost symmetrical façade, north along 14th Street, then turned west on F Street to form an interior courtyard enclosed on the west by other abutting buildings. A C in plan, it could easily accommodate westward expansion toward the Washington Hotel (the open side of the C).

The basic design approach, proposed initially during the 1978 competition by New York architects Hardy Holzman Pfeiffer, was eventually carried out by Washington's Vlastimil Koubek for the Oliver Carr Company. The solution: a contemporary clone job.

The innovative massing of the addition creates a series of pavilionlike, seemingly telescoped volumes stepping up in height from the street as they increase in width. The nested pavilions complete the courtyard space, which connects diagonally to the street. A kind of triumphal colonnade frames the new courtyard's emergence at the sidewalk. Like Peacock Alley inside the original hotel, the courtyard leads pedestrians all the way through the block up to F Street.

On the other hand, the architects and their clients opted for façades stylistically reproducing—but not quite—the original Willard. Mimicking its roof geometry, cornices, brackets, balustrades, pediments, entablatures, ocular windows, and simulated rustication, they created a series of mini-Willards that are cartoons of the original.

It is cute and clever, but is such cloning really the most sympathetic treatment of the venerable Willard? Will it hold up visually and substantively over time? Is this packaging really more compatible with the original than a less imitative set of façades would have been?

The Willard design strategy has proved popular and was certainly approved for tax credit purposes. But I hope it does not signal a trend or suggest that, when faced with adding new to old, the only thing architects can do with confidence is produce clones of originals. To the former rallying cry, "don't tear it down," I would add "don't mock it up."

November 22, 1986

Saving More Than Buildings

A recent visit to several cities in eastern Canada—Toronto, Ottawa, Montreal, and Quebec—reminded me that preserving an occasional historic building from time to time is inadequate as a strategy for historic preservation.

For part of the magic of these cities, especially Quebec, derives from the continued, animated existence of entire neighborhoods or city sections first built in the 17th, 18th, or 19th centuries.

Few buildings of yesteryear emerge as uniquely monumental or exceptionally historic. But collectively such structures and streets form an irreplaceable cultural legacy, an unforgettable architectural experience that fuses past and present.

Canada's municipal, provincial, and national governments undoubtedly had to work together to ensure the survival and maintenance of these sites. Likewise in the United States, urban historic preservation efforts have required city, state, and federal collaboration. However, this is a relatively recent phenomenon.

Historic preservation as a national, civic endeavor acquired momentum and legitimacy in the United States only in the last 20 years. Fortunately, during preceding decades, concerned citizens of towns and cities energetically fought to safeguard the nation's architectural heritage despite the absence of governmental legislation and economic incentives.

One recalls both this heritage and those citizens who sought—and fought—to protect it when walking through historic Annapolis, Maryland; Old Town Alexandria, Virginia; D.C.'s Georgetown; or other urban districts physically rooted in previous centuries.

But there are other reasons to save and use venerable pieces of cities. All of the charm, picturesqueness, and visual enticements of such historic places are not attributable solely to their being historic or aged.

Strolling along 200-year-old sidewalks while looking at 200-year-old buildings, one cannot help but be charmed by the usually intimate, human scale of antique streetscapes. The textures of façades—often composed of brick or stone punctured by familiar patterns of small windows—seem more accessible and personal. User-friendly elements such as porches, entry gardens, low wood or iron fences, and shade trees heighten the streetscape's charm while simultaneously softening hard-edged architecture.

Streets in many historic districts seem dedicated to pedestrians, having been originally laid out to accommodate people, horses, and carriages instead of rapidly moving motorized traffic. Even intensely commercial streets can have a domestic scale to them, their display windows and doors beckoning to passersby who walk or drive along.

Alexandria's royally named streets, Annapolis's Main and Duke of Gloucester streets, and the streets of Georgetown all have proportions, heights and widths, rhythmic architectural elements, and occupancies that are timeless. Their character still can be duplicated using contemporary technology for contemporary purposes.

Indeed, municipal governments have attempted officially to recognize and promote historically reminiscent architectural and urban design values. Many have enacted legislation requiring developers and architects to follow certain design guidelines when undertaking construction in historic districts, whether building from scratch or adding something new to something old.

Preservation-minded codes frequently mandate that existing, dominant design features be respected and maintained. Choices of materials and colors may be prescribed or limited. Types of windows, doors, decoration, or roofs may be subject to regulation, along with setbacks, cornice line heights, planting, and location of parking and drives.

Rarely do design codes actually designate or require a specific style. Alexandria, for example, does not demand that all buildings in Old Town be styled strictly early Colonial, Georgian, Federal, or Greek Revival. What they seek instead is harmony between old and new that transcends literal replication. The goal is to ensure, through law, perceptible compatibility without unduly restricting the design freedom so coveted by architects and their clients.

Nevertheless, architects feel that some design regulations unreasonably limit architectural possibilities. Forced to choose between replicating or caricaturing historic neighbors, designers occasionally end up producing hybrid buildings that lack both the charm and authenticity of older structures. Even with design codes, there is usually just enough flexibility for things to go wrong esthetically.

The most common shortcoming of many historically mandated, contemporary buildings is their distortion of scale and proportion. This results partly from the use of specific elements and compositional motifs—large sliding glass doors and windows, indelicate railings, inappropriate fenestration patterns, oversize brick—that depart substantially from those characteristic of the existing fabric.

Older buildings and streets typically exhibit small-scale details and fine-grained patterns that are subtle yet indispensable to overall visual imagery and spatial identity. If these details and patterns are not echoed in new development, basic streetscape character intended for preservation may be compromised or lost.

Projects sometimes must be built in historic districts that are almost impossible to make fit in. Try a parking garage. In the 1970s, Annapolis had to face a problem encountered sooner or later by every municipality—a critical shortage of parking. The town was growing rapidly, with more government and business activity, boating, and tourism. Its 18th- and 19th-century historic district was increasingly being besieged and choked by automobiles with no place to go.

How could its buildings and streetscapes be preserved if hundreds of cars had to be accommodated? How could a massive parking structure ever be placed in such an environment without seriously violating it, even if vaguely disguised (perhaps behind brick walls full of arched openings or fake double-hung windows)?

The answer was to build a garage within Annapolis's downtown blocks, behind the historic buildings fronting the two principal streets, so that the garage itself had no direct street frontage.

Designed by Washington architect Paul Spreiregen, the parking garage was not obliged to disguise itself in pseudo-Colonial garb. Instead it became a structurally honest, utilitarian, late 20th-century building ingeniously and unobtrusively tucked into Annapolis's 18th-century fabric. And visitors, realizing that Annapolis's narrow streets are meant for cruising on foot, not in cars, quickly found it much easier to park in the garage and walk around town, even to destinations several blocks away.

All of this suggests that preserving historic districts while continuing to build within them is no small challenge. It requires considerable sensitivity and skill on the part of architects, plus a willingness on the part of developers to finance and construct what is appropriate but perhaps unconventional.

Like Annapolis and Old Town Alexandria, communities everywhere feel the need to encourage growth and change while preserving historic neighborhoods. Clearly money, design talent, and public will are essential. Nostalgia, laissez-faire government, and red brick alone are not enough.

September 6, 1986

Preservation and Public Policy

Celebrating the 20th anniversary of the National Historic Preservation Act, signed into law by President Lyndon Baines Johnson on October 15, 1966, was the major agenda item at the 40th National Preservation Conference held in Kansas City.

The National Trust for Historic Preservation, which sponsors the conference, recently reminded its newsletter readers that "the 1966 law set in motion two decades of progress that have brought expansion of the National Register of Historic Places to more than 45,000 listings, creation of historic preservation offices in every state and establishment of the Advisory Council on Historic Preservation to monitor thousands of federal and federally assisted projects."

It further recalls that "the law paved the way for innovative partnerships between all levels of government and the private sector . . . for creation of the National Historic Preservation Fund and a wide variety of regulatory and financial incentives for restoring and rehabilitating old and historic properties."

But today the policies and actions supported by the 1966 preservation act are in jeopardy. Gramm-Rudman and new tax legislation are likely to dampen considerably future preservation efforts.

The balanced-budget amendment, given current fiscal priorities, already is reducing the amount spent by federal agencies for preservation-oriented operations and projects. At the same time, the new tax law curtails or eliminates some tax shelters considered essential for motivating investment in the preservation of historic properties. The real estate industry in general, as well as preservationists, are very nervous about the impact that this legislation might have on future activity.

Most industry experts agree that diminishing tax shelter benefits—some would rather call them incentives—derived from depreciation deductions and investment credits will turn investors away from real estate. The old law allowed investment losses and credits to offset income from any source. The new law's "passive loss rule" permits offsetting only income from the investment itself or from other rental real estate.

Tax reform skeptics foresee property sales and values falling off, declines in new construction and renovation, and even voluntary defaults and foreclosures as limited partners lose tax deductions while being dunned for more cash.

These are undoubtedly serious concerns. But debate about the economic consequences of tax reform has tended to eclipse debate about its noneconomic impact.

Tax policy, as it has evolved over several decades, often has been used to achieve noneconomic goals—primarily social and cultural ones. Among the cultural goals has been the preservation of historically significant buildings, monuments, special sites, neighborhoods, and urban districts.

New tax legislation still offers very attractive tax credits to those who commit funds to the preservation, restoration, and rehabilitation of certified historic structures and places. Congress upheld the assumption that historic preservation, usually a tedious and expensive undertaking, would not occur, that investments would not be made nor risks taken, without special incentives.

In fact, the 1981 tax code revisions pertaining to rehabilitation of historic properties provided almost irresistible tax credits and accelerated depreciation benefits for historic property investment. The availability of this particular tax shelter strategy clearly accounts for much of the surge in preservation-minded real estate development over the last five years.

The rehabilitation and recent rebirth of Washington's Willard Hotel, now the Willard Intercontinental, might never have occurred were it not for the 1981 tax law

modifications. This costly, risky project needed the substantial financial incentives provided by the tax code. Notwithstanding the city's desire for a restored Willard and the Pennsylvania Avenue Development Corporation's commitment to its preservation, only money—in whatever form— could actually make it happen. Thus, an indirect financial tactic directly saved a piece of culture and history.

Now, however, prevailing governmental philosophy is shifting. Today's reformers presumably are seeking to repurify tax policy and regulation so that only economic issues and consequences are addressed in the tax law. Historic preservation, cited by a Senate committee as a "minor issue," will have to be dealt with elsewhere.

But where? While striving to distill tax policy into purely economic fractions, the administration and Congress hardly have considered new policies or laws aimed at ensuring the continued achievement of noneconomic goals so recently deemed worthwhile.

Regardless of one's ideological stance, the future will not be easy. Public expenditures that encourage building are being reduced.

The national economy is stagnant as both budgetary and trade deficits worsen. Many basic industries are seriously depressed, unable to compete in world markets. And according to recent studies, real personal income over the last 15 years actually has been declining.

Meanwhile, in the continuing guns-or-butter debate at the national level, guns seem to prevail. If national defense and cheerleading become the only concerns of the federal government, can states, municipalities, and private business really generate the policies and monies indispensable for other societal missions, of which historic preservation is one?

Saving, rehabilitating, and reusing old structures worthy of preservation is expensive. If destined only for the affluent, incentives and subsidies perhaps would never be required. But this is not the case. Incentives and subsidies, whatever their source, are indispensable. If they are not created through tax legislation, then other means must be found.

Preservation of historically significant buildings and neighborhoods is a legitimate national, as well as local, concern (along with promoting the arts, education, public health, and private commerce). Therefore, national, state, and city governments together must reconsider and adopt new policies affecting investment in preservation in light of today's economic realities and tomorrow's tax laws.

This is not a new idea. The 1966 Historic Preservation Act clearly intended to establish a partnership between private and public sectors, and between all levels of government. Unfortunately, the federal government seems to be pulling out of the deal.

September 13, 1986

8.

The Architect's Task
Shaping the Built Environment

Why Be
an Architect?

What does the word *architect* bring to mind? Is it Gary Cooper playing the incorruptible Howard Ruark in Ayn Rand's *The Fountainhead*? Perhaps it is Mr. Brady of "The Brady Bunch" or Paul Newman interpreting electrical drawings in his office/boudoir atop *The Towering Inferno*.

You might think of the architect as someone who is creative and sensitive, makes blueprints, possesses some technical expertise, lives well, and hobnobs mostly with affluent clients and friends. If you are like lots of people, an architect is really what you always wanted to be.

Paradoxically, architects design much of the physical environment that citizens see, use, or inhabit, yet most citizens do not know an architect, and very few ever have occasion to employ or work with an architect.

Until the 19th century, architecture was not recognized as a distinct, learned profession. For many centuries and in many cultures, buildings were built by knowledgeable artists and craftsmen who had mastery of building technology along with traditions and conventions of design and decoration.

The Industrial Revolution, increased specialization, new technologies, and more rigorous scholarship made architecture a legitimate academic discipline and profession separated from construction contracting, real estate development, and engineering. This has been reinforced by statutory recognition of the architectural profession; all 50 states require that architects be licensed to practice building design.

Civilization has always recognized its architects, some of whom are well remembered for their buildings, ideas, or both. Names like Michelangelo and Frank Lloyd Wright come to mind. But more monuments than architects remain in our collective memories. Who designed the buildings of ancient Greece, Rome, Byzantium, or Gothic Europe? Who conceived the temples of Angkor in Cambodia or the incredible mosques of the Islamic world?

To understand architects today, you must understand more than the services they provide. You must instead look at motivations and goals forged by history, tradition, and circumstances on the one hand, and by attributes of personality on the other.

Developers and contractors are normally motivated by the promise of economic rewards linked to market opportunities. While this is true for some architects, most realize that, contrary to popular opinion, the economic rewards of practicing architecture are modest when compared to other ways of making a living, and especially when compared to equivalent success in law, medicine, real estate development, banking, or contracting.

Why, then, be an architect if indeed it is not the greatest or easiest way to make a living?

The Architect and Client Communicating

Artistic and intellectual fulfillment is one reason. Most architects are turned on by visual rather than literary or political phenomena. They love to draw and express themselves in graphic terms. Like addicts, they are irresistibly stimulated by things visual: events, buildings, spaces, art. Thus, the chance to create art, to explore and experiment, is compelling.

Second, memory and appreciation of great architects and architecture of the past induce some architects to nurture a subconscious (and sometimes conscious) desire for immortality. By shaping buildings and cities, they may influence the esthetic direction that a culture pursues. Ultimately, their buildings and their names as architects might long survive their mortal tenure.

Third, fame may be worth more than money to architects. Some are unabashed in their pursuit of notoriety and public recognition, since it is one way to attract clients for whom the label of a famed designer may be an effective marketing strategy. Unfortunately, fame is often fleeting as fashions and tastes change; very few architects find (or deserve) lasting fame and immortality.

Related to the quest for fame is the desire for professional and peer recognition. While it would be nice to appear on the cover of *Time* magazine, most architects would be content with a reasonable dose of admiration from their colleagues. Such admiration or recognition can take many forms. Having work published in professional journals and winning design awards are probably the most preferred and prestigious forms.

Fifth, many architects are genuinely public-spirited. They seek to make tangible contributions to community welfare and community identity. Motivated sometimes by altruism, sometimes by enlightened self-interest, they apply their talents to projects that offer rewards of satisfaction for helping others in need.

Sixth, architects crusade for the cause of good architecture and good architects. The American Institute of Architects, architectural educators, critics, journalists, and patrons of architecture continually advocate increased public awareness and support of quality design. Sensitizing the architect's constituency—developers, investors, lenders, institutional and individual clients, politicians, government officials, and the general public—to the profession's loftiest values is a significant goal for many designers.

Seventh, serving clients—satisfying their needs, solving their problems—clearly motivates many architects. However, the architect's priorities may not match the client's. For some architects, rendering services is the paramount goal. But for others, it may be subordinate to goals already mentioned. Fortunately, many architects believe that such an either/or choice does not have to be made, that the client's and architect's aims can be reconciled to produce outstanding architecture.

Most architecture firms engage in general practices; they design buildings and the environments of which buildings are a part. This includes new buildings and the preservation, renovation, or restoration of old buildings. It includes the design of landscape as well as interiors.

Projects can vary in functional type and be tiny or gargantuan in size. They can require days, years, or decades to complete. Accordingly, fees for a given project can range from a few dollars to millions, and firms can make or lose money in either case. Moreover, firms must compete for work, since there is no shortage of architects relative to the supply of projects.

Even after getting a commission, architects encounter substantial financial and legal risks. Clients may be slow in paying fees, or refuse to pay. Projects may be delayed or canceled before the architect has billed fees sufficient to cover expenses (mostly labor and overhead).

Fee estimates may have been too low for the amount of time ultimately required to carry out the labor-intensive design work, resulting in a loss. Unfortunately, it is sometimes difficult to predict accurately the amount of work and, accordingly, the requisite fees to complete projects, most of which are one-time-only prototypes. In fact, architects' fee quotations are educated, frequently optimistic guesses. Intense competition also pressures architects to lower their fees, either tempting them to cut corners or forcing them to work diligently but unprofitably.

Architects are at risk when projects far exceed their prescribed budgets. Costly for the client, this is always embarrassing and costly for the architect who may be obligated to redesign for no additional fee. Sometimes, it can cost the architect the commission itself. And architects are always liable for their professional errors and omissions. Like physicians, they can be held personally responsible for damages by anyone—a client or third party—who experiences loss or injury due to architectural acts of negligence.

Despite the risks, most talented architects practice architecture for love and glory, not for money or power. While architecture is just a job to some, many others are dedicated to designing built environments that transcend the pragmatic. If they are successful enough, they too may become transcendent.

November 24, 1984

The Ideas of Design

n an architecture school studio late one night, a fellow design student, borrowing from Shakespeare's "King Richard III," cried out, "An idea, an idea, my kingdom for an idea!"

With little time remaining to complete his studio project, the student was still searching desperately for some elusive insight that would allow him to formulate an architectural statement. Like generations of architecture students preceding and following him, he was struggling with the often mysterious act of design.

How do architects design? The search often begins with givens that define the project mission and constraints:

- The program (a description of needs, activities, and space requirements) plus a project budget, which represents the economic resources available;

- The site, which presents geometric, topographic, geological, climatic, scenic, and other natural characteristics along with characteristics of the built environment—the context of existing buildings and neighborhoods, streets, utilities, and other constructed forms;

- Regulations applicable to the project and site, mostly contained in zoning ordinances that limit building use and size and building codes that prescribe safety criteria for design.

But if you had a computer capable of absorbing the preceding data, the computer, like the architectural designer, would still face the potentially infinite number of design solutions that could prove functionally satisfactory. Thus, to make architecture, analysis of all the givens and their priorities is necessary, but never sufficient. The design act needs something more.

Architectural ideas are needed that go beyond pragmatic problem solving. But where do these ideas come from, and how do architects manipulate them? The list of sources or rationales is long, but most relate to one or more of the following:

- The technology of construction and its formal expression can produce an architecture where methods of assembly, materials, structure, mechanical systems, and other building components constitute the primary visual language.

- Abstract geometrical form making employs familiar figures or solids (squares, cubes, circles, cylinders, triangles, pyramids, hexagons). These figures can be used literally, as pure shapes, or deformed, eroded, and combined to configure buildings.

- Functional diagramming inspires some architects to design buildings whose exterior wrapping reflects the uses, spaces, and circulation elements within. Corridors, stair and utility cores, activity zones, specially shaped spaces, and even bathrooms may emerge and manifest themselves in or on the façade.

- The architect may decide to make a building "look" like something else via metaphoric reference. The something else can be almost anything (a machine, an animal, a plant, a molecule, a piece of swiss cheese) and be chosen for any reason, so long as the client is willing and the design is lawful.

The Architect's Quest for Inspiration

- By historical reference, the architect can adopt as a model some precedent building or place that seems appropriate for the current project. Appropriateness may be predicated on functional analogy (same-use type), but some architects may be more interested in purely visual or cultural transplants. Revivalists may be literal in replicating the precedent, while others might borrow only parts of the precedent idea and motifs. Some interpret and transform substantially the historical precedent and its design vocabulary so that the new project alludes to, but does not copy, its forerunner.

- Contextual reference, the good-neighbor approach, entails borrowing or extending design ideas and motifs from adjoining buildings, neighborhoods, or regions. Projects so designed "fit in" with their surroundings by sharing attributes such as color, materials, height, massing, decoration, door and window type, and overall "style," perhaps appearing to have been there all along.

Common to all of these idea sources is the inescapable notion of preconception, which everyone brings to the design act. Our cultural traditions and experiences—what we have grown up with, seen around us, and learned—color our beliefs and expectations. Architects in particular are expected to have large, refined repertoires of preconceived notions and images enabling them to design architecture that is rich in ideas and well composed.

In fact, compositional skill is indispensable to implementing the architect's intellectual and emotional conceptions, for good ideas can be badly composed just as bad ideas can be beautifully composed. Compositional strategies include the use of grid patterns, axiality, symmetry and asymmetry, rhythm, repetition, and proportioning systems. *Juxtaposition, overlapping, layering, interpenetration*, and *modulation* are among the words architects utter when discussing their tactics for composing spaces, volumes, surfaces, and sites.

Thus, the architect must somehow take all the givens, plus his or her preconceived ideas, and, through graphic experimentation, perhaps compose a new idea. Because the number of variables is so great, the conflicting criteria so many, and the com-

positional possibilities so limitless, design is always a challenging but fascinating undertaking. It is both a "Cook's Tour" and a "Lewis and Clark Expedition." You know generally where you want to go, yet you are never certain how you are going to get there or what it will be like until the trip is over.

By drawing hundreds and hundreds of sketches, the architect develops design ideas while exploring thousands of design variables, but only a few at a time in each sketch. Through overlays of tracing paper, successive sketches become transformations and refinements of previous ones.

Drawings show how a site could be occupied and landscaped, how a building could be massed volumetrically, how the plan could be orchestrated using rooms, circulation spaces, courtyards, columns, and walls. The designer draws sections, elevations, and perspectives to show horizontal and vertical relationships, structure, interior spaces, wall surfaces, and exterior façades.

Scale models show the three-dimensional forms and architectural character being proposed. As the design evolves, drawings increase in size and specificity. The design idea may have appeared first in a series of very small, diagrammatic sketches. But it culminates after hundreds or thousands of hours of labor, in numerous detailed documents—plans and specifications—that are unambiguous about what is to be built and how it will look.

During this evolution, the architect does not work alone. The effort is collaborative. Many meetings with the client, who must understand and approve the work, influence the design. Jurisdictional authorities are often consulted for code and sometimes esthetic reviews.

Once basic architectural outlines are established, structural engineers begin designing foundations and structural members. Civil engineers tackle grading, utilities, roads, and tunnels. Mechanical engineers design heating and airconditioning systems, while electrical engineers worry about electrical distribution and lighting, plus communication, security, and fire protection systems. These engineered systems must be anticipated and coordinated in the architect's design to make sure that they all fit together without conflict.

The history of a project's design is a history of trial and error, of testing and modifying, of analysis and intuition. It is at once science and art. It demands that esthetic risks be taken and willful decisions be made reflecting the tastes and biases of architect and client. Above all, it takes time and dedication to do it well—and money helps too.

Nevertheless, final results will be architecturally successful only if the client remains committed to design quality, and if builders care about craftsmanship when they carry out the design.

December 1, 1984

The Massing
of Buildings

As one of its projects, my architecture school class designed the Pan American Health Organization building on the triangular site bounded by Virginia Avenue, 23rd Street, and E Street N.W., just north of the State Department in Washington, D.C. Built in 1964, it had been the subject of an inter-American design competition.

Each of us in the studio struggled primarily with one major issue for several weeks: how to "mass" the building, given the site's three-sided geometry, constraints of zoning, and the client's list of programmatic requirements.

None of the solutions we proposed looked at all like the building that stands there today—a curving slab with vertical fins, convexly facing Virginia Avenue, while its concave side faces southwest to form a backdrop for the circular auditorium building at the corner of E and 23rd.

Most of our schemes filled the site and conformed to D.C.'s prevalent street and block pattern. Our façades lined the sidewalks and streets on all three sides, and the interior of the mass was removed to create a trapezoidal courtyard. A few designs were L-shaped, the legs of the L being along 23rd and E, leaving an open triangular-shaped court facing Virginia Avenue.

Each scheme within the class exhibited differences in dimensions, height, façade treatment, and small-scale volumetric moves. Some of us further subdivided our large building masses in ways that made the project appear to be an assemblage of smaller volumes. In each case, however, there was a conscious attempt to "control" every square foot of the site.

Building siting and massing are among the first design questions that an architect must consider when undertaking a project, whether for a new building or an addition to an existing building, the latter being sometimes an even more difficult problem.

At the outset of a siting and massing design study, perhaps during the feasibility determination stage, owner and architect establish a general program for the project reflecting its purpose, size, relationships between activities, budget, and other requirements that might affect the design.

Simultaneously, the characteristics of the site are analyzed, since they too will influence the building's shape and location. These include the site's natural features—configuration and orientation, topography, hydrology, soils, and microclimate (patterns of prevailing wind and sun).

Important as natural factors are, however, they alone rarely determine a design solution. Existing buildings on or adjoining the site must be accounted for. These built contextual elements have their own massing and architectural characteristics, relationships to streets, to each other, and to abutting open spaces. Relative to the project site, they may be neutral, confining, high, low, continuous or discontinuous, axial, orderly or disorderly, simple or complex. Judgments must be made about how these contextual pressures apply.

WHAT THE SITE OFFERS...

WHAT ZONING ALLOWS...

WHAT SOME NEIGHBORS WANT...

WHAT THE DEVELOPER REQUIRES...

WHAT THE ARCHITECT DREAMS...

WHAT WAS FINALLY DONE!

ROGER K. LEWIS

Then there is zoning, invisibly fingering and sculpting the still inchoate mass. Zoning works in two ways. It constrains on the one hand by setting maximum limits for building use, height, size, and lot coverage while setting minimum limits for yard dimensions and parking. On the other hand, it can relax certain limits as an incentive for special design amenities.

In the face of all this, the architect must somehow take that unformed, metaphoric lump of clay, whose volume is roughly analogous to the building volume representing the client's program, and ascertain if, where, and how it can fit on the site.

This architectural act of assimilation and invention usually combines accident and intent. The designer and client may have a preconceived notion about the siting and massing of their building; on infill or otherwise constricted lots, such matters may be effectively prescribed by zoning. But often these notions evolve unpredictably as the

architect continually imposes his or her compositional will, along with the constraints provided by nature, technology, the marketplace, the client, and the law.

Initial massing studies, undertaken with sketches and models, are a process of trial and error. The architect must understand the scale and size of the project, even while conjuring up abstract patterns or searching for appropriate imagery. The clay stays lumpy as it is modeled and tested.

Questions are asked and ideas postulated (and often rejected) relating to overall building geometry, plan and space patterns, height, programmatic organization, and cost. Should there be an atrium? Should the building stretch horizontally or vertically? Should the center or corners be volumetrically accentuated? Should the roof height vary, step down, or step up? Should the building be perceived as one mass or three masses? Should the main façade wall be in one plane or several?

These early design decisions are obviously critical ones, particularly from an urban design point of view. They vitally affect the streetscape and the quality of public spaces next to the project. Yet fundamental siting

and massing decisions do not begin to complete the architectural picture. In fact, the architectural design task is just beginning.

For the site/massing concept, however original or elegant it may be, is still only a three-dimensional diagram for a building. It must be transformed into architecture through hundreds or thousands of hours of additional study and refinement leading to a precise, constructable artifact. Detailed floor plans, elevations, cross sections, landscape plans, and interiors must be developed. The artfulness with which they are designed will determine the project's ultimate architectural character and quality, even more so than the massing concept.

Compare, for example, two well-known Washington buildings whose siting and general massing are similar, but whose architectural characters contrast sharply—the Treasury Building and the Old Executive Office Building flanking the White House.

Or consider the old-plus-new Willard Hotel on Pennsylvania Avenue. The complex massing of the set-back, stepped-down, midblock addition contrasts strongly with the simple, corner-turning massing of the original hotel. Their relationship to one another is cemented by replicative roofs, decorative details, and the entry courtyard.

Across the street at National Place, much subtler massing occurs through changes of plane and carving away parts of dominant volumes that nevertheless fill most of the block's envelope. These tactics, plus changes in materials and window types, impart an entirely different character to this block of the avenue by comparison with the adjacent Willard.

Clearly, the perceived style of both the Willard and National Place projects would be altered radically by changing only surface treatments and fenestration, with no changes in basic massing. The same applies to hundreds of downtown office buildings whose massing is generally undistinguished.

Much more distinguishing is the massing of the National Gallery's East Building and that of the Guggenheim Museum in New York City. Likewise, many suburban buildings and custom-designed homes flex massing muscles to achieve their expressive imagery.

In New York, Chicago, and other highrise cities, architects are again exploring more complex massing for office buildings, especially at their bottoms and tops. Although this may lead to increased perimeter skin area, greater energy demands, fewer standardized floors, and higher costs, developers are becoming convinced that such image-rich buildings, if well designed, eventually result in classier tenants and higher rents.

The next time you drive down the street, look at the massing and siting of buildings, not their skin and stylistic elements. You may see things that you never noticed before.

June 29, 1985

Marrying Structure and Form

As you read this book, you may be sitting in your wood-frame house unaware of your home's framing pattern, unsure about which parts of the house are structural and which are not.

Most wood-frame houses exhibit little visible evidence of how they are held up. Conventional "balloon" or "platform" framing allows builders to shape homes in almost any configuration, to place walls in any location, to use almost any kind of roof, and to cover the exterior with almost any material.

Whether outside or inside, you get little sense of where major or secondary supporting beams, columns, or bearing walls are located. Are roofs made with rafters or trusses? In which direction do ceiling or floor joists span? How is the frame braced to resist lateral forces? Generally, the structural system of such houses is subordinated totally to the composition of volumes, rooms, and finished surfaces.

At the other extreme are buildings whose structural systems are visually dominant. Primary structural components—trusses, beams, arches, floor slabs, piers, columns—not only are visible but also regulate the shaping of rooms within the building along with exterior massing and façade composition. Office and apartment buildings, schools, large single space buildings (such as factories or air terminals), and other special-purpose buildings frequently typify this design strategy. The Washington Monument obelisk, for instance, is the pure embodiment of "column," of compressive stresses increasing toward the earth, of hewn material firmly resisting the forces of nature.

Few edifices rival the magnificent 13th- and 14th-century French Gothic cathedrals when it comes to expressing the marriage of structure and form. They are tours de force in the use of powerfully articulated columns, arches, vaults, and flying buttresses to constitute both structural frame and enclosing shell all at once. That they were carved entirely of stone is even more remarkable.

The Gothic cathedral's structural system corresponds perfectly with the building's spaces. Structural elements define, contain, and impart rhythmic modulation to church nave, side aisles, transept, and choir. Even elaborate, decorative stone carvings do not mask the soaring, ethereal order of structure, space, mass, and surface.

However, most buildings stand between the extremes of Gothic cathedral and balloon-frame house. Their structural system geometry is only partially apparent. Often, concealed building skeletons are revealed implicitly through patterns of windows and façade treatment. Clues to structural order may come from emerging pilasters, porches, colonnades, or arcades.

Indeed, it is an ancient but timeless idea to design buildings so that their visual order derives partly from their necessary structural order. Many neoclassical buildings in Washington, from the White House to Union Station to the Pentagon, exemplify this mode of structural expression.

By contrast, the Hirshhorn Museum on the Mall has a structural system entirely subservient to its arresting, circular geometry.

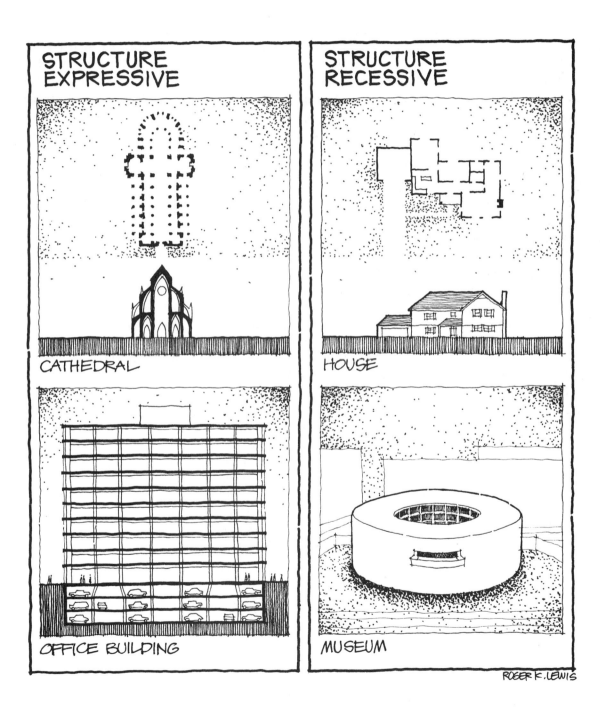

STRUCTURE
EXPRESSIVE

STRUCTURE
RECESSIVE

CATHEDRAL

HOUSE

OFFICE BUILDING

MUSEUM

ROGER K. LEWIS

Despite the presence of massive piers supporting the inscrutable, truncated cylinder overhead, it is difficult to comprehend the latter's structure. In fact, structural framing was probably not significant in determining the Hirshhorn's shape, proportions, or interior space configurations.

The National Gallery's East Building derives its framing patterns from a plan and massing geometry generated by the trapezoidal geometry (resolved into two triangles) of the site. Unlike the Hirshhorn, the East Building's shape responds to the city's street pattern, but the triangular patterns of its structural system, intimately linked to the shapes of spaces inside, are not imprinted on its exterior façades.

In many office buildings, an unseen force, unrelated to lot configuration or the city's street pattern, orchestrates column grid patterns: underground parking. Designing such buildings is a planning puzzle; to solve it, the architect must create a network of columns to accommodate cars and driving aisles. Zoning regulations in D.C. stipulate that parking spaces be at least 9 feet by 19 feet (8 feet by 16 feet for compact cars) with access aisles at least 20 feet wide.

These requirements lead to underground garages with column grids typically forming bays measuring approximately 20 feet by 20 feet. In turn, the garage column grid pattern dictates the office building column grid pattern above, since columns must be continuous vertically from roof down to foundation. Minor shifts in column placement in the above-grade office structure are sometimes accommodated in underground garages by using now familiar, but still visually bizarre, leaning columns.

D.C. office buildings often have structural frames and façades based on "flat plate" or "flat slab" reinforced concrete construction, ideally suited to 20 by 20 column grids. A continuous concrete slab, normally about 8 inches thick, spans both directions between columns without any girders or beams below the slab.

As a result, the overall depth of the floor structure is minimized, reducing floor-to-floor dimensions. In high-density zones, these dimensional savings may add up sufficiently to allow an extra story to be squeezed in under the height and floor area ratio (FAR) limits specified for the zone. The floor-to-floor height saving also reduces the amount and cost of façade surface per story, an economic benefit appealing to developers.

The structural systems of most buildings represent a surprisingly small percentage of overall project investment. Labor and materials to construct foundations and superstructure may be less than 10 percent of total development expense (including land, financing, and fees) and rarely exceed 25 percent of all construction contract costs.

Consequently, even a substantial variation in structural system cost may affect project capital cost by only 2 or 3 percent, making a building's structure a relatively fixed development budget component. And from a public safety point of view, the structure is clearly not the place to scrimp or take short cuts, since it alone keeps buildings standing and stable.

Building structural systems can be subdued, passive, invisible. Or they can influence dramatically how buildings look and how you feel about them. Even without structural expertise, your intuitive assessment of, and response to, the structure of any artifact can be both correct and compelling.

The Washington Monument looks structurally logical and comprehensible. Yet, if we wanted, we could build it upside down, poised wondrously on its pyramidal apex, or leaning over like a giant stone spear thrust into the landscape. But your instincts probably would tell you that something was amiss, inappropriate, perhaps even upsetting about such provocative propositions.

The structural systems of buildings can carry messages as well as forces, and it is satisfying, as well as safe, to see them transmitted properly.

October 19, 1985

203

Putting Up a
Good Front

A façade, says Webster's dictionary, is "the front of a building." But in Webster's inimitable and succinct way, its second definition states that a façade is "the front part of anything—often used figuratively with implications of an imposing appearance concealing something inferior."

How often the reverse is true when an otherwise respectable building is compromised by an inferior façade.

Most architects would admit that it is often easier to develop a good set of plans for a project than to create a good set of façades. Deciding how to mass and site buildings, organize them spatially, and modulate their structural systems can be less challenging than composing their elevations.

Designing building façades nevertheless can be the most exciting piece of the architectural action (for many office buildings, it is the only action). The enclosing planes of buildings offer the greatest esthetic opportunities for compositional exploration and expression to which the public has direct visual access. Exterior walls of buildings come closest to being like a painter's canvas stretched over a frame, awaiting the artist's hand. Façades, not floor plans or even massing, are where most designers imprint their signatures.

However, building façades hold other meanings for those who create and use buildings. To a developer, the exterior walls of buildings represent a substantial part of the cost of construction. For example, in office building construction, the exterior skin can cost from $20 to $40 per square foot of skin area. And that is just the basic curtain wall, exclusive of insulation, structural supports, and interior finishes. In a typical project, the exterior wall system may be as much as 20 percent of the total construction budget.

Naturally, owners and architects expect exterior walls to keep out rain, wind, dirt, insects, unwanted sunlight, and intruders. Thermal comfort must be ensured by wall insulation that resists the transfer of heat between inside and outside. Vapor barriers must stop the movement of moisture. Façades should resist the transmission of outside ambient noise (from jet aircraft, autos, sirens, and unruly mobs) into the interior, unless a window is opened for ventilation.

Building occupants like windows in their exterior walls. Windows can ventilate and admit natural daylight, which, if properly controlled, can lower electric lighting costs. Windows admitting winter sunlight can conserve energy and reduce heating costs, something appreciated by both landlords and tenants.

Windows offer views to the outside world, allowing occupants to check the weather, peek in on neighbors, observe changing landscapes, or generally watch whatever goes by. And windows, with the light they bring, make us more conscious of the wall itself—its dimensions, perhaps its materials—and the interior space bounded and shaped by the wall.

Façades are also obligated to provide security and safety. They must be structurally capable of supporting their own weight while resisting the lateral surface pressure and forces generated by wind or earthquakes. They should be fire resistant as well. Except for private homes, low-density housing and small buildings of limited or no public assembly, most building codes require that exterior walls of buildings be assemblies of noncombustible materials—glass, metal, masonry, concrete, tile, or stucco.

Finally, façades must be buildable. Contractors must have access to the materials, labor, and equipment needed to construct them. The more exotic the façade design and materials, the more costly will be erection, particularly if it requires highly specialized craftsmen, installers, scaffolding, or cranes.

Perhaps you take most of this for granted, but architects cannot. For even with the incredible functional, technical, and eco-nomic demands placed on the exterior walls of buildings, designing façades remains an art more than a science. If one could computerize all of the performance requirements just summarized, there would still be an infinite number of possible design solutions—distinctly different façade compositions—that could satisfy presumably objective equations.

Focusing on building façades, consider the many esthetic variables that the architect and client must ponder:

- What overall imagery should be conveyed by the combination of massing and façade design decisions affecting the building's character—its stylistic and cultural associations? Façades can be high- or low-tech, playful, witty, sober, sedate, inscrutable, chaotic, orderly, awesome, bizarre, historically allusive, storytelling, or any combination of these.

- To achieve desired imagery, what should be the dominant and secondary patterns of: windows, doors, and other openings that affect solid-to-void relationships; materials and joints between materials; and colors and textures?

- How many materials, and what types, should be used, putting aside purely technical and economic considerations?

- Which window shapes, sizes, proportions, and types (e.g., single-pane, sliding, casement, metal, wood) should be used? Windows can be oblong (vertically or horizontally), square, round, half-round, oval, triangular, or diamond-shaped, and can be subdivided, in turn, into smaller units.

- How can façades be enriched three-dimensionally by: changes of plane (e.g., between wall and window planes); creation of multiple layers of walls, colonnades, or screens; wall thickness (thick, thin, or even diaphanous); addition of subordinate volumes (bays, towers, balconies, canopies, overhangs); or penetrations by other elements?

- What decorative and ornamental elements should be applied—fasciae, friezes, bases, belt-courses, window and door trim, mullion trim, columns and pilasters, spandrels, railings, medallions—and how? These decisions are obviously part of overall pattern-making and image-making decisions.

In grappling with these questions, architects operate simultaneously in objective and subjective realms, relying on both rational thought and intuition, on analysis as well as feeling. Their "eye," as much as their intellect, makes purely visual judgments related to scale, rhythm and repetition, symmetry and asymmetry, opacity and porosity, among many other attributes. And buildings do not have to be just one thing or possess only one set of attributes.

Façades are conceived as whole, three-dimensional things composed of smaller parts that, in themselves, may constitute whole subfaçades. Thus, façades may acquire central and flanking "pavilions," atticlike tops, multistoried middles, and baselike bottoms through changes in wall plane and massing, or by manipulation of surface patterns. Subfaçades with their own self-defined orders can be organized around major entrances or other significant points within a larger façade order.

A piece of a façade's backside, let us say a section of wall with three windows in it, can serve simultaneously as the interior façade of a room. Those three windows should not only enhance and contribute to the architectural form of the room, but they might also be positioned on the exterior façade in such a way as to accentuate a doorway below or participate in a sequence of windows forming a distinct pattern seen from a great distance.

Façades can also express a building's use and telegraph to the outside world the spaces and structure behind, much like a skin revealing the organs and skeleton of the architectural body. Or they can mask what is contained within, instead deriving compositional cues from other sources— the surrounding context, distant architectural precedents, or the designer's whim.

Building imagery, determined essentially by façade composition and massing, is what we most readily recall about architecture. But we are still only just scratching its surface.

July 13, 1985

Roofitecture

How roof conscious are you? Do you recall parents reminding you to be grateful for having "a roof over your head"?

The universal role of roofs as providers and symbols of shelter has changed little since human beings first made buildings, whether primitive huts or sophisticated domes. But like façades, roofs also influence how we perceive cities and buildings, contributing more to the architectural experience than just keeping out the rain and snow.

Roofs shape the silhouettes of buildings, streetscapes, neighborhoods, and cities. The configuration, detail, proportions, color, and texture of roofs clearly affect a building's overall image. Certain roof types have historical and cultural associations. And most important, roofs define and give form to the spaces contained under them.

Some roofs are no more than a horizontal plane behind parapets or gravel stops on a building's top story. Many flat-roofed office buildings, schools, apartments, shopping centers, and factories depend primarily on their floor plan geometries and façade elaboration for attaining esthetic character. Their roofs simply do not participate symbolically or formalistically in the exterior composition.

However, flat roofs do not have to be neutral. The great French architect Le Corbusier saw the flat roof as a special opportunity, another site in the form of a new piece of constructed, horizontal real estate given free of charge. His vision, and many of his buildings, transformed flat roof planes into lofty terraces and landscapes, usable like a beach or patio. As if making a microcosmic village, he positioned skylights, penthouses, stair towers, ramps, trellises, and railings on roofs and transformed the profile of his cubistic buildings.

Roofs can become entire buildings, dramatic and all-encompassing. They can diminish or even eliminate the presence of façade walls. An Indian tepee or the A-frame vacation house represents such

forms. Eero Saarinen's Dulles International Airport is a roof constituting a building, as are arched-roof airplane hangers and Quonset huts.

On the campus of Washington's Mount Vernon College are chapel and dormitory buildings whose most sculptural façades are in fact sloping roofs that come nearly to the ground. The roof planes are penetrated by openings that admit light to the chapel sanctuary and to individual dorm rooms. Light enters both directly and indirectly, brightening and bouncing off other surfaces before being diffused in the interior spaces.

Thus, roofs can have windows. *Clerestories* occur between two roof surfaces displaced vertically from one another. *Dormers* with their own miniroofs can punch through sloping roofs to bring light into attics. Skylights in a variety of shapes can penetrate

roof surfaces, and entire roof structures can be glazed. With premeditation, rich and constantly changing patterns of light and shadow can paint a building's interior.

Children (and perhaps adults) drawing a house will usually draw a simple shape topped by a peaked roof as viewed from the "gable" end, like Monopoly game houses. This undoubtedly represents our quintessential roof memory, the symbol of "home."

Sloping roofs have *ridges* at their top edges, and their bottom edges are frequently defined by a fascia and gutter. *Valleys* occur where two sloping roof planes intersect concavely. Roofs turning corners convexly are *hipped*, and a roof plane sloping only one way is a *shed* roof. Many buildings appearing to be flat-roofed actually have very shallow sloping roofs. Conventional sloping roofs cover rectangular volumes and spaces most easily, but with appropriate ridging, valleying, and hipping, almost any geometry can be fitted.

Roof overhangs, or their absence, are dictated by climatic demands, construction customs, tastes, and desires for symbolic expression. In one-story buildings, overhangs protect walls and windows from both sun and dripping rainwater. But designers often stop roofs at the top edges of façade wall planes. Without overhangs, a roof appears to be part of the cladding system, conforming to the surfaces and edges of the building volume. By contrast, an overhanging roof can dominate and obscure such geometry and solidity. Some roofs resemble removable brimmed hats, hovering over and casting shadows on façades.

Compare houses designed by Frank Lloyd Wright and Hugh Newell Jacobsen, which illustrate different roof strategies. Wright's Prairie houses use cantilevered, overhanging, horizontally expressive roof forms, along with projecting balconies and terraces, to claim and control both exterior and interior spaces. Inside ceilings become outside ceilings (soffits). From the interior, dominant roofs compress and squeeze views horizontally outward, stressing connections to the landscape in metaphor and in actuality. But from outside, it is hard to comprehend the volumes comprising the whole building.

On the other hand, some of Jacobsen's houses clearly expose and dramatize the pristine quality of simple, white, cubic volumes ingeniously juxtaposed. Roof surfaces are differentiated only by slope, texture, and color—roof as skin. Not only are there no overhangs, there are no gutters visible; they are concealed within the roof over the exterior wall. Only inside does the space-making power of Jacobsen's roofs become manifest in rooms with "cathedral" ceilings.

The dome is one of architectural history's most wondrous shapes. Usually combined with other roof geometries, domes and cupolas almost always surmount buildings and significant spaces for purposes of grandeur and exaltation, to demarcate and proclaim. Even when small in scale, they can monumentalize and enrich otherwise mundane buildings. Domes have been idealized for centuries because of their geometry, their centrality and axiality, the techniques of their construction, and their ability to soar vertically while spanning large spaces.

In Rome, Florence, and Istanbul, domed churches and mosques are among the great landmarks and skyline determinants. In D.C., the domes of the Jefferson Memorial, the Library of Congress, the Museum of Natural History, and the National Gallery of Art complement the Capitol dome as profile makers. A beautifully tiled dome also caps the Byzantine-styled Shrine of the Immaculate Conception at Catholic University.

Mansard roofs, popular during the 19th century, are often really parts of façades, inclined walls that surround attic stories. Since we habitually perceive the bottom edge of a roof as the uppermost edge of a building's rectangular mass, the mansard roof can lower the apparent scale and height of a structure. The actual, normally invisible roofs of many contemporary mansard-roofed buildings are nearly flat.

Washington Harbour's roofscape, designed by Arthur Cotton Moore on the Georgetown waterfront, is a veritable exposition of roof forms—flat, shallow-sloped, mansard-sloped, domed, vaulted, terraced, chimneyed—as if a new elevated Potomac minicity and skyline were created. Like it or not, it is an unforgettable silhouette.

Architects must worry not only about how a building and its roof looks, but also about resisting the forces of gravity, the transfer of heat, the penetration of water, and the threat of fire. No wonder people look up to well-designed roofs.

August 3, 1985

9.

Assembling Architecture
Building Systems

Weaving Building Systems

Do you find that buildings under construction look at least as fascinating as they do when completed? Perhaps you believe some buildings look even better when all you see is their skeletons and metabolic innards, before they are masked by sometimes less than wonderful façades.

There is something undeniably intriguing about the indispensable systems of support, supply, and control used to fashion buildings. Yet you may take these systems for granted, not noticing in a conscious way their shape, their relationships to other architectural phenomena, or their inner workings.

In fact, you may become keenly aware of building systems only when they fail. This was illustrated dramatically and tragically when Mexico City's earthquake collapsed hundreds of buildings. Soon thereafter, the U.S. Eastern Seaboard suffered damage to structures and loss of electrical power as hurricane Gloria swept northward.

People who own or occupy buildings, long after architects and engineers have designed them and contractors have built them, presume that building systems serve unambiguous, essential purposes—to provide unobtrusive support, uncompromised safety, and uninterrupted comfort. Little wonder then that when you feel secure in a building, without being too hot or too cold, your systems consciousness is likely to be minimal.

The public's interest and values concerning its "health, safety, and welfare" have been translated into public policy and regulatory legislation. Building codes establish threshold criteria for the design and construction of buildings, particularly related to structural stability and fire safety.

Although most codes require acceptable margins of performance, they do not require ideal or esthetically pleasing designs. Much is left to the discretion of architects, engineers, regulators, and fabricators. And market-oriented developers look for building systems to satisfy both codes and consumer expectations. They want cost-effective, trouble-free, easy-to-construct buildings that keep tenants happy.

Specialized structural, mechanical, and electrical engineers, often consultants to or associates of architects, carry the burden of actually designing in detail most building systems. They, too, share the concerns of building owners and the public. However, they also must consider the nationally adopted standards and methods of their own professional discipline, which may advocate more conservative and costlier design, along with the aspirations of the architect, whose systems priorities can be more esthetically motivated.

To some architects, building systems are nothing more than service elements, functional components to be designed quantitatively by engineers after a building's architectural form has been determined. Feeling obliged only to provide poetic "delight" (budget permitting), such architects rely on engineers for the provision of adequate "commodity" and "firmness."

On the other hand, many architects exploit building systems as inherent form-giving elements. From the outset of design, when basic concepts are first being explored, they may manipulate certain of these necessary building ingredients to regulate space, volume, and surface. Ultimately, composing and coordinating building systems may lead to desirable visual order and expressiveness both inside and out.

What are the fundamental, behind-the-façade building systems and their respective roles, regardless of project size or type?

Structural Systems. A building's structural skeleton resists the forces of gravity, occasional wind-induced uplift, and lateral forces caused by wind and earthquake movement. Designed to remain in "static equilibrium" as loads change over time, a building's structural frame collects and transmits all forces to the earth through foundations. Among all building systems,

the structural system most affects, and is affected by, the architectural shaping and patterning of buildings.

Mechanical Systems. This set of subsystems (frequently referred to as the HVAC system—heating, ventilating, airconditioning) artificially tempers the atmosphere within buildings and renders spaces inhabitable. Air is supplied and returned via ductwork connected to air handling units. Heating, refrigeration, humidification, and filtering equipment adds or removes heat, moisture, and particulate matter. Buildings themselves may also contribute passively to atmospheric control, energy conservation, and comfort through their inherent geometrical characteristics, independent of mechanized systems.

Plumbing Systems. These consist of independent networks of piping that perform multiple tasks. One network, connected to the public water supply system or wells, distributes water under pressure throughout a building for purposes of drinking, cooking, washing, and, in many buildings, fire suppression. A separate network of slightly larger pipes relies on gravity to collect waste water and lead it down and out to public sanitary sewer systems or on-site

septic systems. Another network of pipes carries natural or propane gas from distribution mains or tanks to gas-fueled equipment—furnaces, water heaters, and stoves. Buildings heated by distributing steam or hot water have piping loops that connect boilers to radiators or convection units.

Electrical Systems. Comprised of networks of cables, wires, transformers, switches, and meters, electrical systems distribute electrical power in assorted circuits and voltages throughout a building to energize lighting fixtures, lamps, and electrically powered equipment and appliances.

Conveyance Systems. Elevators and escalators are the most visible mechanical conveyance devices found in multistory buildings. However, from an architectural point of view, stairs are equally essential conveyance devices. Likewise, ramps and corridors are nonmechanical components of a building's complete system of conveyance for movement of people and goods.

Communication Systems. These are low-voltage electronic networks and equipment used for transmitting conversations, data, and control signals originating or terminating within buildings. The telephone is the most common and familiar of such systems, along with fire detection and security systems.

Interior Enclosure Systems. Once a building is framed and weather-proofed by roof and exterior cladding, and after some of its other systems are "roughed-in," nonstructural partitions and ceilings can be installed and finished. So-called integrated, suspended ceiling systems can combine overhead lighting, air supply and return, and acoustical control.

Each of the preceding systems is engineered, fabricated, furnished, and installed by separate manufacturers, suppliers, and subcontractors. Nevertheless, they all must be carefully and artfully integrated by the design architect, who cannot treat them as separate and independent elements.

Like interrelated systems of the human body, building systems must be woven together to form a single organism, something greater than the sum of its respective, functional parts. Indeed, they can be orchestrated and assembled in ways that make environments beautiful and orderly, as well as safe and comfortable. This is one goal that architects, engineers, owners, investors, and the public can willingly share, even though it is not written in the codes.

October 12, 1985

217

How Structural Frames Work

Comprehending how structural systems work to support and stabilize buildings can be interesting, possibly useful, and not nearly so difficult conceptually as you might believe.

To concoct mentally a simplified model of a structural framing system, imagine two folding-leg card tables stacked on top of one another and sitting outside on the ground. Pretend further that you are sitting on the lower table. The legs of the table above, your metaphoric roof, are securely attached to the four corners of the table top on which you sit.

Assume it is a windless day. Everything seems motionless. Chances are that the system will remain stable as it transmits your weight (the live load), plus the weight of the tables themselves (the dead load), down to the ground.

But despite the appearance of stability and lack of motion, a closer look reveals that, in fact, some movement has occurred. The thin, tubular legs of the bottom card table may be pushing their way gradually into the earth, since all the weight from above is being concentrated in four small points. To prevent the legs from settling farther into the ground, you know intuitively that you must reduce the stress (pounds per square inch) between leg and ground by spreading the weight over a larger area.

A footing is needed. It must be large enough so that the soil below it can carry all of the weight from above without allowing the footing to penetrate. It must also be thick enough so that the card table's leg would not break or punch through the footing itself. Thus, a dictionary under each leg would work better than a thin piece of slate or cardboard.

Putting the footing on top of the ground might be all right in Florida or southern California where it rarely freezes. But in colder climates, freezing and thawing cycles cause the ground to heave, to move alternately up and down. Therefore, the footing should be in the ground below the frost line to keep the above-grade structure from heaving also.

Even with firm footings, the card table top on which you sit does not remain level. It moves too, deflecting noticeably because of your weight. Common sense suggests that to reduce this deflection and bending, you must either stiffen the whole top or decrease the dimensions it spans. *Beams* could be added below to strengthen the edges, and a series of *joists* could span between the stiffened edge beams. Or additional legs and footings could support the table top at more points from below.

The table top and its edges are analogous to the floor slab and beams in a building. They must be strong enough to carry superimposed live loads as well as their own dead load. Bending, deflection, and stresses from overloading can result in excessive deformation, fracture, and eventual collapse.

Assume optimistically that the card table top, your imaginary system's *floor*, is sufficiently strong and stiff. Yet the legs, the system's *columns*, could be bowing slightly, a phenomenon known as *buckling*. It occurs when relatively slender structural members carry enough compressive force to make them bend, just like a piece of paper bends suddenly when you hold each end and push steadily toward the middle.

The remedy: stiffen or fatten the column. The card table leg (assume it is a metal tube) could be made of heavier gauge steel, or its diameter could be increased, making its proportions less slender and therefore less susceptible to buckling.

Visualize again your imaginary framing system as a whole. Each part has been made strong enough to carry both live and dead loads down columns that are not buckling to footings that are not settling. But the wind starts blowing. Despite adequately reinforced horizontal and vertical

components throughout the system, the entire frame nevertheless is deforming. Rectangles are becoming parallelograms as 90-degree angles between table tops and legs enlarge or diminish slightly.

What is happening now? The structural frame, while able to resist satisfactorily all of the forces arising from the pull of gravity, is still unstable when subjected to horizontal forces that tend to push it sideways, overturn it, or twist it around its vertical axis. For complete stability under all conditions of loading, including horizontal forces arising from wind or earth movement, at least one of three tactics could be employed.

First, all the joints and connections between each table leg and each top could be rigidified. Think of transforming the folding card tables into "parson's" tables with thick, solid legs and edges. Both steel and reinforced concrete buildings can rely on the stiffness of columns, beams, and column-to-beam connections to stabilize the whole structure when the wind blows or the earth trembles.

Then there is triangulation. A triangle is the only polygonal figure whose shape cannot change without changing the length of

one of its sides; a rectangle can be transformed into a parallelogram with no change in the dimensions of its sides. Therefore, rectangular frames can be rigidified by installing structural members that subdivide rectangles into triangles. In our mental model, diagonal braces attached to each side of each card table would make the whole two-story system rigid.

Buildings stabilized with this type of diagonal bracing usually do not expose their triangulation to view, instead concealing it within opaque exterior and interior walls. However, there are exceptions, the John Hancock tower in Chicago being among the tallest and most familiar. And you see triangulation routinely all around you—in bridge trusses and transmission towers.

Finally, vertical wall planes, referred to by engineers as *shear* walls, can stabilize a potentially wobbly framing system. Imagine sheets of plywood fastened to each of the four sides of the card table assembly. A sheet of plywood, while bending easily when forces perpendicular to its surface are applied, strongly resists deforming when forces are applied parallel to its surface. Very rigid within its own plane, it can stiffen any skeletal framing plane to which it is attached, much like diagonal bracing. Even when some of the plywood (but not too much) is cut away to make openings for windows or doors, the remaining material can still provide sufficient rigidity.

In many buildings, continuous vertical shear walls of reinforced concrete or masonry stabilize the overall structure. They may be exterior façade walls firmly attached to or supporting the skeleton, or party walls between abutting buildings. Other shear walls can be inside the building envelope, frequently formed by reinforced concrete enclosures rising around stairways and elevator cores.

Contrary to appearances, exterior brick surfaces seen on residential and commercial structures are not always shear walls. The brick is frequently a veneer, and, as the name implies, it is hung or supported like a curtain over the real structural frame behind. Diagonal bracing or sheathing (such as plywood nailed to studs) is the source of skeletal rigidity, not the brick.

Having constructed mentally this intuitive, backyard "model" of a building frame with its respective parts, perhaps now you can better appreciate what is happening when your table, your house, or your office shakes a bit from time to time—or when they do not shake.

October 26, 1985

The Arch and the Dome

Among Washington's most memorable architectural features are domes and arches, ancient structural forms that gracefully cover monumental spaces, orchestrate loggias and arcades, or span boldly over rushing rivers.

Of course, D.C. is full of buildings with structural systems composed predominantly of rectilinear framing elements: vertical columns supporting horizontal beams, trusses, and slabs. But it is not a city whose image is one of soaring framed towers like Chicago, or towers and suspension bridges like New York.

Arches, vaults, and domes are structural forms found in nature. A cave can exist because its ceiling and sides approximate an arch in cross section. Likewise, the shells of walnuts, coconuts, and turtles are natural domes whose curved surfaces provide great structural rigidity.

How does an arch behave in comparison to a post and lintel framing system? Consider first how a lintel, or beam, works.

Envision a small stream with a log spanning it. You and your companions are crossing the stream atop the log. The log bends and curves downward slightly, its point of greatest deflection occurring in the middle. A close look reveals that, in bending, the bottom of the log stretches and elongates; the top of the log simultaneously shortens and compresses.

What is happening inside the log, composed of millions of tiny wood fibers? The stretched fibers along the bottom of the log are in tension and are being pulled apart from one another. The fibers along the top of the log are in compression, being squeezed together and shortened. If you and your companions are evenly spaced along the top of the log, the greatest compressive and tensile stresses will occur in the topmost and bottommost fibers at midspan, the point of maximum deflection.

This fundamental "beam behavior" occurs irrespective of whether a beam is made of wood, steel, concrete, stone, or any other material. However, the coexistence of compression and tension within a beam requires a material that is capable of resisting equally both compressive and tensile forces.

Wood and steel have this capability; brick, stone, and concrete do not. Concrete, although very strong in compression, has almost no tensile strength. When stretched, it breaks immediately, explaining why steel-reinforced concrete was invented. Reinforcing rods are placed within concrete beams, slabs, columns, walls, and footings wherever engineers predict that tensile forces will develop. Without tension reinforcing, all concrete structures would crack open and collapse.

This is also why ancient builders in Greece and Rome could not go very far with stone lintels. They could span between door and window jambs, and between closely spaced columns. But stone beams could not span across large spaces, a feat easily accomplished with tension-resisting wood framing or, as the Romans learned, with masonry arches, vaults, and domes.

The structural virtue of the vault, the arch, or the dome is that all the forces in their constituent elements are compressive. Ideally, there is no bending or "beam" action.

Pretend now that your imaginary stream is spanned by a simple bridge consisting of a circular brick arch, in lieu of the straight log. Each brick in the arch will be in compression, squeezed into an infinitesimally smaller volume by compressive forces transmitted by adjacent bricks. The greater the superimposed load, the higher will be the compressive forces and the tighter the arch's bricks will be squeezed together.

In effect, a vault is an extruded arch, and a dome is an arch rotated about its vertical axis of symmetry. The profiles of arches, vaults, and domes are often semicircular, but they can be less than half a circle. When their profile is only a small segment of a circle, they are considered "flat." The flatter the profile, the greater becomes the outward horizontal thrust at their bases.

Arches, vaults, and domes also can be configured to follow other geometric shapes such as parabolas and catenaries (the curve made by a cable freely suspended from its two ends). St. Louis's freestanding arched Gateway to the West, designed by Eero Saarinen, is a catenary arch. McDonald's Restaurants' twin golden arches seem to approximate catenaries as well.

Looking at Washington, you see countless examples of arched forms. The flat arches of Memorial Bridge skim gracefully across the Potomac. A short distance upriver, Key Bridge vaults across the Potomac with two rhythms. Its semicircular arcades of varying height support the roadway while sitting atop the bridge's major arched spans. Massive arches of stone and concrete support bridges spanning Rock Creek and along the George Washington Parkway lining the Potomac River.

Arched arcades and windows occupy the façades of many D.C. buildings, particularly along their bases where stores or entries demand more expressive, nobler demarcation. Sometimes, buildings have arched openings only at significant points of entry, or above such points, with rectilinear openings everywhere else. Look carefully at the selective use of arched openings on the U.S. Capitol and White House façades, on the façades of many Federal Triangle buildings, or on the entrance pediment at the Museum of Natural History.

Washington, like Paris and Rome, is a city of architectural domes. Domes sit atop many of the Mall's buildings, the most prominent and famous being the Capitol's. The domes of the Jefferson Memorial and the National Gallery of Art were inspired by the shape and proportions (but not the dimensions) of one of history's most famous domed buildings, the Pantheon in Rome, built nearly 2,000 years ago.

Not all the arches and domes that you see are structural; many do not use compressive, masonry arch technology. Conventionally framed buildings often contain rooms with suspended ceilings shaped like vaults or domes. Curtain walls or other nonbearing walls can have arched openings cut out of them, without the arches being genuinely structural.

The dome of the U.S. Capitol, completed during the Civil War, is framed structurally by two curved shells, one above the other, made of triangulated cast-iron trusswork. The visible exterior dome, as well as the interior coffered and painted ceiling domes covering the Rotunda, are actually veneers supported by the concealed iron framework.

Arches, vaults, and domes have always had more than structural significance. Their geometry is based on the circle and the sphere, figures considered by many cultures to be universal symbols of the ideal, of completeness, unity, and perfection. Philosophers through the ages have ascribed cosmic and theological connotations to them, recognizing that they are omnidirectional, yet focal and centered. It is therefore not surprising that architects historically have used circular geometries for special, sacred places.

Standing beneath a dome, you sense immediately the power of its form, its ability to span and contain centralized space. You also comprehend intuitively its innate structural stability. But domes suggest something beyond themselves. Perhaps humans always have perceived, consciously or subliminally, inexplicable connections between the circular structures they build and the intangible universe they did not build.

November 2, 1985

Building Walls...
A Shell Game

In the 1950s, an unforgettable television episode of "Amos 'n' Andy" concerned a two-story, suburban house façade about six inches thick. Erected on an attractive subdivision lot as a background set for shooting a movie scene, it looked genuine.

The irrepressible Kingfish, having assumed the role of real estate agent, set about to market this "unique" property to his favorite customer Andy. The most memorable scene occurred when Andy, accompanied by Kingfish, admiringly approached the house, opened the front door, and stepped in. He immediately found himself in the back yard. Meanwhile, Kingfish was extolling the virtues of the property—how quickly one could reach the garden from the inside, how little effort was needed to keep its compact rooms clean, how wonderful to have so much yard space.

Andy kept walking back and forth through the façade, puzzled that he could get from back to front yard so quickly, at the same time barely noticing the spaces within.

Kingfish kept focusing Andy's attention on the façade and the yards, suggesting that the building's spatial contents were of little consequence.

In retrospect, this bit of comedy seems to be an appropriate commentary on architectural perceptions. Indeed, your visual memory of the environment consists largely of the outer layers of inches-thick façades that you see. But what is exposed to Mother Nature on the outside may reveal little about the exterior wall itself, much less about the building's contents.

How are such walls made? Until the 19th century, buildings of consequence were always constructed of solid masonry—brick, natural stone, cut granite or limestone—mortared together and finished on the inside with paint, plaster, or, budget permitting, marble. In most cases, walls were monolithic and quite thick, being obliged to support their own weight plus the weight of all floors above.

Although apparently strong and permanent, monolithic masonry readily conducts heat and allows water to infiltrate, dampening interior surfaces. Water also penetrates into small cracks caused by seasonal expansion and contraction, gradual shrinkage

of mortar, and structural movement (primarily foundation settlement). Eventually, through erosion and freezing/thawing cycles, the wall can deteriorate or even collapse as mortar and particles of masonry wash away.

Wood is a much better natural thermal insulator than masonry, and wood structures can absorb slight dimensional changes without coming apart. Nevertheless, wood swells when wet, shrinks as it dries, warps, and splits. Susceptible to rot and appetizing to termites, it also burns enthusiastically.

Although wood is stronger in tension than masonry, which has almost no tensile strength, masonry is much stronger in compression. Therefore wood, used routinely for houses, barns, and other modest buildings, has rarely been used for tall structures. This engineering reality, coupled with wood's rustic associations and vulnerabilities, continues to account for its being judged inappropriate for monumental Western architecture.

During the last 100 years, metallurgy, chemistry, and chemical/petroleum engineering gave rise to unprecedented new products for building construction, changing the way buildings are shaped. Structural steel, 20 times stronger than masonry and producible in a variety of shapes from thin sheet to round tubes, permitted open-frame, highrise building. Steel and aluminum could be rolled or extruded to make lightweight wall panels, studs, window frames, and sashes.

Evolving synthetics industries invented and manufactured plastic and rubber compounds that could be squeezed out of tubes to fill and seal construction joints. Continuous, amazingly thin sheets of plastic, rubber, aluminum, or copper could be fabricated for use as moisture barriers. Mineral and glass industries devised new fibrous insulations in which millions of tiny air pockets, each resisting heat flow, are entrapped.

Clearly, traditional ways of designing exterior walls of buildings became questionable. Architects realized that, in an age of increasing specialization, the façade's many tasks could be performed by separate, specialized products and systems that nevertheless could be combined to make a lightweight, unified wall assembly. They also realized that these new technologies allowed much greater compositional freedom than had been possible when walls could be made only of heavy, compressive masonry.

Consequently, most 20th-century building façades are not monolithic, but are, rather, sandwiches composed of several distinct layers of materials. These layered sandwiches are placed in or hung on independently structured steel or reinforced concrete skeletons that support all the building's weight (called *dead loads*) plus all superimposed loads (*live loads*) arising from occupants, furnishings, equipment, wind, and earthquakes.

Imagine a cross section of a generic curtain wall with the outside to your left, the inside to your right.

Exposed directly to the weather on the left is the finish *siding* or *cladding*, the outside veneer. It can be brick, metal panels, stucco on lath, terra-cotta, precast concrete, cast stone, limestone, granite, or marble. Veneers are expected to provide desired exterior color and texture, impermeability to water, resistance to staining or discoloration, durability, and ease of maintenance. Usually presumed to last as long as the building, veneers can be less than an inch in thickness. They contribute little to a building's structural stability.

Veneers are backed up by and fastened laterally to a layer of compressed mineral sheathing board, typically ½ to ¾ inch thick, attached to the outside of 3- to 6-inch vertical studs spaced 16 to 24 inches apart. Or concrete block, 4 to 12 inches thick, may be used as a backup wall.

Stud or block backup assemblies, connected to the building structure, provide curtain wall rigidity. Glass fiber insulation, slightly less than the stud thickness, resides between studs. For block backup walls, 1- to 3-inch-thick rigid foam insulation is laminated to one side.

An air space, or *cavity*, between the veneer and the sheathing or block backup wall provides an important thermal break. The cavity ventilates the wall, allowing water vapor and condensation trapped within the wall eventually to migrate out via *weep holes* or thin drainage slits.

At the right in our generic wall section is the interior finish—typically ½-inch gypsum board (*drywall*)—applied directly to studs or to *furring* strips, ¾ or 1½ inches thick, attached to concrete block walls. Drywall's paper surface may be painted, or additional wall finishes—ceramic tile, wallpaper, fabrics, plastic coverings, wood paneling—can be added.

On the room side of the insulation is a vapor barrier, often aluminum foil or polyethylene. Its mission is to prevent water vapor generated inside the building (e.g., from cooking, bathing, humidification) from penetrating into the exterior wall. During cool weather, this vapor can condense upon reaching a layer in the wall sandwich where the temperature is at or below the dew point. Condensation can saturate insulation, destroying its effectiveness, and ultimately damage other wall materials.

A wall can be as thin as a few inches, or as thick as a foot. Its overall dimension is simply the sum of the dimensions of each layer chosen—cladding, air space, sheathing, and studs (or block wall backup) with insulation, and interior finish. In general, the greater the floor-to-ceiling distance the wall must span, the stronger and thicker the wall must be to achieve sufficient lateral stiffness. But the designer may also thicken a wall for other reasons, either esthetic or technical.

Remember that a building's façade is really three-dimensional. Thus, our exploration is not finished. For what happens when the architect cuts or garnishes the façade sandwich?

July 20, 1985

Magic Materials
Forming Façades

designed a house a few years ago for some clients who were skeptical about using synthetics—polystyrenes, polyurethanes, polyvinyls, polysulfides, and other such compounds—on or within the exterior wall sandwich.

They felt that these new materials—gigantic long-chain molecules of carbon, hydrogen, oxygen, nitrogen, sulfur, chlorine, or silicon atoms—have been around and tested for too little time. Would they endure for decades or even centuries the way good architecture built with traditional materials should endure? My clients knew that sunlight's ultraviolet radiation eventually can break down the molecular bonds of plastic and rubber compounds, causing them to become brittle, lose strength, and decompose. Moreover, some emit poisonous fumes when burned.

Undaunted, I pointed out that, in certain respects, architecture had been revolutionized by such chemical innovations and that tens of thousands of buildings have been put together during this century utilizing synthetics. And they are still standing, although few are maintenance-free. Indeed, I suggested that many structures could not have been assembled at all without these special adhesives, sealants, coatings, insulations, gaskets, putties, and paints.

Look closely at buildings, and you will see that synthetics are particularly indispensable to making latter-day façades. Modern technology and materials enable architects to design almost anything that does not violate the laws of physics or the client's budget. Compositional innovation and rapidly changing standards of taste have engendered new façade "freedoms" made feasible by 20th-century substances.

For example, we can increase window area to the point of covering buildings entirely with gasketed glass, practically eliminating any trace of exterior mullions, trim, or solid wall. Electric lighting and mechanical ventilation allow buildings to be sealed hermetically, without operable window sash. Or, in the *Brave New World* style, windows can be eliminated altogether.

We can create structural spans and cantilevers of substantial mass and dimension while slipping wall planes back and forth without needing to support them on bearing walls below. We can butt and glue together both exotic and traditional materials to create unprecedented surface effects. Brick walls can be made to drape, fold, fly, or otherwise defy gravity.

Nevertheless, certain façade conditions and requirements cannot be denied. Whenever there are penetrations, openings, or discontinuities in exterior walls—for windows, doors, emerging structural elements, ventilators, changes of material, or expansion joints—very careful detailing is necessary to ensure that the façade will do its duty, whether or not it looks good.

The control of moisture is the thorniest challenge. Rainwater, especially from wind-driven rain, always seeks to invade joints in walls or to penetrate porous surfaces. To

keep it out, exterior waterproof coatings (e.g., silicone or acrylic) can be applied to seal large, permeable surfaces such as brick or exposed concrete block, which love to suck up water.

Inside the wall sandwich, horizontal wall *flashing*, usually made of aluminum, galvanized metal, copper, rubber, or plasticized fabric, catches water forced inside and behind veneers. Installed over window and door heads, or at other critical points in the wall, L-shaped flashings divert water to the outside where it drips away, sometimes through weep holes.

All exterior joints (excluding mortar joints between masonry units) must be tightly gasketed or caulked to seal—forever, it is hoped—the constructed cracks through which water can easily migrate. Critical joints occur between window glazing and sash, between window or door frames and masonry or concrete wall surfaces, between precast concrete panels, and between abutting dissimilar materials. If joints are sizable (more than ¼ inch), compressible fibrous fillers or backing *rods* of flexible polystyrene foam are used to pack the joint behind the caulking.

Having kept out the rain, walls must also provide thermal insulation, difficult to achieve with all-glass façades having little or no solid wall to contain batts of glass fiber or foam.

Special glazing has been invented to absorb or reflect infrared radiation, though not all of it, so that the summer cooling load on glassy buildings is reduced. Two or three parallel sheets of glass separated by a small, evacuated layer of space create an insulating window unit that resists heat transfer from inside to outside in the winter.

Instead of heat-absorbing glass, the architect can use clear insulating glass combined with summer sun shading devices built into or onto the wall, thus admitting solar radiation into the building's interior in the wintertime when it is desirable for space heating and energy conservation. Such shading devices, best installed outside the thermal envelope of the building, can include awnings, overhanging roofs, balconies, screens, louvers, and other projections. Blinds, louvers, or drapes on the interior are less effective because they deflect or absorb radiation only after the radiant heat already has entered the building's thermal envelope.

Window and door frames are crucial to the thermal picture during cold weather. Wood frames are natural insulators; their interior surface remains close to room temperature. But aluminum or steel frames conduct heat readily, staying frigid in winter despite the indoor temperature. This results in all-too-familiar condensation dripping down windows and jambs, eventually staining wall and sill finishes and causing deterioration inside the wall. On very cold days, ice can form on the window and frame.

Calling upon synthetics again, manufacturers now make metal frames with built-in rubber or plastic *thermal breaks*. Thin gaskets divide the extruded frame into interior and exterior halves, with each half isolated thermally from the other.

In properly designed buildings, most of the exterior wall sandwich assembly, including the insulation layer, lies outside the column-beam-floor slab system. This keeps all of the building's primary structural components at or near interior room temperature, minimizing thermal expansion and contraction of the structural skeleton at the building's perimeter. This also prevents heat loss through the structural frame itself. Even when you see what appears to be a building's structural columns and beam faces exposed on the façade, you are not usually seeing the actual skeletal elements, but rather a thin veneer of nonstructural components paralleling the load-bearing frame behind.

Each assembled material in a façade has its own unique rate of temperature expansion and contraction, its own unique strength and elasticity (the ability of a material to deform without breaking and then return to its original shape). Intuition tells you that glued-together pieces of glass, rubber, aluminum, steel, and concrete, under the same conditions of loading and climate, will change their respective dimensions differently.

Moreover, buildings as a whole move, flexing or twisting when the wind blows. On sunny days, south façades will expand while north façades contract and compress slightly. Foundation settlement at one corner may not be the same as at another corner.

Therefore, buildings must accommodate differential movement. Fitted together too tightly, without compressible or stretchable sealants, or without attachments that permit slight slippage, façade components can be stressed to the point of fracture. Previously sealed joints can break open, or new ones can form, allowing water to penetrate. Panes of glass gripped too tightly by their frames can break. In large buildings, stress-relieving expansion joints cut through the entire structure.

The next time you are near a building's exterior wall, consider the many different pieces, materials, joints, and openings that are visible, plus those you cannot see. You may gain new insight into how architects synthesize façades to provide "commodity, firmness, and delight."

July 27, 1985

Going Through the Roof

According to a recent publication of the American Institute of Architects, roofs of buildings are the number-one source of complaints and litigation against architects, engineers, and contractors. And the number-one problem is roof leaks.

If creating "roofitecture" is among the most exciting parts of design for the architect, coping with leaks is among the most frustrating. Troubleshooting roofs is also not a very inspiring activity for building contractors, owners, and tenants. However, if one thing holds true in the world of building, it is the certainty that all roofs will indeed leak somewhere, sometime.

To keep water out, the roof "sandwich" begins with a waterproof covering, the roofing. Note that *roof* and *roofing* are not the same. The *roof* is the entire assembly of materials and structure covering the top of a building and contributing to its characteristic visual image and silhouette. *Roofing* refers only to the outermost layer of shingles or membranes.

Most sloping roofs are covered with thin, light, inexpensive asphalt shingles finished in a variety of colors. If the budget permits, heavier, fancier asphalt shingles, fabricated to look like slate or wood shakes, can be used. Unfortunately, asphalt shingles do not last forever, 7 to 15 years at most. On the other hand, slate shingles can last for a building's lifetime if properly installed and maintained.

Machine-cut wood shingles or rougher, thicker split wood shakes, usually cedar, are popular for residential use. When treated to be fire-retardant, they too can be expensive. Occasionally, you may see noncombustible cement shingles or red terracotta tile roofs, the latter more prevalent in warmer climates.

Roofers apply the first row of shingles to the lowest edge of the sloping roof plane and then proceed upward row by row. Nailed to the roof sheathing covered with moisture-resistant building paper or felt, each row overlaps the row below so that water must run several inches uphill to get under the shingles. Unfortunately, this can happen with enough wind or wintertime ice damming along roof edges.

Sloped roofs can also be covered with rustproof metals—copper, lead, zinc, tin, and special alloys. Standing seams between each metal sheet are folded over tightly and anchored to the sheathing by metal cleats within the folded seam. More visually prominent battens may be used to fasten and cover joints. Metal roofs, available today in a multitude of colors, are also more expensive than conventional asphalt shingles.

How steep should a sloping roof be? Most shingle manufacturers will not guarantee the performance of their product if used on a roof whose slope is less than about 20 degrees (measured from the horizontal). Metal-covered roofs can be more shallow. The steeper a roof's pitch, the more

quickly and positively it will shed water, but this can also be a problem for gutters and downspouts sized too small. Surprisingly, snow can stick tenaciously to well-insulated, very steep roofs.

For flat roofs, which should be pitched slightly for drainage, two kinds of roofing are commonly used today. The five-ply built-up roof is the most widely employed and consists of alternating layers of mopped-on bitumen and asphalt-impregnated roofing felts. After all plies are installed, a layer of gravel or white marble chips is imbedded in the top coating of bitumen to reflect sunlight and protect the roofing plies from damage.

The second type of roofing consists of thin, synthetic rubber sheets applied to roof decks to form continuous, water-impervious membranes. Lapped joints are chemically "welded" or glued together with special solvents. Once in place, a "ballast" of gravel or insulation boards is put on top of the membrane to hold it down and protect it from sun and impact.

What comprises the rest of the roof sandwich? In wood-frame structures, the continuous sheathing or decking to which roofing is applied can be plywood or wood planks. These in turn are supported by structural roof joists, beams, or trusses.

Steel or concrete frame structures support decks or slabs several inches thick. Decks are often composites of corrugated steel sheet and concrete poured on top of the sheet. For domes and vaults, the structural shell may be reinforced concrete, steel, cut stone, or brick over which roofing is applied. The roof on Washington's Dulles International Airport is a suspended cable structure that supports prefabricated decking with a continuous roofing membrane on top.

Insulating a roof properly in temperate climates is even more critical than insulating exterior walls. Unlike walls, roofs receive intense and direct solar radiation throughout the day in summertime. In winter, rising heat in a building can be lost through the roof by conduction and radiation, especially at night. Thus, adequate roof insulation keeps summer heat out and winter heat in, conserving energy and reducing fuel costs.

Rigid insulation, such as boards of dense polyfoams, can be installed between synthetic membrane roofing and the decking layer. On flat roof surfaces, it also can be placed on top of membrane roofing, maintaining the waterproof membrane at a more stable, moderate, year-round temperature. With either flat or pitched roofs, glass or mineral fiber insulation can be installed on top of the finished ceiling, with a vented attic or air space between the top of the insulation and the roof decking.

Venting the air spaces between insulation and roof decking is essential, for it lets water vapor escape and reduces the risk of condensation. As with walls, moisture can get into roof or attic spaces from inside as well as from the exterior, so that vapor barriers on the underside of the insulation are needed.

Ceilings under roofs, whether drywall, plaster, or some other material, can be attached directly to roof or ceiling joists, or they may be suspended from the roof structure. In some buildings, the underside of the roof structure and decking is left exposed. In this case, because there is no attic space, the only place for roof insulation is on top of the decking.

Making a continuous sandwich of roofing, decking or sheathing, insulation, vapor barrier, and ceiling seems straightforward enough. This gets tricky only where we must penetrate the roof or form its edges. For almost all roof leaks occur when parapets, walls, chimneys, skylights, pipes, and ventilators interrupt the continuity of the roofing surfaces.

Appropriate roof flashing is supposedly our salvation. Thin sheets of copper, lead, aluminum, galvanized steel, or plastic are generally folded and lapped so that water cannot enter the building except by flowing uphill or rising to a level well above the roof plane. Asphaltic or synthetic sealants may also be used to caulk or cover joints, especially around skylights.

At chimneys, façade setbacks, penthouses, parapets, and other roof-wall intersections, continuous or lapped flashing is embedded in the wall several inches above the roof plane. It emerges and turns down the wall until it reaches the roofing surface, where it again turns to be integrated with the roofing itself. In effect, a waterproof metallic curb is created. For pipes, special circular collar flashings are used.

There are many reasons why flashing details fail—faulty design or faulty installation, differential movement of building components, shrinkage and deterioration of sealants and other materials, to name a few. But sometimes nature can overwhelm a roof's defenses. Severe and prolonged thunderstorms or abnormal amounts of ice and snow can produce levels of precipitation and pressures that push moisture over and behind roof flashings. As on walls, sealed seams can eventually open up when caulking compounds dry out, shrink, and lose elasticity.

It may sound apologetic, but the ideal roofing system has yet to be invented or built. We can make roofs beautiful, but we can not make them perfect—yet.

August 10, 1985

Tempering the Indoor Environment

To real estate developers, "location, location, location" is a favorite motto. Architects like to talk about "commodity, firmness, and delight." But as a building occupant, your greatest interest might be "health, safety, and welfare."

All would agree that the interior environments of buildings should be reasonably hygienic and comfortable. This is not always easy to achieve. Since the 1800s, industrialization and its by-products—from atmospheric pollutants to radioactive contaminants in water and soil—have compromised the quality of the earth, air, and water, believed by the ancients to be the fundamental elements (along with fire).

Today, you may wonder whether you are better off indoors or outdoors. Should you open or close your windows? Should your house be tightly sealed or slightly leaky?

Inside buildings, you could be assaulted by invisible, carcinogenic fibers that otherwise keep you warm. Radon could be seeping up from the ground, or all the synthetics around you could be emitting complex gaseous compounds molecule by molecule. Cigarette smoke, molds and mildew, and radiation from microwave ovens or computer video screens may be zapping you.

Outdoors, automobile exhaust fumes, smog, pollen, dust, countless bacteria, and more fibers await. Even the sun's ultraviolet radiation can be harmful.

Back inside, your concerns include not only the cleanliness of the air but also its temperature, humidity, and movement. Few climates provide natural, year-round comfort conditions that make buildings inhabitable without heating or cooling.

Until the 19th century, environmental control technologies were very limited, but straightforward. In winter, space heating was provided directly by fireplaces or stoves. Heat was conserved by wearing ample clothing, sleeping under piles of blankets, and closing doors and windows in thick, uninsulated masonry or wood walls. And dampness was always a problem.

In summer, clothes were loosened while doors and windows were opened to admit breezes and encourage cross-ventilation. Roofs, walls, and shutters kept out the hot sun, but not the oppressive humidity.

The Industrial Revolution brought advancements in engineering, especially metallurgy and thermodynamics, leading to "mechanical" heating systems. Boilers could burn wood, coal, or oil to produce steam distributed through pipes to room radiators.

As steam cools and condenses, its heat transfers to metal radiator sections. They in turn transfer heat in two ways: by infrared radiation from the metal radiator surfaces to other surfaces in the room; and by direct conduction of heat to air touching the radiator. Air warmed by conduction then *convects* upward as cooler air falls downward (a *convection loop*).

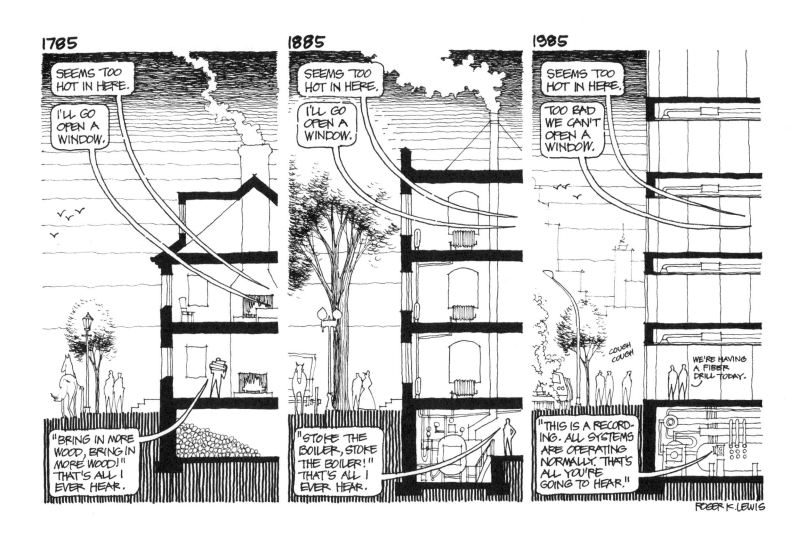

Steam heating systems had limited impact on the exterior appearance of buildings. But inside, they necessitated a sooty boiler room in the basement, a network of clattering pipes attached to the building structure, and radiators located under or adjacent to windows, which were invariably obstacles to laying carpets, placing furniture, and hanging drapes.

Radiators were also noisy, leaky, rusty, and often made rooms too warm and too dry, or not warm enough. The only control consisted of a valve regulating the quantity of steam entering each radiator, obliging occupants to act as human thermostats. Periodically, boilers would break down, valves would stick, or pipes would burst, usually during severe cold spells.

The turn of the century witnessed the advent of commercially produced electricity, electrical controls and motors, and refrigeration. Engineers realized that they could control completely the interior environment of a building. Indeed, with electric lighting, windows suddenly seemed optional.

Designers dreamed of creating idealized, sanitized, automated environments requiring little or no human intervention. Buildings could be enclosed hermetically with curtain walls and windows that did not have to open, keeping out unwanted "ethers." In fact, human intervention seemed undesirable because it could upset the delicate balance and performance of centralized, mechanized, finely tuned systems.

Thus, several generations of hermetic buildings were erected, a few before World War II, but most since the war. Architects, engineers, building owners, and occupants shared a common faith in the reliability of motors, fans, furnaces, ducts, compressors, filters, humidifiers, and thermostats.

Until the 1970s, this design credo was reinforced by its economic feasibility. Energy was cheap and plentiful. Conserving energy through judicious building design was of low priority, even though mechanical systems—the "hardware"—represent a substantial portion of a building's construction budget, sometimes more than any other single system.

Fuel (or electricity) costs for heating and cooling are proportional to the amount of heat supplied to a building in winter and removed in summer. This in turn depends on:

- The comfort level desired by owners and occupants;
- The building's "skin" area, determined by its basic geometry;
- The amount of insulation in the skin (walls and roof);
- The quantity of exterior glazing and its insulating value;
- The building's tightness and resistance to air infiltration;
- The efficiency of the building's mechanical system in transferring heat.

But for many decades, fuel costs were not serious economic constraints on design. Architects and their clients willingly and generously glazed buildings, primarily for expressive, esthetic reasons. Building compactness, double-glazing, extra insulation, and solar shading were not considered necessities.

Orientation also affects heat gain and loss. North sides of buildings are coldest in winter and coolest in summer, when south and west sides are hottest. Yet these differences were often disregarded in designing façades. Standardization, repetition of modular wall components, and belief in the potential of the universal "skin" became part of the modern design ethic. Such an ethic, appropriate or not, depended in part on the existence of energy intense, mechanized, environmental control systems.

In Washington, D.C., New York, Los Angeles, Chicago, Houston, Miami, or any other American city, you see countless modern buildings with windows that do not open. There are thousands of buildings each of whose façades are identical, regardless of orientation, buildings which consume large amounts of energy to heat and cool. And when fuel costs rose dramatically in the 1970s, operating costs and rents climbed correspondingly.

Over the past dozen years, designers have become more sensitive about methods and costs of comfort control. Buildings now are better insulated, with insulating glazing almost standard. Glass is used more sparingly. Orientation and solar conditions frequently influence the composition of façades.

Central heating and cooling systems have been decentralized, allowing occupants to control air temperature at many different points within a building. Thermostats can be programmed to maintain acceptable comfort conditions only during selected periods of building use.

Some mechanical systems provide simultaneous heating and cooling. Heat can be removed from one part of a building, in need of cooling, and transferred to another part of the building where heating is required. Recapture of heat generated by electric lights, and capture of heat from the sun, can significantly reduce energy demand. A building's structure, plus water or other dense elements, can store heat in winter.

Still, conserving energy, cutting fuel costs, and creating climatically responsive architecture do not complete the environmental picture. Questions about atmospheric pollutants, biochemistry, fibrous carcinogens, and background radiation remain. If the power fails, it is nice to be able to open a window to maintain comfort. But is it always healthy?

November 9, 1985

Mechanical Systems ... Costly, Unseen, Imperfect

There is one thing you can always count on when it comes to mechanical systems in buildings: they never work perfectly.

No matter how carefully designed and constructed, mechanical climate control systems cannot provide every space in a building with exactly the right amount of air at the right temperature, humidity, and velocity. Furthermore, if two people occupy a space, there will be at least three opinions about what constitutes desirable comfort conditions.

Environmental design is a statistical exercise, since people's body systems vary widely. *Psychometric response* in human beings, as the term implies, is measured primarily through perception. Feelings of comfort are influenced both by physiological factors—body metabolism, body mass, physical activity, fatigue—and by psychological factors—season of the year, level and quality of light, time of day, size and character of space occupied. Even intellectual and emotional expectations or frame of mind affect sense of comfort.

Statistical data predict ranges of temperature and humidity in which most (but not all) people will experience acceptable (but not necessarily ideal) levels of comfort.

With this in mind, architects and engineers design buildings to maintain indoor temperature and humidity within a limited "comfort" range. This range spans approximately 10 degrees, centered around 70 degrees (Fahrenheit). In summer, buildings must accommodate outdoor-indoor temperature differentials up to 25 degrees (100 degrees outside, 75 degrees inside), while winter differentials can be 70 degrees (-5 degrees outside, 65 degrees inside).

Probable, maximum temperature differentials in each season, along with insulating properties of walls and roofs, determine maximum rates (British thermal units—BTUs—per hour) of heat gain or loss for a building. These in turn dictate the size and cost of system equipment and components.

If outdoor temperatures go beyond those assumed, indoor temperatures in the comfort range cannot be maintained.

Most of today's mechanical HVAC (heating, ventilation, and airconditioning) systems include the following basic components:

- For heating, furnaces or boilers burn fossil fuels; electric heat pumps compress, condense, and vaporize a refrigerant gas. Electric resistance elements produce heat directly, though expensively, like a hair dryer.

- For cooling, gas absorption chillers produce cold refrigerant circulated through heat transfer coils. A heat pump, gaining BTUs on one side of its refrigerant gas loop while losing them on the other, can be used for airconditioning as well as heating. Heat removed during airconditioning must be dissipated or recycled for other purposes.

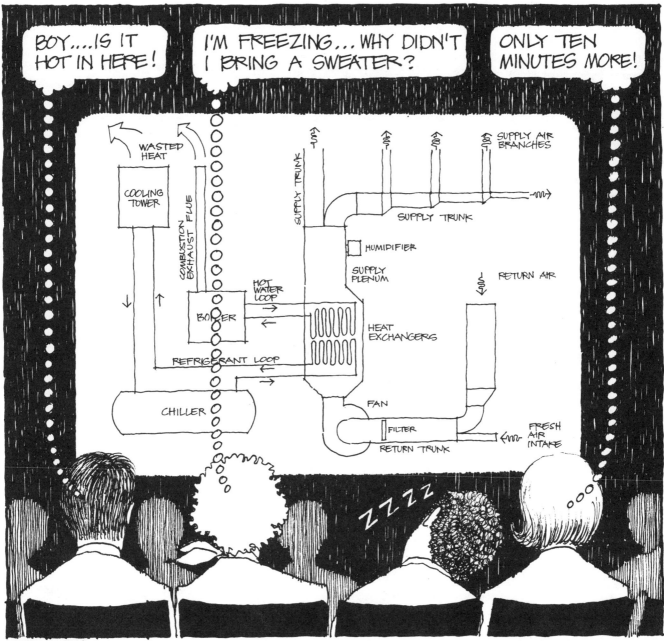

ROGER K. LEWIS

- In central air systems, centrifugal blowers are connected to return air ducts that draw in "old" air from individual spaces throughout buildings, or from a few central locations in smaller buildings. Fresh air may also be ducted into the return side of the system. After passing across heat transfer coils on the output side of the blower, heated or cooled (and dehumidified) air flows through supply ducts to room registers located at or near the perimeters of buildings where most heat is lost or gained.

- Air filters, normally on the return side of blowers, trap particles suspended in the air stream, particularly fibers and dust. Most are effective, but if they are not cleaned or changed periodically, the buildup of trapped particles will impede air flow and seriously reduce the system's operating efficiency.

- On dry winter days, humidifiers can inject water vapor into the warm, supply air stream for the benefit of both people and indoor plants. However, without insulating window glass, humidification can lead to interior condensation and frost. In summer, dehumidification occurs when moisture in warm, humid air condenses on airconditioning coils.

- Instead of carrying large volumes of tempered air through sizable and lengthy ducts, some systems distribute centrally heated or chilled water through pipes to dispersed air-handling or *fan-coil* units. A centrifugal blower and heat-exchanging coil in each unit supply heated or cooled air to discrete zones or spaces. Individual units can be located under windows or above suspended ceilings. When fan-coil units only temper air recirculating within zones or rooms, a central ventilation system introduces fresh air while exhausting stale air.

- Networks of ducts, supported by the structure, must thread their way vertically and horizontally through buildings to carry air to its destination. Most ducts consist of thin, galvanized steel sheet formed into rectangular or round sections. As air volume decreases, duct size decreases accordingly. Main supply and return trunks connecting to air-handling units are the largest, diminishing progressively in cross-sectional area as they subdivide into separate branches and zones.

- Ducts are wrapped with insulation when exposed to outdoor temperatures and should be lined with insulation for interior noise abatement near air-handling units. Flexible, accordionlike connectors isolate main trunk ducts from machine vibration, while resilient hangers isolate ducts from building structure.

- At the end of each branch of a supply or return air duct is a register, the interface between the mechanical system and the spaces it serves. Some registers have adjustable dampers to control the volume of air flowing through them and, presumably, to permit "balancing" of the system. Unfortunately, after a few personal adjustments are made, balance may be lost. Also, registers are often easy to spot because of gray smudges on adjacent ceilings, walls, carpeting, and drapes.

- Thermostats do one basic thing, despite latter-day refinements. Sensing the temperature in a zone, they tell the unit they control either to turn on or off. Contrary to occasional popular belief, setting a thermostat to a high temperature will not make a furnace produce warmer air. It only makes it run continuously until the thermostat signals it to stop.

What are the architectural implications of such systems? Clearly, rooms must be provided in buildings for chillers, boilers, furnaces, and fans, plus all the sheet metal ductwork, plenums, and pipes. A building may contain one equipment room or several.

Ideally, equipment should be accessible for routine servicing, yet noise, vibration, and products of combustion should not reach inhabited spaces. Often, central mechanical rooms are located in basements, but equipment may also be housed on roofs, potentially affecting a building's silhouette.

The major design challenge, apart from ensuring comfort, is integrating mechanical components and networks with a building's structural skeleton and system of enclosure. Here lies the greatest potential for conflict. There is not a contractor alive who does not delight in recounting stories about architects' and engineers' plans that show ducts, columns, and beams occupying the same space at the same time.

Coordinating the patterns and geometries of ductwork, piping, and structural elements is a three-dimensional design act requiring careful communication between architect, mechanical engineer, and structural engineer. Lack of coordination can lead to costly field revisions and change orders, not to mention unplanned bumps, bulkheads, pilasters, or columns.

This is why many office buildings, designed for interior partitioning flexibility, employ ceilings hung below the bottom of each floor's structure. Systems coordination is greatly simplified, since almost everything running horizontally can be routed easily within this utilitarian space sandwich.

Perhaps the increasing cost and complexity of mechanical systems, coupled with the integration challenge, led designers in the 1960s to explore the possibility of exposing and expressing systems architecturally. Why spend all that money to be comfortable, and then hide it? With a bit of imagination, a building's "metabolics" might contribute to its visual order and even say something about the meaning and esthetics of technology. It was an idea that had to be tried.

November 16, 1985

Systems as Architecture

What child has not been fascinated by the intricate innards of human fabrications? How often were you tempted to remove the backs of radios or to dissect clocks, mechanical toys, or other devices, just to see what made them work?

Many adults continue to be fascinated, if not intimidated, by what is under the hood of a car, disbelieving that such a jumble of stuff could possibly function together smoothly to produce unified motion. Perhaps you can appreciate the esthetics of a quarter-mile dragster, a wheeled and motorized framework bristling with chrome-plated pipes, even while admiring the elegant, streamlined body of a Porsche or Ferrari.

The esthetic potential of "innards" and technical systems has not escaped the attention of architects. In fact, the beauty of unpackaged machines, whether farm tractors or steam engines or oil refineries, began to interest designers in the 19th century as the Industrial Revolution transformed society and technology.

Speculation about buildings as machines intensified in the 1920s and 1930s, when the principles of modern architecture became more explicit and were more stridently advocated. After centuries of discourse about the composition, proportioning, and decoration of façades, and about the relative appropriateness of one historical style versus another, Modernists changed the architectural agenda completely. Denying the need for design expression rooted in history and tradition, they believed that architecture should express the culture and technology of the period during which it is created. Even an idealized future could be anticipated through design.

Thus, the functionally natural and honest "look" of ships, airplanes, factories, and machines represented a new design ethic. These unmasked forms, shaped by operational and technological necessity, were seen as intrinsically beautiful, precursors of a new esthetic for a new culture.

Buildings, likewise born of necessity in a technological age, could reflect the same values and expressive intent. Covering modern artifacts with Greek, Roman, Byzantine, or Gothic skins seemed to be, by reciprocity, the moral equivalent of glazing the Parthenon to keep out the weather.

Not until after World War II did architects fully explore and popularize this esthetic idea. The exposing of mechanical systems was an especially radical concept, much more so than expressing building function (through massing and fenestration) or structure. After all, the latter was nothing new, as seen convincingly in the Gothic cathedrals of the Middle Ages.

As an architecture student in the early 1960s, I clearly recall the first time I saw a mechanical system used expressively anywhere in a building. I was visiting New York City's United Nations complex, completed in 1951, a project whose structures are wrapped with smooth, systematic veneers.

But to my surprise, the ceiling of the Economic and Social Council chamber was a giant collage of exposed ductwork, pipes, conduit, and structural appurtenances. To unify it all visually, everything overhead was painted dark gray. Sheet metal had been elevated to art, and at little cost; the ductwork had to be there anyway to heat, cool, and ventilate the space. I wondered: Could the look of the New Jersey Turnpike be the wave of the future?

Indeed, many buildings have been designed since then with their metabolic systems exposed, primarily on the interior. In the absence of suspended ceilings, occupants can see patterns of structure, ductwork, piping, electrical conduits and light fixtures woven together overhead to make a kind of complex, horizontal mural. Parts may be painted different colors to signify their respective purposes, or simply to create independent chromatic patterns.

Avant-garde architects in Europe and Japan pushed this notion to the limit in the megastructure days of the 1960s and early 1970s. Visionary, often unbuildable projects were drawn on an unprecedented scale. At a time when we were going to the moon, ambitious schemes to construct new cities over Tokyo Bay or the English Channel seemed perfectly reasonable.

Invariably, the "architecture" of these huge, metabolic proposals consisted of networks of structure filled with cellular modules for habitation, mass transportation conduits (mostly monorails and automated roadways), public utilities, elevators, escalators, and mechanical services.

Of course, if you can not suddenly build a city, the next best thing is a building. So architects tried to test their ideas in microcosm whenever a willing client and appropriate project came along. Nowhere is this more apparent than Japan, where hundreds of buildings embodying this kind of metabolic imagery have risen over the last 20 years.

However, the most famous and expressively uncompromising of such visceral buildings is the Georges Pompidou National Arts and Cultural Center at Place Beaubourg in Paris. Designed in 1971 by Renzo Piano and Richard Rogers pursuant to an international competition, it was completed in 1975. The building houses a modern art museum, an industrial design center, a center for music, and a library, plus related visitor services.

The Pompidou Center is described by its architects as a "flexible container and a dynamic machine" that "reveals its internal mechanism to all." Each rectangular floor level, measuring approximately 48 meters (157 feet) by 170 meters (558 feet), is spanned by trusses and uninterrupted by any fixed, vertical elements, either structural or mechanical. All interior partitions are movable.

The six-story, prefabricated "inside out" building is intended to demystify its workings by locating all of its support and service systems—columns, diagonal bracing, mechanical equipment, ducts, plumbing, roll-up fire and sun shutters, escalators, elevators, stairs, and corridors—transparently on the outside of the building.

Vivid colors—blue, green, red, yellow, orange—accent metabolic components. Shades of white and gray, plus chrome, cover the latticework of structure. Virtually all enclosing skin is glass infill. Transparent glass tubes enclose walkways and escalators, which seem to be crawling diagonally up the building like a giant see-through worm.

Stylistically, the Pompidou Center disregards its neighboring mansard-roofed, stone-faced row buildings constructed in the 17th, 18th, and 19th centuries. Its noncontextual design would probably never be considered if the competition were held today. Yet, like it or not, this technologically aggressive edifice is visually arresting, a gutsy building that lets it all hang out for the edification of visitors. As its architects state: "There is no façade."

November 23, 1985

10.

Buildings from Factories
The Limits of Prefabrication

Industrialized Building . . . Is There a Future?

In 1968, the National Commission on Urban Problems, chaired by the late Senator Paul Douglas, asked Boston architect Carl Koch to prepare a report, which was titled "Roadblocks to Innovation in the Housing Industry."

Koch was a pioneer in the postwar design and development of prefabricated housing systems, his most enduring and well known being the Techbuilt House. I had been a student and employee of Koch's, and he asked me to assist in the study, a survey of the history of factorymade housing in the United States.

We began at the turn of the century with architect Grosvenor Atterbury's precast concrete, panelized system at Forest Hills, Long Island. Atterbury had begun his research in 1902, built a prototype at his own expense, and finally, with the support of the Russell Sage Foundation (who acted as developer), erected the first rowhouses at Forest Hills Gardens in 1910.

The Forest Hills system used 8-foot-high wall panels composed of two 1½-inch-thick, unreinforced concrete membranes separated by a 6-inch airspace and stiffening ribs. Decorative patterns were cast into the concrete at the factory so that the panel, once erected, formed a complete, prefinished wall system inside and out. Abutting panels were grouted together.

Although Atterbury's prototypes were technically and stylistically acceptable, they were costly. Large trucks and cranes were needed to transport and erect the heavy concrete panels. Molds and other manufacturing equipment represented substantial capital investments that had to be amortized. Only if prefabricated and constructed in great volume could the system prove itself economically feasible. This was never to be.

The Sage Foundation completed Forest Hills Gardens with houses designed by Atterbury but built conventionally and less expensively. Even many years later, in 1943, the New York City Housing Authority rejected Atterbury's proposal for constructing thousands of low-cost, prefabricated concrete housing units. Despite potential economies of scale afforded by volume production, the city still favored conventional construction.

Immediately after World War II, pent-up demand for new homes was accompanied by a consensus among designers that housing prefabrication and industrialization were at last achievable. Just as space-age technical progress in the 1960s had fueled the optimism of architects, engineers, and builders, similar wartime advances in methods of production and technology had inspired their predecessors in the 1940s.

Among the first postwar prefabrication attempts was Carl Koch's Acorn House, a two-bedroom home whose 24 feet by 35 feet shell could be folded up to form a single 8 feet by 24 feet "core." Supported on exposed steel beams beneath the floor, the core contained the factorymade kitchen, bathroom, and mechanical equipment. With its room wings folded, the compact house could be transported easily.

The Acorn House was built like an airplane. Its walls were stressed-skin, paper honeycomb sandwich panels, making the house light and durable. Interior wall sur-

faces were plywood. In one day, four men could move it from its trailer to a prepared foundation, unfold it, make necessary bolted joint and utility connections, install the "innards," and turn it over for occupancy.

In 1949, the Acorn House was projected to cost $6,000 to $7,000 FOB, of which less than 15 percent was factory labor. Adding approximately $1,000 for transportation and erection costs, plus 10 percent profit, brought the selling price (excluding the lot) to just under $10,000. Estimates in 1951 anticipated that eight houses per day could be produced with 125 hours of labor per house, plus 9 hours of labor for indirect labor and supervision. To achieve this level of productivity, $325,000 had to be invested in machinery, tools, and equipment. On paper, the idea appeared sound and straightforward.

However, there were problems. Our Douglas Commission report noted "how vastly different the Acorn was from what people were used to. In appearance . . . it was rather unobtrusive and demure, but with respect to . . . methods of plumbing, framing and foundation, it was probably in violation on fifteen or more counts of the building codes of every town in New England." Authorities wondered about wall studs—codes required two-by-fours no more than 16 inches apart—but the Acorn House had no studs at all.

Lenders balked at mortgaging prefabricated houses that could be folded up and moved (were they really real estate?). In New England, people worried about lack of a basement and heating a structure with paper in its walls. Smaller than many conventional houses, the Acorn House seemed too big and well equipped to be marketed as a vacation cottage. And perhaps most critically, its $10,000 selling price was about the same as many comparable builders' homes on the market at that time, whose price *included* the lot.

Despite good press coverage (*Life* magazine did a spread on Acorn), the lack of guaranteed continuous sales and mortgage financing made plant financing difficult. Without a plant, dealerships, and steady sales, there was no cash flow. Thus the project remained only a noble experiment.

A decade later, the Alside Corporation, an aluminum siding company, developed an innovative factorymade building system based on a 12 feet by 14 feet by 8 feet repetitive space module. Formed by a black, steel frame of tubular columns and beams, modules could be joined in a variety of ways to make different house models. Stressed-skin sandwich panels, made of polystyrene cores faced with aluminum, were fabricated in several colors to compose exterior walls. All parts, including floor and roof panels, kitchens, bathrooms, appliances, and mechanical equipment, were manufactured in the plant and shipped in kits to dealers.

Like the Acorn House, the only work done outside the factory was site preparation and foundations, atop which a crew of five could assemble the complete house in one week. In 1959, the crisply detailed, internationally styled Alside House was priced to sell for about $9 per square foot to compete with conventional builders' homes.

Having built a new automated factory using tape-controlled milling and high-speed data processing ($10 million was invested in tooling), Alside seemed both committed and destined to make its mark in the American housing industry, but it failed. Despite sophisticated design, a network of dealers with model homes to show, and acceptance by consumers, the Federal Housing Administration, labor unions, and building code officials, Alside was unprepared for the cyclical, erratic, localized nature of the real estate and mortgage markets. Financially unable to keep houses in inventory, dealers naturally placed orders only when customer orders were firm.

With purchase orders coming in unevenly, Alside had to slow down production and distribution, in turn driving up its per-unit costs and ultimate selling price, which then made its houses less competitive. Alside was trapped in a vicious circle from which it could not escape. Sales continued falling as dealers hedged and prices rose. Factory production slowed further. Having barely begun, the plant soon closed its doors.

What do these cases, among others, illustrate? Problems associated with prefabrication or industrialization of housing are not necessarily technological or even esthetic. There is no secret to designing houses, acceptable to a large share of the market, that can be produced efficiently in a factory.

The real roadblocks relate to marketing and financing in volume, and to the uncertainties of national and local economic conditions. If sufficient numbers of people can not afford to buy on a continuous basis, if mortgages and working capital are unavailable or too expensive, or if there is no concentrated, large-scale housing procurement program, then no amount of creative design or industrial efficiency will make the factorymade house preeminent.

January 25, 1986

A Bit of History...
The Lustron
House

Following the end of World War II, a persuasive engineer named Carl Strandlund developed the famous and ill-fated Lustron House, still one of America's most interesting and ambitious attempts to mass-produce factorymade housing.

The Lustron House was a one-story, 1,025-square-foot bungalow framed in steel and faced with porcelain-enameled steel panels (like gas stations). Houses were to be manufactured and finished totally on a factory assembly line, then shipped and installed on any one of millions of vacant lots throughout the United States. Sold through dealer franchises, the steel houses would be marketed for about $7,000 to the young, employed, expanding middle class.

In 1946, postwar Congress had authorized the Reconstruction Finance Corporation (RFC) to make loans for producing industrialized housing. Strandlund borrowed $15.5 million, the capital initially thought necessary for the scale of plant and equipment envisioned. His early estimates soon proved too low.

The first Lustron prototype was constructed in 1947. Technically innovative in almost every respect, it used a new, low-temperature process for fusing porcelain enamel to cold-rolled sheet steel. All its roof, wall, and floor sections were formed by cold rolling or die pressing. Automatic welding and enameling machines shaped, cleaned, color coated, baked, and assembled house components—steel studs, trusses, and interlocking panels—to form the complete shell. Strandlund also introduced what was then a new insulating material—fiberglass—along with radiant heating panels in the ceiling to offset the high thermal conductivity of the porcelain-enameled, rust-free, no-maintenance steel.

Subsequent design refinements proposed by architect Carl Koch improved the initial Lustron prototype, which had too many small components, joints, and gaskets. Number of site-assembled parts was reduced from 3,000 to 37, primarily by eliminating two-feet-square panels clipped to studs in favor of larger, floor-to-ceiling, gasketless panels. Preassembled plumbing and storage walls were introduced.

Strandlund was equally innovative in dealing with labor. He wisely invited the American Federation of Labor and craft unions, traditional opponents of prefabrication, into the plant and convinced them that year-round, indoor, steady employment was preferable to uncertain, often uncomfortable field conditions. Lustron made an international agreement with the carpenters', plumbers', and electricians' unions to guarantee in-plant employment in return for limiting construction jurisdiction to these three trades. Thus, organized labor, in its own interests, supported Lustron.

By the time the Lustron Corporation was fully tooled up and operating, $33 million had been invested in the enterprise. Lustron's impressive new plant was built on a former Curtis-Wright plane factory site in Columbus, Ohio. Only one year after starting tool design and installation, 23 acres of equipment were ready to produce over 100 houses daily using a conveyor moving 20 feet per minute. Lustron could

make a finished house every 14 minutes; annual sales revenue could reach $150,000,000 per year.

The May 1949 issue of *Architectural Forum* commented that Lustron "is the first real plant demonstration of the seductive theory that houses can be turned out like automobiles. But it also means that somewhere in the United States a house customer must arise, waving his mortgage papers, every 14 minutes."

Architectural Forum noted further that for Lustron to fail would be "one of the biggest busts in modern business, a bust that would rock Washington and probably end the question of a factorybuilt house within our lifetime."

Lustron hit the market in early 1949, just as economic recession had set in and much of the postwar peak housing demand already had been met. Nevertheless, people liked the low-cost, precision-detailed house, and orders started to come in from Lustron's network of dealerships.

Out from the factory went the houses, designed to be erected with 350 field hours of labor. With 280 hours of factory labor, the Lustron House theoretically consumed a total of only 630 hours of labor. A comparable, conventional house required about 1,600 hours, a saving of nearly 1,000 hours, easily offsetting the costs of transportation from the factory.

But the labor savings were hard to achieve right away because of inexperienced field crews and variable field conditions. After purchasing the house from the factory for approximately $6,000, dealers had to add these unpredictable on-site costs to the lot cost, plus overhead and profit. The result was a $10,000 to $12,000 product, not $7,000 as originally intended. In 1949 dollars, this was no longer low-cost housing. And out-of-factory cost variables made it difficult for Lustron to advertise its product pricing nationally, the way automobile "sticker" prices are publicized.

Other minor impediments were encountered. Lustron's copper piping, today the norm, was still not permitted by some local building codes married to cast iron. Lustron homes could not be built in Chicago or Detroit, which mandated brick veneer.

The Federal Housing Administration (FHA) was inconsistent, as always, in its regional underwriting reviews, even though its technical division in Washington had issued the appropriate bulletin of approval. State FHA offices had different requirements and appraisal criteria, a serious problem when marketing nationally a standardized factory product. For instance, in Tennessee, the FHA office insisted on a door between the kitchen and dining room, while other FHA offices accepted an open, doorless (and therefore less costly) plan.

But Lustron's most serious problems were not architectural. The major roadblocks were economic:

- Lustron needed working capital of $5,800 per house (every 14 minutes) to maintain production and service its debt.

- Dealers needed interim construction financing of $6,000 per house, payable FOB, for each house ordered. To sell 20 homes a month (only 5 hours of factory production), a dealer needed at least

$120,000 in continuously available working capital, excluding capital required for lot acquisition and improvement.

- Despite FHA loan insurance commitments, lenders insisted on "dribbling" out construction loan disbursements as houses were assembled on the site, refusing to finance a "prefab" package in one disbursement transaction.

- Neither Lustron nor its dealers had the money or space to stockpile houses and house trailers. As soon as houses were manufactured, they had to be delivered immediately to their ultimate sites and customers. Thus, dealers ordered houses only upon receipt of firm commitments from qualified buyers.

Even with a production break-even point of 35 houses per day, Lustron realized that it could survive only if it received volume orders in addition to its fragmented, sporadic dealer orders. In fact, Lustron further subdivided its dealer franchises to increase their number and distribution.

Larger contract orders finally began coming in. Venezuela ordered 60 houses, a group of Cleveland insurance companies planned to build 3,000 Lustron homes, and, perhaps most promising, the military was considering the Lustron House as its national standard. Here at last was a large, concentrated, annual market whose fulfillment could save taxpayers' money, in contrast to the military's normal procurement practices.

But time was running out. Expenses were rising faster than income. Just as Lustron was focusing on new mechanisms for dealer and customer financing (including creation of a credit acceptance corporation analogous to those in other industries), RFC officials became nervous and began pressuring Lustron's management. An adverse political climate made matters even worse. In March 1950, the RFC foreclosed on Lustron's short-term loans, then in default, which the RFC previously had promised to consolidate into a single long-term loan.

Without continuing capitalization, Lustron was doomed, notwithstanding increased orders for units. After selling 2,700 homes, the bankrupt company closed its doors. Despite pleas and testimony supporting the value of Lustron's concept and product, the administration ordered the plant converted to aircraft production. All of Lustron's equipment was junked or sold off.

At the 1951 hearings before the Senate Committee on Banking and Currency, former Lustron dealer and home builder Arthur Padula stated that "we are . . . destroying the last remnants of a $37 million investment in a new industry, which was never given the chance to succeed. The technical problems of manufacturing had been overcome. . . . The only thing wrong with it was that it could not be merchandised."

February 1, 1986

Industrialized Building in Europe

On a bitterly cold, gray February day in 1968, Boston architect Carl Koch and I left our Moscow hotel for a field trip. Led by our congenial guide, we were to visit a housing factory and several housing projects in the Soviet capital.

This chilly venture was part of our study, "Roadblocks to Innovation in the Housing Industry," for the National Commission on Urban Problems. Our mission was to compare the goals, methods, circumstances, and achievements of European housing innovation with those of the United States.

What we saw and learned was impressive. Motivated by crisis-level shortages of housing after World War II, postwar European governments had undertaken or supported massive programs of housing production. Building in high volume had become a national priority for many countries, an unquestioned necessity in the face of severe urban overcrowding and citizen demand for immediate remedies.

In the Soviet Union, factorymade housing had seemed to be the logical answer. Questions of architectural merit or esthetic values were secondary, if considered at all. The objective was output, to produce as many individual dwelling units as possible, as quickly as possible, regardless of other compromises or considerations.

At the time, the Soviet government had built over 1,000 plants to prefabricate housing components, mostly panels or box-like modules of concrete, to meet their goal. Indeed, they were erecting 300 units per day in Moscow alone. Nationally, over 2 million dwelling units were constructed annually; nearly 85 percent were factory produced.

Prefabricated dwellings in Moscow were small by American standards. Tiny one-, two-, or three-bedroom apartments were stacked in walk-up or highrise buildings. These slablike structures in turn were arranged regimentally in new, high-density districts looking much like public housing projects built in the United States during the 1950s and 1960s. Minimally landscaped open spaces, appearing forlorn and lifeless in midwinter, separated and surrounded buildings.

Reinforced wall panels, typically insulated, prewired, preplumbed, and prewindowed in the plant, had rough and uneven finishes. Decoration, if any, was marginal. Ornamental ceramic tiles sometimes were cast into panel surfaces at the factory, but these were frequently misaligned and regularly fell off during or after installation. Precast elements aligned only approximately; level planes, plumb lines, and flush joints were rare.

Yet despite such design and construction shortcomings, vast quantities of new housing, ugly but structurally sound, were being supplied. Young married couples, previously obliged to share cramped quarters with parents and other relatives, at last could rent or cooperatively purchase a place of their own, no matter how modest. Citizens were grateful for whatever privacy and personal territory they could claim, never doubting the appropriateness of the government's efforts to meet quantitative goals first. Quality would come later.

261

Before arriving in the Soviet Union, we visited Sweden, where conditions were obviously different. Sweden's housing industry, unlike Russia's, is not nationalized, although the government both collaborates with and regulates private enterprise. Sweden, too, faced nationwide housing shortages, which might have suggested sacrificing quality for quantity. But the country has a centuries-old tradition of quality craftsmanship, along with its traditions of private home building and manufacturing.

In Malmö, a quick hydrofoil passage from Copenhagen, we visited a plant making the Heart Unit. This was a completely prefinished, three-dimensional, rectangular concrete box containing a kitchen, bathroom, hot water heater and furnace, and laundry. Everything was plugged into a common central wall with built-in plumbing and wiring. Delivered by truck to the site, Heart Units were lifted by cranes and placed on prepared foundations or structural frames. They only needed to be connected to in-place utilities, after which the rest of the house or apartment could be assembled around them.

In effect, the manufacturer was implementing part of Buckminster Fuller's 1927 Dymaxion House concept—the house as a "machine for living," a service core at its center. With specialized, standardized tradework concentrated in the factory, these appropriately named service modules nevertheless could be incorporated into a wide variety of flexible dwelling types.

In contrast to factories and housing seen in Russia, Sweden's were exceedingly refined, neat, and well detailed. On plant assembly lines or construction sites, Swedish workers rigorously maintain craftsmanship standards of care and precision. Heart Units were pristine, beautifully designed, consistently dimensioned, and finished. Before leaving the factory, everything was in place and checked, ready for use. There was even a roll of toilet paper in the toilet paper holder.

Since our visit to Sweden in 1968, industrialization and energy consciousness have accelerated. According to the recently published *Coming in From the Cold: Energy-Wise Housing in Sweden*: "The share of single-family houses assembled from factory-built elements has grown from 40 . . . to 90 percent." Yet construction performance, quality, and consumer acceptance of prefabrication have grown with it. Sweden's housing producers simply have

moved most of their construction indoors. Likewise, customers go enthusiastically to factories to select and inspect their products as they are manufactured.

Sweden believes that the provision of adequate housing is a matter of national policy and purpose. Its government works closely with designers, manufacturers, builders, and consumers to reach consensus on all major issues affecting the supply and quality of Swedish housing. National construction standards and performance codes are mutually established; technical research is advocated, funded, and applied; and virtually all home mortgages are subsidized. This public policy, a product of the continuing partnership between government and private interests, has yielded a stable housing market accompanied by consistent levels of employment.

In marked contrast to Sweden and the Soviet Union, American housing markets and construction are extremely cyclical, regionalized, fragmented, and chronically undercapitalized. Home building is an "industry" primarily in name.

Mass production of housing on a scale comparable to Europe's would require the action of centralized housing authorities capable of committing economic resources for hundreds of thousands of units annually. Vertical integration of all phases of production would be needed. Regional and national land-use policies, along with nationally accepted codes and standards, would have to be adopted. Or perhaps there would have to exist a relatively homogeneous national market with few differences in design taste, income, climate, building practices, technology, or local politics. These clearly are not conditions characterizing the United States.

Only the mobile home industry has achieved continuous factory production of a low-cost dwelling at a substantial scale. Yet mobile homes are still not a "mainstream" form of housing, being located typically in rural or urban fringe areas, and mostly in sunbelt states (often, it seems, where tornadoes touch down). Mobile homes are still considered unacceptable as principal residences by a large majority of the population and the building industry.

In a geographically dispersed, diversified, free enterprise system such as ours, only concerted actions by governments—city, county, state, and federal—are likely to transform the nominal housing industry into an actual industry. Whether this in fact is desirable poses another, more ideological question, one that certainly has been answered no for the moment.

February 8, 1986

Technology Meets Reality

The year before NASA's project Apollo reached the moon, the U.S. Department of Housing and Urban Development (HUD) launched Operation Breakthrough. Its intentions were to mobilize American space-age technology and management for the purpose of revolutionizing the design and production of housing and new communities.

Many were convinced that the nation's housing problems could be solved, and the housing industry transformed, by advanced technologies never before applied rationally to home building.

HUD solicited and evaluated proposals from every conceivable source—manufacturers, contractors, developers, architects, engineers, universities. There were hundreds of responses. Proposals were reviewed, selected, funded, and tested in one of the most ambitious programs of design and building experimentation ever devised and carried out in the United States.

Surely, it was believed, this shotgun approach would yield the innovations hoped for, whatever they might be.

But Operation Breakthrough, and the short-lived excitement accompanying it, only reconfirmed what some skeptically suspected. New and exciting designs, new construction methods, new materials, new site-planning strategies, and other technical innovations, directed at product enhancement or construction cost reduction alone, could not alter significantly the basic process by which American housing is financed, built, and marketed.

The skeptics' vindication was inevitable. They knew, both from personal experience and familiarity with history, that technology was not the key to making breakthroughs in housing. They knew that the critical path in housing production meandered through quagmires that technology could not eliminate.

Look at the development process. Most of the housing that you see in cities and suburbs is created by independent acts of private entrepreneurs responding to perceived local markets. Developers must acquire or assemble land—either as raw acreage or already improved lots—to build on. The land has to be zoned for residential use, and, in some cases, zoning itself can preclude design innovation.

Builders and their consultants then have to prepare plans for sites or subdivisions, engineer roads and utilities, and design buildings and related landscape. Even here, architectural or technological innovation may have low priority; the driving forces are predominantly economic and legal. Market satisfaction and development budget objectives are paramount. Statutory regulations must be met, along with loan underwriting standards.

The developer must obtain funds sufficient to pay for land, design, permits and miscellaneous fees, construction, financing costs, marketing, and operating overhead. Typically, most of these funds are borrowed in the form of short-term construction loans disbursed by lenders as construction proceeds. Moreover, the

developer must hope that cost projections are both accurate and achievable. If not, he or she can go broke or end up with an overpriced, unmarketable product.

Finally, developers and their customers must have access to permanent, long-term mortgage loan funds that pay off short-term construction loans when construction is completed. Most important, prospective housing buyers must be able to afford such permanent mortgages and related down payments, demonstrating stability and steady employment to qualify as borrowers.

Developers and lenders know that ultimate success in selling or renting housing is linked inextricably to general conditions in financial markets and to consumer household income. If economic circumstances are unstable or unfavorable, no amount of ingenious planning, breakthrough design, or wishful thinking will produce housing and convey it to waiting purchasers. Even

extreme cost-cutting measures—reducing lot and unit sizes, amenities, or quality—may prove inadequate, if not unacceptable, to the market.

In a rapidly changing or unpredictable economic climate, home builders assume extreme financial risks. And unlike some industries threatened periodically by foreign competition, obsolescence, or changing tastes, the fragmented housing industry has little or no control over its own destiny, so inexorably is it tied to local, regional, and national economic forces.

Perhaps this explains why home builders, while interested in technological and design innovation, are much more attracted to programs and policies that produce economic stability, employment, and capital formation. In fact, many would argue that economic instability is itself a primary deterrent to design and technical innovation. Sticking to the tried and true, they reason that going farther out on a limb for the sake of experimentation only exaggerates their risks needlessly.

By contrast, recall what can occur when favorable financial and market conditions, public policy, and private entrepreneurship are synchronous. In the late 1940s, postwar demand for housing, especially by vet-

erans, was enormous. Unemployment was under 5 percent. Simultaneously, the means for producing housing—skilled labor, materials, new techniques, available land, and accumulated savings—were in great supply.

Congress had increased Federal Housing Administration and Veterans Administration home mortgage insurance authorizations. Loans were made with 5 percent down and interest at 4.5 percent. Automobiles, not tanks, again were being produced on a massive scale, while roads were being planned and built for them to drive on. Suburbia was about to sprawl in earnest as housing starts rose from 326,000 in 1945 to 1,023,000 in 1946.

Housing developer William J. Levitt clearly saw the opportunity for innovation arising from these circumstances. He would industrialize the process of building houses, not in a factory, but in the field. Started in 1947, his first Levittown arose on Long Island and eventually contained over 17,000 homes on 5,000 inexpensive acres.

Levitt created the residential version of the Model T, constructing as many as 150 homes per day. They were built with conventional materials, and all were basically the same, conventional-looking house. By varying colors, window placement, roof lines, and setbacks, Levitt made buyers feel that each house was somewhat unique. Architecturally undistinguished, Levittown houses nevertheless proved to be just what the public wanted.

But the building process was anything but conventional. Levitt realized that the selling price of a home included many profit and overhead markups that go into the pockets of a number of different individuals—suppliers, subcontractors, land sellers and subdividers, brokers. To lower his selling price, he decided to integrate the process vertically and reduce the number of separate participants and markups. Levitt purchased raw materials directly from factories, used mechanized tools, precut lumber, and preassembled wall panels and plumbing trees. Specialized crews would sweep across the site from house to house, performing only one set of tasks in sequence. It was, in effect, a static mass-production assembly line.

Levitt's innovative thinking had focused on the process, not the product. Yet he knew Levittown was feasible only because there were employed people in need of shelter who could secure the financing to buy it. And such financing was available, first, because there was a pool of capital that could be invested continuously in home mortgages and, second, because the federal government was willing to insure such mortgages.

Today, you can still obtain a mortgage and mortgage insurance to buy a house. But you might not qualify any longer with only the income of a returning veteran. For many Americans, the costs of housing and house financing have outstripped their incomes. As economic uncertainties persist, home builders once again are less concerned about technological innovation, instead wondering if the next generation seeking shelter will be able to afford anything at all.

February 15, 1986

11.

Regulating Land Use
Planning and Zoning

Land . . . Owning and Zoning It

What does it mean to "own" land? How has the use of land and its regulation affected the look of Washington, D.C., and, by way of comparison, other cities as well?

For thousands of years, owning land really meant controlling it. Just like animals instinctively occupying and guarding their territories against competitors seeking to drive them out or devour them, our ancestors could assert ownership claim only to those lands they could defend. Even today, this is still true in some parts of the world.

As human civilization and laws evolved, the method for acquiring and holding land changed. With consolidation of Europe's kingdoms and colonies, monarchs could grant land to nobles or colonizers who could in turn grant it to others. Such grants of lands within recognized realms were evidenced by a land grant document or title stating clearly that the subject property had indeed been given by the grantor to the grantee.

Grantees could continue to subdivide and grant parts of their estates to subsequent property owners, with the preceding chain of ownership (back to the king) being cited as proof of the right of conveyance. It became traditional to inscribe such transfers of title in church records, which were seen as both public and institutionally permanent. This set the precedent for publicly recording real property title transactions.

But ownership of land meant more than the rights of possession and conveyance. To own land implied freedom to do with it as one pleased, without interference. True dominion and control entailed rights to use and improve land, to cultivate it, to build on it, to bequeath it, to encumber it by pledging it as collateral, or to lease it to others. These perpetual rights could be taken away only by consent.

Yet absolute, unencumbered private control over the use of land was curtailed as societies began to urbanize. Living close together required that certain compromises be reached between private and public interests. Even in the most primitive cultures, tacit understandings existed about what was acceptable or unacceptable to the community regarding land use.

Before and during the 18th century, European cities had well-established civil codes regulating the type and size of building that could occur. Paris had controlled the height of its buildings since the 16th century, a fact well known to Pierre L'Enfant, George Washington, and Thomas Jefferson.

With the creation of the American republic at the end of the 18th century, two things happened that would interact significantly in the future to shape Washington, D.C., and most other cities in the country as well. One was the adoption of a federal constitution that entitled government to pass laws and take actions needed to pro-

tect the public's "health, safety, welfare, and morals." The other was the establishment of the new federal city in accordance with a grand plan conceived by L'Enfant.

Both events were expressions of public policy. Most important, the constitutional provision would ultimately justify the right of government bodies to adopt, implement, and enforce plans for cities. Further, such plans would take precedence over precious economic and private property rights for which so many Americans had battled during the American Revolution.

Even when the District of Columbia was being mapped and laid out, private interests were subordinated to public interests when it became necessary to tear down Daniel Carroll's partially built house—it interfered with the prescribed street plan.

Urban historian Ruth Ann Overbeck points out that George Washington, as a matter of public policy, defined the types of buildings that he thought should be erected, their height (two to three stories), their materials (frame, brick, stone), their relationship to

the street and to other buildings. However, enforcing these stipulations was occasional and haphazard.

No government agency was officially charged with policing construction, something left mostly to the ad hoc initiatives of land speculators and city commissioners. Platted lot sizes depended on whether lots faced a street or avenue. Deed restrictions imposed time constraints; a lot title could be forfeited if construction did not proceed by a certain date.

Agricultural uses were supposedly disallowed, and buildings containing "nuisance" uses ran the risk of being torn down. A unified, overall plan was required for the construction of rowhouses, along with proposed street grades.

But President Washington himself had waived the height regulations in 1796, a precedent followed by others. In 1818, President James Monroe rescinded the regulations altogether. In 1822, the city council outlawed wooden houses higher than 20 feet and reinstated some of the previous regulations. Later, the wood building height limit was again abandoned.

As the century progressed, lot-by-lot deed restrictions imposed by developers and subdividers continued to control land use

and construction more than any overall public plan or ordinance. Some of these lot restrictions concerned light and air, types of use (residential, commercial, or industrial), building materials, or the sale and use of alcohol. Some restrictions were unabashedly social, racial, or economic in intent.

With the advent of the renewed commission form of government and Boss Shepherd in the 1870s, another set of comprehensive building regulations was passed for the District. Businesses could not locate in residential blocks, although this, too, was not strictly enforced—dwellings mixed with shops continued. Wooden buildings were generally limited to three stories, and buildings without fireproofing could not exceed 75 feet, except churches.

In 1897, a fire downtown destroyed 22 buildings in one block. This prompted Congress to enact still more piecemeal regulations affecting yards and setbacks for light, air, and access. Certain streets were designated specifically for commercial or residential use only, and allowable building heights were determined by street widths:

90 feet on residential streets, 110 feet on commercial streets, and 130 feet on avenues.

By the turn of the century, the "city beautiful" movement was in full swing. The McMillan Commission was doing its work to rediscover and implement the monumental and esthetic intentions of the L'Enfant plan, and Congress continued to tinker with D.C.'s height regulations. Meanwhile, New York City was moving toward the adoption of a citywide zoning ordinance, an example soon to be followed by Washington and other cities.

Indeed, in 1920, Congress empowered the District to draw up and adopt a comprehensive zoning ordinance similar to New York's. The commissioners hired planner Harland Bartholomew, assisted by staff from the Army Corps of Engineers. They conducted land-use studies and prepared a zoning proposal dividing the District into residential, commercial, and industrial zones with associated use, height, and building bulk restrictions.

Bartholomew's effort amalgamated the 1916 New York ordinance, with its three categories of use, and the St. Louis ordinance, which had several subcategories. Washington's first zoning code was a 5- by 7-inch document about 20 pages long, of which 3 pages were definitions.

Not everyone thought zoning was a good idea. In fact, since the city's beginning, many citizens denounced any and all such regulations as arbitrary, unfair, and, above all, compromising of their inalienable private property rights. And most were convinced that the U.S. Constitution was on their side, despite Congress's interpretation of it.

Likewise, Americans outside of Washington believed that zoning was a clear case of government's abrogating individuals' rights in favor of rights of the collective. Not surprisingly, six years after the adoption of D.C.'s first zoning act, the very concept of zoning would be tested legally in the U.S. Supreme Court.

April 27, 1985

The Powers and
Pitfalls of Zoning

Northeast of Cleveland, near the southern shore of Lake Erie, stands the town of Euclid, Ohio. Like New York, Washington, D.C., and other American municipalities, Euclid in the 1920s had adopted and attempted to enforce a zoning ordinance.

A local landowner, frustrated because regulations prevented his residentially zoned property from being used for commercial purposes, sued the municipality. In *Village of Euclid* v. *Ambler Realty Company*, Ambler sought to have Euclid's zoning ordinance declared unconstitutional on the grounds that it was an unreasonable exercise of government's police power.

The claim was that zoning amounted to a de facto taking of property without due process of law. It was confiscatory, Ambler asserted, depriving land of its value and its owners of rights and liberties guaranteed by the Constitution.

Euclid insisted that zoning was a legitimate use of police power to prohibit potential "nuisances," even if such nuisances did not yet exist. The public interest, they argued, took precedence over private interests. Protection of public "health, safety, welfare, and morals," the police power specifically granted to government by the Constitution, justified zoning.

The right of government to exercise its constitutionally mandated police power was, of course, the preferred basis for zoning. If property values fell because of a zoning action, affected owners did not have to be compensated. By contrast, when government takes land through its power of eminent domain, it must compensate owners fairly for such losses.

The case went to the U.S. Supreme Court, with every zoned community and city in America watching. The stakes were high. If Ambler prevailed, then no zoning ordinance in the country would be legal. Further, since the legal issues under consideration were broad rather than narrow, a pro-Ambler decision would effectively preclude any future zoning ordinance from being enacted and enforced anywhere.

In 1926, the Supreme Court ruled in favor of Euclid. Zoning was declared to be a legitimate use of the police power of government so long as it was reasonable, nondiscriminatory, and nonconfiscatory. The Court recognized that zoning regulation could be abusive. But it said that only in individual cases, where specific circumstances supported such contentions of abuse, could zoning be overturned.

Recall that zoning ordinances really prescribe more than allowable land uses—residential, commercial, industrial, or otherwise. They also regulate the intensity of use by setting limits on lot sizes, lot coverage, yard sizes and setbacks, residential density (sometimes expressed as numbers of dwellings per acre), building height, and building size.

Allowable building size, or bulk, is often stated as the ratio between the building floor area (the total of all floors above

grade) permitted on a lot and the lot area. It is commonly referred to as the FAR, the floor area ratio. For example, in a zone where a FAR of 10 is permitted, 1,000 square feet of building floor area can be constructed for each 100 square feet of lot area. The FAR allowed in a given zone is clearly a major determinant of both architectural form and economic value.

After the landmark Euclid decision, cities, towns, and counties in every state proceeded to write and adopt similar zoning ordinances. In fact, to this day, most such ordinances are referred to as examples of "Euclidean" zoning (not to be confused with Euclidean geometry), reflecting the 1926 legal event that made it all possible and sustainable.

Traditional Euclidean zoning ordinances have three components: a list of definitions considered necessary to make clear the exact legal meaning of words such as *one-family dwelling, front yard, floor area, lot width, alley,* or *light industry*; written regulations describing each zoning category with its allowable uses and physical development limitations; and a zoning map dividing the subject jurisdiction into various land-use zones governed by the written regulations.

Those charged with drafting zoning ordinances faced inevitable conflicts. Most cities, like Washington, already had well-established patterns of development and land use prior to adoption of zoning. Thus, zoning maps and regulations had to take into account and largely follow such existing patterns. In this regard, much early zoning was destined initially to reinforce rather than direct urban land-use patterns.

Yet zoning would clearly influence future growth and real estate investment returns. Property owners, for instance, who thought that one day someone might enrich them by purchasing their land for an office building or commercial center, suddenly found themselves owning land indelibly marked for rowhouses, or less.

Many zoning ordinances were drawn up by attorneys, surveyors, and civil engineers, not by architects or urban designers. Therefore, zoning laws and maps rarely embodied concepts for the conscious, comprehensive shaping of urban form, city silhouette, streetscape, transportation, and other patterns of use with three-dimensional, visual implications.

Zoning was mostly a two-dimensional mapping exercise determined by previous usage, demographic growth predictions of questionable reliability, and, not incidentally, current and potential real estate values. Moreover, the fundamental policy assumption characterizing all Euclidean zoning in the United States was that *homogeneity* (of use, of economic and social levels, of building type and quality) was *always* desirable. All things being equal, the status quo was to be preserved.

Even ardent supporters of zoning worried about its inflexibility, about its dependence on fixed boundaries and codified constraints. People on all sides realized that circumstances change over time, that tomorrow's goals and values will differ from today's just as today's differ from yesterday's. They also recognized that, in specific cases, conditions could justify departing from strict application of current standards.

Therefore, zoning ordinances typically contain provisions for three kinds of departure or change: the variance, a form of administrative relief, minor in nature, from some particular requirement of the regulations whose enforcement would constitute a hardship for the owner (for example, a slight variation in a setback dimension might be allowed); the exception, usually an additional use allowed under special circumstances (such as a private school or a nursing home in a residential zone); and the zoning map amendment, the most radical change, through which a specific property or area becomes reclassified or rezoned for new uses not previously permitted.

None of these changes can be effectuated routinely. D.C. and other jurisdictions have zoning boards appointed by mayors and/or legislative councils. Boards are empowered to hear formal requests or petitions for variances, exceptions, and rezonings in accordance with articulated procedures and evaluative criteria. Most procedures involve public hearings and also require that zoning agency staffs prepare reports and recommendations for action by the zoning board.

Despite these protocols for flexibility, there is a natural tendency for owners and developers to undertake improvements fully in conformance with existing regulations (matter-of-right development). This saves time, avoids public exposure and controversy, and minimizes risk and expense. But it may not result in the most appropriate use of the property. And it may not reflect the property's potential fair market value or represent the best interests of the public.

Over the last 60 years, both developers and governments have come to recognize that zoning can do more than just protect the status quo or impose burdensome restrictions. It can be a tool for city building, a catalyst rather than a deterrent for innovation in design and development. Private and public interests do not always have to be at odds.

May 4, 1985

From Zoning to
Master Planning
... and Back

Zoning was instituted in the early part of this century to restrict "nuisance" uses of privately owned land. However, long before such restrictions were judicially tested and declared constitutionally legal, it was clear that government intended to regulate land use for other reasons.

More than 100 years prior to passage of Washington's first comprehensive zoning ordinance in 1920, the height of D.C.'s buildings had become a matter of esthetically motivated public policy. America's Founding Fathers were much taken by the "look" of Paris, particularly its low buildings and spacious streets where sunshine and air were in ample supply. Keeping the city's profile low was a conscious decision about urban image as well as a matter of safety, access, light, and ventilation.

In October 1954, the U.S. Supreme Court again confirmed its view that government could control private land use. Congress had empowered D.C.'s Redevelopment Land Agency to condemn property in Southwest occupied by "miserable and disreputable housing." Upholding the right of eminent domain for slum clearance in *Berman* v. *Parker*, Justice William Douglas wrote:

"The concept of the public welfare is broad and inclusive. . . . The values it represents are spiritual as well as physical, esthetic as well as monetary. It is within the power of the legislature to determine that the community should be beautiful as well as healthy, spacious as well as clean, well-balanced as well as carefully patrolled. . . . If those who govern the District of Columbia decide that the Nation's Capital should be beautiful as well as sanitary, there is nothing in the Fifth Amendment that stands in the way."

Accompanying this enlarged conception of land regulation has been the advent and growth of highly institutionalized city, county, and regional planning efforts. Almost all local jurisdictions in the United States now have planning commissions and agencies staffed by professional planners, as well as zoning commissions and boards appointed by legislative councils.

Planning commissions and planners make "master plans," a phrase conjuring up visions of grandiose utopian designs, authoritative maps of a destiny not to be denied. Master plans, like zoning maps, are attempts to reconcile the known past with the transient present and uncertain future. Compromised by the urban history that preceded their creation, they try to anticipate land-use needs—housing, business and commercial, industrial, recreational, educational, institutional, open space, and transportation—and to pin down their future locations, configurations, and characteristics.

Land-use plans take on many graphic forms, but the most typical ones are colored mosaics overlaying a base map of the jurisdictional area being planned. Each color represents a different type of land use, and there may be additional symbols for special purposes or sites (such as a transportation center).

Master plans are based on studies of demography and population growth trends, economic activity, existing and projected infrastructure development (roads and utilities), traffic patterns, and ecological factors (topography, geology, soils, hydrology, climate, vegetation). Planners also consider existing neighborhood patterns and characteristics, taking note of underdeveloped areas or areas perceived to be decaying that may be marked for renewal.

How do master plans relate to zoning, and what is their legal status? In most cities, zoning preceded master planning. Original zoning maps were drawn up to reflect already established patterns of land use and to create additional reserves of zoned land, usually extensions of existing patterns.

Zoning is law. But a master plan, even though created by an official planning commission and adopted by a legislative council, is a statement of goals and policies about land use, not an ordinance or set of specific, enforceable regulations.

In fact, long-range master planning always poses a dilemma: how to allow for flexibility, circumstantial discretion, and inevitable change tomorrow while committing to a specific and unambiguous land plan today.

Moreover, local governments can ensure implementation of master plans only through the powers of eminent domain or zoning. Having decided that certain kinds of uses might be desirable for a given area in the near or distant future, mayors and councils are obliged to rezone property, condemn it, or hope for the best.

Idealized master plans, despite extensive research and analysis, often disregard property ownership patterns. Yet the chain of ownership and lotting patterns imposed on urban land are powerful determinants of the look of cities and neighborhoods.

It seems easy to take colored markers and paint large tracts of land red, blue, yellow, or green at will. Indeed, it may be good theoretical planning to brush over and conceptually unify an area comprised of dozens or hundreds of small lots belonging to as many different owners. But implementation of the plan may prove impossible without concerted action. Ironically, after decades of subdivision, much new urban development depends on the ability to reassemble small lots into usable parcels.

Land owners and developers often take the initiative and petition for rezoning of property. Justification is usually predicated on at least one of three legal arguments: that the character of the neighborhood has changed substantially; that the original zoning was erroneous or inappropriate; or that the proposed new zoning is clearly in the public interest and, most important, in conformance with adopted master plans.

The economic and physical implications of all this can be dramatic. Favorable rezoning can instantaneously increase land value and can change radically the architectural character of development—building type, size, and density.

For example, suppose you owned a piece of property zoned for single-family houses at a density of two dwellings per acre. If lots of this size in this location were generally selling for $10,000, then your land would be worth about $20,000 per acre.

But if it were rezoned for apartments at a density of 40 units per acre, and if the going price for multifamily property were $2,000 per apartment unit, your property would suddenly become marketable for $80,000 per acre, a 400 percent increase in value!

If you owned 10,000 square feet of downtown property zoned for 65 feet of height and an FAR of 5, you could build a 5- or 6-story building containing 50,000 square feet. With comparable property selling at $60 per square foot of allowable building area, your lot would be worth $3 million. Rezoning to a height of 110 feet and an FAR of 10 yields a 10-story building of 100,000 square feet and a lot worth $6 million!

Thus, decisions about rezoning are susceptible to pressures unrelated to prevention of nuisances, demonstrable neighborhood changes, esthetics, or master plan fulfillment. Fortunes can be made overnight on a council's rezoning vote or a commission's affirmative recommendation. Political and economic considerations can influence deliberations, along with the subtle exchanging of gifts or favors.

A sometimes questionable zoning practice, perhaps reinforced by master plans, is premature spot zoning. This occurs when a particular property or group of contiguous properties is rezoned to a category of use unrelated to surrounding land uses. Some more intensive and potentially lucrative use seems to have leapfrogged across the landscape onto a "chosen" spot. Setting a new precedent, spot-zoned sites invariably pave the way for subsequent rezoning proposals within the changed neighborhood.

Initially a means for safeguarding property values, zoning statutes have become complex, voluminous sets of constraints and opportunities that both entrepreneurs and governments can exploit. Yet even under the best of circumstances, elaborate planning and zoning measures do not guarantee quality architecture or a rich urban environment.

May 11, 1985

Expanding the Power of Zoning

To many Washingtonians, a *floating zone* may sound like an innovative defensive strategy employed by the Redskins.

Rather, it is one of many zoning strategies that have been adopted by cities and counties during the past couple of decades with the intention of facilitating innovative, flexible land development and design.

In the 1950s and 1960s, conventional Euclidean zoning, with its emphasis on strict separation of homogeneous uses and precisely prescribed geometrical constraints, seemed too obstructive for increasingly sophisticated planning, architectural, financial, and market concepts.

Zoning and master planning were accepted as legalized instruments of public policies only distantly related to protecting "health, safety, welfare, and morals." Achievement of economic, social, and esthetic goals was legitimate grounds for zoning, and for new zoning tactics.

In fact, many communities, especially suburban ones, had tested the bounds of zoning legitimacy. Exclusionary zoning had effectively separated socioeconomic classes by limiting subdivision lots to one, two, or more acres. Low- or moderate-income homes were unlikely to be built since the costs of acquiring and improving such large lots were substantially greater than improving lots containing 5,000, 10,000 or 15,000 square feet.

During the 1960s and 1970s, judicial actions overturned exclusionary zoning in specific cases and locations. Plaintiffs argued that such zoning was clearly discriminatory, and effectively reinforced existing patterns of segregation by race as well as by economic and social status. No protection of the public interest, they claimed, could be shown.

But local governments could use zoning for positive economic purposes. By encouraging and enabling certain types of development to occur in a community, government could augment its property tax base, increase business and employment activity, and thereby enhance economic opportunity and growth.

Of course, more intense land use or higher density does not always lead to improved fiscal conditions. Sometimes, new development can result in greater demand for municipal services—schools, roads, road maintenance, police and fire protection, utilities, trash collection, and other administrative support. If the additional costs of providing these services exceed the additional tax revenues generated, the fiscal impact is negative.

For example, neighborhoods with townhouses and homes of modest size are likely to attract young, middle-income families with school-age children. Because public education is usually the largest single item in a city or county's budget, this type of development will have greater fiscal impact than zoning targeted for singles, couples, the elderly, or the affluent. As a result, many jurisdictions have tried to shape their zoning ordinances to control the demand for and cost of urban services.

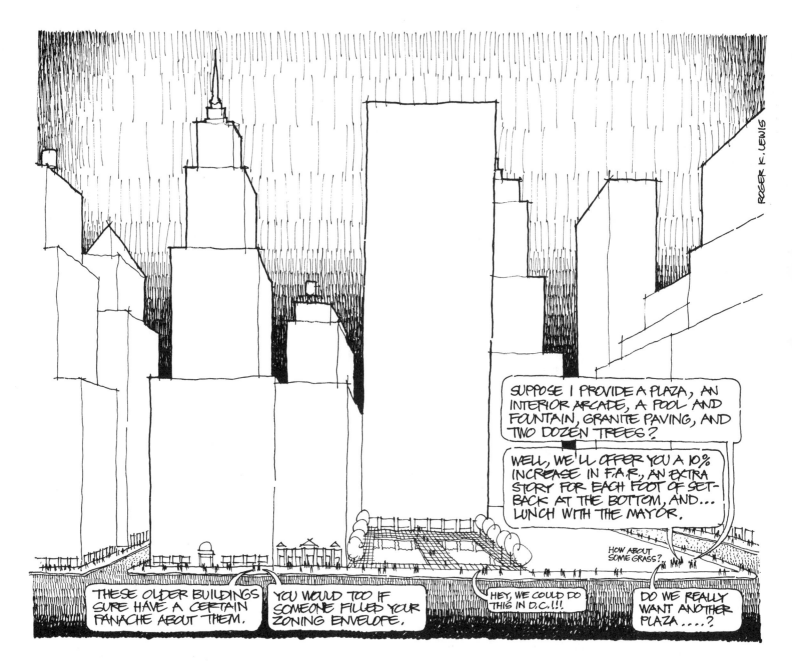

283

Industrial parks, office buildings, and certain kinds of retail activity usually produce a net positive fiscal benefit. However, they can generate new and serious traffic and parking problems whose costs are indirect. For some neighbors and travelers-by, the nuisance deficit may outweigh the tax surplus.

Much recent zoning reflects esthetic policy. Developers, architects, planners, and government officials believed that imaginatively written ordinances could provide incentives for designing and constructing better environments. Most were convinced that this was virtually impossible with traditional Euclidean zoning based solely on constraint.

Once again, New York took the lead. After World War II, Manhattan's skyline and skyscrapers were characterized by the "wedding cake" look. Buildings rose straight up from the sidewalk at the property line, then stepped back incrementally as they rose higher and higher, to an often

exuberant silhouette or spire. This was a direct expression of the mandated zoning envelope, intended to ensure adequate light, air, and sky view.

Setting back the whole building could create a public plaza, an amenity perceived to be lacking in New York's canyon country. But the developer would have to sacrifice leasable floor space, for the building's footprint and gross area would be smaller.

So planners and zoners came up with incentive or trade-off "bonuses." As motivation and in return for making a plaza and a thinner building, it seemed both fair and economically indispensable to allow such buildings to reach higher and contain even more square footage with increased FARs.

The presumption was that certain amenities—plazas, arcades, courtyards, atria—would rarely be included by developers seeking to maximize their investment returns on traditionally zoned property by filling the zoning envelope.

Thus, if the body politic could reach consensus as to which amenities were worth having, then zoning could become a quid pro quo process. In effect, zoning commissions and agencies could negotiate with

developers and architects. Traditional constraints—on density, height, setbacks, lot size and shape and, most importantly, allowable uses—could be relaxed in exchange for dedication of open space, easements, extra roads, elaborate landscaping, preservation of historic structures, or special facilities for selected population groups.

Incentive zoning appears to serve both public and private interests. But to maintain control over final results, most jurisdictions impose a multistep process to finalize the private-public "deal." Unlike matter-of-right zoning, which allows building to proceed without special reviews and approvals, most flexible zoning requires that the developer submit site plans and building designs for review prior to zoning approval and issuance of building permits.

This entails considerable risk. First, it can be costly and time-consuming, depending on numbers of reviews, notice periods required for public hearings, workloads of planning and zoning staffs, and the schedules of planning and zoning boards or commissions. In some jurisdictions, final action may even depend on approval of the legislative council. And, after months or years of work, the final vote may be negative.

Second, there is the "too many cooks stirring the broth" risk, design by committee that yields camels instead of horses. At each step in the process, developer and architect are subjected to input from reviewers, who willingly make suggestions about design characteristics of the project for which zoning is sought.

What are some of the zoning categories that typify incentive zoning yet normally require layers of approval?

- Planned-unit-development (PUD) zones, which allow a mixture of uses and buildings to occupy a single parcel of land.

- Cluster zones, which allow housing units to be aggregated rather than spread out on a tract of land so that the overall density of the tract remains unchanged; constructed density and infrastructure efficiency are increased, along with common open space.

- Floating zones, which are usually of intense and mixed uses not assigned in advance to particular lots. As if floating freely in space, they come down to earth only when applied for by an owner or developer for a particular property.

- Conditional zoning, which has been adjudged illegal by some state courts, grants zoning to properties contingent on the applicant meeting specific, agreed-upon conditions for development of the property.

- Special or ad hoc zoning, which is created by a legislative act establishing a new zoning category only for specific projects that otherwise could not be implemented under existing zoning.

Zoning has come a long way since the 1920s. Pamphlet-size zoning ordinances have turned into weighty sets of statute books. Specialized attorneys handle zoning cases. Architects spend dozens of hours researching, reading, and interpreting zoning regulations to figure out what they can and can not design.

One sometimes wonders if it is all necessary, if the end results justify the means. What might our environment look like without zoning? No pun intended, but zoning may have its limits.

May 18, 1985

... And You Must Know About Houston!

Houston, Texas, the fourth largest city in the United States, has no zoning ordinance.

Every few years, Houstonians turn back attempts by local Texas "liberals" to enact zoning and land-use regulations, still viewed by many as one step away from socialism or communism.

Born and raised in Houston, and later having struggled with zoning ordinances in D.C., Maryland, and Virginia as part of architectural and planning practice, I frequently look at Houston and wonder if its lack of zoning has resulted in a city whose form and function are unique, either for better or worse.

Houston has an abysmal semitropical climate—usually too hot, sometimes too cold, and always too humid. Occupying a flat, featureless coastal plain sliding ut of the Gulf of Mexico, it has a network of shallow bayous, drainage ditches, and a ship channel leading to one of America's major ports.

No more than an outpost nearly a century after L'Enfant planned Washington, Houston had a main street (still named "Main Street") centered in a grid of unpaved, muddy streets. Galveston had been the port city, but with construction of the ship channel and development of the oil industry after the 1930s, Houston was clearly destined to outgrow its original skin.

Under Texas state law, incorporated cities can annex surrounding county lands almost at will. Therefore, Houston was able to increase both its size and population dramatically by expanding its borders and encompassing subdivision after subdivision, even wrapping itself around already existing municipalities such as Bellaire.

This process of land annexation made Houston one of America's fastest growing cities. With virtually no land-use or zoning constraints, developers could acquire county land anywhere, subdivide it, construct on-site roads and utilities, build and sell houses, and then await annexation by the city.

Once annexed, residents then looked to the city for urban services—schools, police and fire protection, trash collection, and street maintenance. Many of these subdivisions began as wholly self-contained water and sewer districts when first developed, evidenced by the many freestanding, elevated water-storage tanks scattered about the landscape.

With no zoning, developers themselves imposed restrictions through deed covenants. These restrictive covenants usually precluded commercial use of residential lots and prevented further subdivision. Prevailing building sizes and setbacks had to be maintained. In some neighborhoods, deed covenants openly (and illegally) restricted ownership by race and religion.

But any tract of land or lots without such covenants could be developed as their owners saw fit. Land use, land prices, and density were determined by the free market alone.

Houston became the world's energy capital and home of the National Aeronautics and Space Administration's manned space center. While "government" made D.C. run, Houston ran on oil. Between 1950 and 1980, the city tripled in size and built a network of freeways. During the 1970s, it was boasted, 1,000 people per week moved to Houston.

The economic boom spurred by the jump in oil prices and energy-related business produced record levels of home building, office construction, and shopping center development. Unfortunately, it also produced the world's worst traffic congestion on freeways and major arteries.

Developers were able to acquire and assemble lots in older, closer-in subdivisions whose covenants had expired. These former residential lots soon contained millions of square feet of new commercial space, highrise condominiums, hotels, or shopping facilities, sometimes built next to existing single-family homes.

Houston's overall low residential density and extraordinary area limited mass transit possibilities. The bus system is used almost exclusively by domestic workers to get from one side of town to another. For most Houstonians, the automobile is indispensable, along with airconditioning. Recent attempts to plan and implement a citywide rail transit system were rejected by voters, who refused to approve needed taxes or bond issues.

Despite all of this, Houston's urban fabric is surprisingly like many other cities, especially those of the sunbelt—Phoenix, Denver, Salt Lake City, or Los Angeles. The central business district is typical of many 20th-century downtowns with its skyscrapers full of offices and banks, its underground garages and shops, and its sidewalks deserted during evenings, weekends, and summers. Its sprawling suburbs are accretions of linear shopping strips, shopping malls, highrise and lowrise office buildings, parking lots, apartment and townhouse complexes, and acre upon acre of subdivision homes.

Interestingly, intermixing of land uses does not seem to be the disaster feared by so many in other cities. Contrasting, abutting uses coexist peacefully when intrusive nui-

sances are avoided. Thus, one sees neighborhoods with apartments next to townhouses next to patio homes next to single-family homes next to branch banks and even service stations.

So, you might ask, why have zoning? To dampen growth? Zoning certainly has not mitigated or eliminated traffic and parking problems in other cities. Zoning does not ensure that beautiful buildings will be designed and built. It has not precipitated more innovation in design and real estate development than in Houston.

Yet Houston has serious problems, and they stem partly from the absence of land-use planning and development controls. After booming decades of unconstrained, unmanaged growth, the oil industry recession has created unprecedented vacancies in "see-through" office buildings, shopping strips, and housing.

In addition to transportation and traffic problems, Houston suffers from water supply shortages, inadequate sewage treatment capacity, poor drainage, periodic flooding, and land subsidence (water table depletion and land settlement). Can anyone deny that some measure of comprehensive planning, regulation of growth, and infrastructure development was lacking?

By comparison, Washington, D.C., is a more mature city whose traditions—concerning its history, land-use patterns, building heights and styles, public tastes and sensitivities, and the respective roles of citizens and government—are firmly established. On the other hand, Houston is still manufacturing its identity while shedding remnants of an inferiority complex vis-à-vis older urban cultures of the Eastern Seaboard.

Can we learn anything from Houston? Clearly, abdication of planning and regulatory initiatives to the private sector is questionable. Cities must shape themselves, coordinate and build needed infrastructure, and advocate the public's interests. Yet entrepreneurs must be encouraged to pursue concepts not envisioned by previously made plans or legislated zoning.

Perhaps Washington, D.C.'s, Comprehensive Plan Act of 1984 will eventually prove to be a policy model for urban design and development, a strategy that reconciles public and private interests more effectively. It is too early to tell, but the act's 10 overlapping and interrelated plan "Elements"—on land use, downtown, preservation and historic features, public facilities, urban design, transportation, environmental protection, housing, economic development, and human services—may indeed produce something other than a zoning code to map the city's future form.

May 25, 1985

12.

The Development Process
Risks and Rewards

So You Want to Be a Developer?

L'Enfant and his successors created a great plan for a great capital city, but plans mean little until transformed through building into three-dimensional reality. If good buildings are not made as a plan is implemented, then the urban and architectural results will be mediocre, no matter how brilliant the plan.

Buildings provide shelter and space for human activity. Through the artful language of architectural design, they also convey ideas about civilization, culture, and technology. But buildings get built for reasons that often lie outside the realms of esthetics and technology.

Throughout history, most nonmonumental building has occurred in response to perceivable and measurable needs or markets. Recognizing the potential for building something, someone must then undertake to satisfy the need or market. This "someone" is the developer or project sponsor, the entrepreneur or owner.

When the government needs a new office building, the sponsoring agency and General Services Administration are the developer. If the Smithsonian needs a new museum, the Smithsonian is the developer. If you remodel a kitchen or add a room to your house, you the homeowner are the developer. If it is believed that the community needs more office space, retail space, recreational facilities, hotel accommodations, or housing, and if there appears to be an economic basis for the demand, then private entrepreneurs undertake development.

Economic demand implies that there is a sufficient number of customers—tenants, buyers, and users—in the community who have both the desire and the financial means to constitute a viable market. Frequently, there is desire but no resources. In the case of governmental and institutional projects, need and marketability are confirmed only when sponsors convince budget authorizers, funding entities, or contributors to provide financial support.

But even if the need for a project is genuine and financing is available, many hurdles stand between a beginning idea and a finished building. If you have never undertaken the development of a project, how-

ever modest in scope, it is difficult to appreciate the tasks and risks that most developers face.

The public sometimes views real estate developers stereotypically as well-heeled, insensitive opportunists. While some may be, many developers would rather describe themselves as enlightened capitalists who serve the public, stimulate the economy, and promote architecture by engaging in one of the most difficult and complex of all business ventures.

How difficult is it? Developing a project, no matter what its purpose, demands successful completion of a number of interlocking activities before construction can commence:

- Verification of both present and future need through market analysis and preliminary leasing or sales commitments. This must be done whether for a convention center or a housing project.

- Economic feasibility studies based on market assessments and projections of probable income, development costs, financing costs, and operating expenses.

- Control of a site through preexisting ownership, contract purchase, or land lease—no site, no project.

- Organization of ownership structure—legal form of ownership (corporate, governmental, limited partnership, individual or joint ownership, joint venture) and decision-making protocol (who does what, to whom, when, and for how much).

- Raising equity funds needed for development costs not covered by borrowed funds. Equity funds are at risk and come from the pockets of individual owners or limited partners in the case of private development, from budget appropriations for government projects, and from assets held or money raised by institutions (such as churches or private schools).

- Obtaining loan commitments from lenders who must be repaid in the future (unlike equity investors) regardless of the success or failure of the project. Typical lenders include commercial banks, savings and loan associations, insurance companies, real estate investment trusts, and mortgage bankers. Projects sponsored by state, county, and city governments may be financed through underwriters' selling bonds to individual and institutional investors who become, in effect, project lenders.

- Design of the project by architects selected and retained by the developer, who prescribes the program requirements and budget. Project design often requires the services of structural and mechanical engineers, civil engineers, landscape architects, land surveyors, interior designers, and other highly specialized consultants—with the architect normally coordinating all of the design-related activities.

- Obtaining governmental approvals, of which there can be dozens required prior to issuance of a building permit.These can involve reviews for zoning compliance, petitioning for zoning changes or variances, accommodation of traffic or parking, building code compliance, life safety and fire protection, es-thetic acceptability, labor and employment practices, and compliance with environmental or other regulations.

- Construction estimating, bidding and contract (or subcontract) negotiations with selected contractors who will provide the on-site labor, materials, and management needed to construct the project in accordance with the architects' and engineers' plans and specifications. Some developers undertake construction themselves or with a selected contractor, whereas most government contracts are awarded to qualified contractors chosen through competitive bidding.

- Active marketing directed at those who will lease, buy, or otherwise use the project. For commercial projects, this involves real estate brokers and leasing agents, plus promotional advertising and aggressive selling campaigns.

When all of the preceding are accomplished—need and market verified, site acquired, design completed, approvals and building permits granted, contract awarded, equity and construction financing secured—then construction of the project can commence. It normally proceeds under the continuous scrutiny of the owner/developer, the architects and engineers, various governmental building inspectors, the lender who is disbursing construction loan draws, and, last but not least, neighbors and passersby.

Except for projects built for sale, property management and maintenance become developer/owner responsibilities once construction is completed and the project is put into use. This involves repairs, capital improvements, continual leasing efforts, provision of utilities and housekeeping services, and administration of building staff and functions. Owners sometimes hire property management companies specializing in this activity.

Finally, with all the contracts and legal considerations, and all the number crunching, remember that no developer would be without a good lawyer and a creative accountant.

We now see that a public or private developer must orchestrate and pay for the efforts of a multitude of project participants in order to build. And some of these participants contribute directly to determining the ultimate physical form and economic success of the project.

Unfortunately, scores of pitfalls and unavoidable risks may still jeopardize well-planned projects. Encountered before construction, they can delay or kill projects. During and after construction, they can lead to economic disaster.

To be a developer requires more than a desire to make a profit or satisfy a great community need. It demands patience and stamina, diligent management, a gambling instinct with a willingness to lose or fail, a strong stomach, optimism about the future, and an undeniable portion of good luck.

October 27, 1984

Profit or Loss . . .
A Calculated Risk

Nothing ventured, nothing gained." "A penny saved is a penny earned." These are mottoes that profit-motivated developers might proclaim as guides to successful building.

What are the risks and rewards expected by developers and investors who build office buildings and other commercial properties?

Before construction, any one of the following occurrences could stop a project and result in a loss of all funds expended up to the point of termination:

- The site proves technically unfeasible for building because of unforeseen subsurface conditions too costly to remedy. Unstable soils, excessive rock, or poor drainage and groundwater conditions may be discovered only after extensive testing, and sometimes even after construction begins.

- When land is being acquired, unclear titles, recalcitrant sellers, lingering claims, or easements not previously revealed can stall or prevent development.

- Governing authorities may refuse to approve requested zoning variances, exceptions, or changes required to build the project as designed. The project might not meet building code criteria.

- Public utilities may become unavailable, particularly sewer hookup authorizations—many people still recall the necessary but costly sewer moratoria of the 1970s that delayed or stopped millions of dollars of new construction in the D.C. area.

- Unacceptably high construction bids can result from uncontrollable general increases in labor and material costs, material and labor shortages, overdesign by architects and engineers, an insufficiently competitive bidding climate (when contractors are busy and not "hungry" enough), or increases in scope of work caused by additional government regulatory requirements or market needs.

- Legal actions by neighbors, community groups, or others opposed to the project can be initiated and delay or kill the development.

- Project financing may be inadequate to cover all costs. Investors might back off, perhaps because of excessive risk or insufficient return. Lenders might refuse to provide permanent and construction loans on acceptable terms, demanding interest rates, loan fees, and other provisions that a developer could not live with economically. Or there might not be any offers to provide financing if lenders question the project's soundness.

Once construction is under way, new risks appear. Unforeseen construction cost overruns, those annoying extras caused by factors previously cited, can precipitate serious cash flow problems requiring the investment of more money, either out-of-pocket or borrowed. Without offsetting increases in income, investment return may disappear altogether. In some cases, developers run out of funds before project completion, ultimately burdening project lenders with finishing and marketing the project.

Development Vignettes

Delays, for whatever reasons, can add significantly to both administrative and financing costs. Time is literally money when the loan interest clock is running. If delays are substantial, a developer may miss crucial leasing or selling opportunities while experiencing unanticipated development cost increases for interest and overhead.

However, even after all these risks are run, commercial developers must still pass the market test. Two basic questions must be affirmatively answered. First, are there enough tenants out there looking for space at the location where it is being provided? And, second, are those tenants willing to pay at least enough rent to cover operating expenses (real estate taxes, utilities, management and maintenance, housekeeping, insurance) and debt service (loan interest and amortization)?

If the development fails the market test by not attracting tenants, then the developer must obviously make up the deficit, since those expenses and debts have to be paid regularly. When funds are exhausted, default and foreclosure may ensue.

Poor market absorption and intolerable vacancy rates may be caused by mistaken assumptions and projections arising from erroneous market analysis data, underestimation of competition, or questionable location. Contrary to popular real estate lore asserting that the three most critical factors for success are "location, location, location," a great site, while necessary, is not sufficient.

Timing is a major factor. Conditions may have changed rapidly during the development period, which can easily last three to four years or more. Interest rates may have risen, or a general economic recession may have set in. Rents that looked realistic 30 months ago may be unrealistic today.

Now, you may ask, why take all these risks? The economic rationale is profit. The economic technique is leverage.

Leverage allows developers and investors to own and control an asset of great value with a relatively small amount of equity. Thus, even a small percentage return on the total asset value can represent a large percentage return on the invested equity.

Real estate investment returns consist of several components. Cash revenues from a project may exceed cash expenditures, leaving a distributable cash surplus at year's end. Tax laws permit noncash depreciation deductions. For tax accounting purposes, these may result in net losses being generated by projects yielding cash surpluses. But these can no longer shelter other income that would otherwise be taxed in the absence of such losses.

Appreciation in the value of real estate over time, amortization of project debt, and the conversion of current ordinary income into future capital gain income represent another form of potential return. But this can backfire. A sale at the wrong moment can produce enormous, negative tax consequences and cash outlays, not bankable profit. Or tax laws can change.

Real estate is often owned by limited partnerships consisting of a managing general partner backed up financially by passive, limited partner investors. Such limited partners may be more interested in tax shelter benefits than in additional cash income. Nevertheless, their ultimate motive for investing is to become wealthier by keeping more of their income.

This risk and reward system shapes cities and buildings by influencing decisions about how, where, and when money is invested. Today, in cities like Washington or Houston, office space remains vacant because investors, developers, and lenders overestimated the market. Some misjudged the strength of tenants' locational preferences and the persistence of competition from other parts of the city and suburbs.

Buildings exhibit more amenities as developers struggle to compete with each other for choice occupants. But greater architectural amenities—better finishes, high-tech security systems, increased landscaping, interior atria, sophisticated environmental controls—imply higher capital costs. With high interest rates and land costs, extraordinarily high rentals and occupancy levels are required just to break even.

Moreover, recent years have witnessed the inflow of foreign investment capital attracted by the security of American real estate. Thus, projects have been built as capital repositories without necessarily being sound economic performers. Coupled with aggressive, tax-motivated real estate investment, this has distorted the office-building market.

Eventually, marginal locations in the city become desirable locations. Empty buildings fill up. If the current owner does not make money, perhaps the next one will. However discouraging today's outlook may be, things will improve tomorrow. For developers, it is in the blood.

November 3, 1984

Building Without the Profit Motive

I once had a client who was an official with a local government agency that had jurisdiction over matters of real estate development. At the same time, in the community where he lived, he had volunteered to head the effort to build a new neighborhood nonprofit recreational facility.

When the project was finally completed, he told me that his attitude toward developers had been forever changed. Having been a seeker rather than a giver of approval, he had experienced most of the unforgettable trials and tribulations associated with all building development.

Much of the built environment is comprised of buildings that were not built as investments by profit-motivated companies or entrepreneurs. Governments and other societal, nonbusiness institutions—church organizations, schools, community groups, cultural organizations—sponsor them.

Their financial life is not directly dependent on specific economic markets. Instead, they depend on the desire and will of constituents who support their development and who, in some way, will benefit from them.

Washington is a city amply supplied with such buildings, many belonging to the federal government. When Uncle Sam needs to build something, usually at the request of some specific executive agency, Congress and the president must ultimately approve it and appropriate money for it. Thus, while the private developer must make a convincing case with investors and bankers, federal agencies must convince the Office of Management and Budget plus the House of Representatives and the Senate.

While the private developer must often negotiate for and acquire title to property on the open market, the government may already have usable sites. Or it may acquire them through condemnation, paying the former property owner the hypothetical fair market value based on independent appraisals.

Local government agencies frequently acquire sites for public facilities—parks, schools, plazas, pedestrian and vehicular rights-of-way—from developers who convey such public-purpose sites for little or no money. Rather, these concessions are usually granted in return for zoning benefits or other needed approvals and sanctions that may result in increased densities or more intensive development rights.

Like their private sector counterparts, public sector and nonprofit developers must justify the need for projects they contemplate building. Churches, school boards, museums, foreign ministries, trade associations, and government agencies must all prepare and defend specific programs and projections supporting their arguments for funds to build. The research and documentation involved may well be comparable to the marketing efforts required of a commercial developer.

The Conception and Realization of the Washington Monument

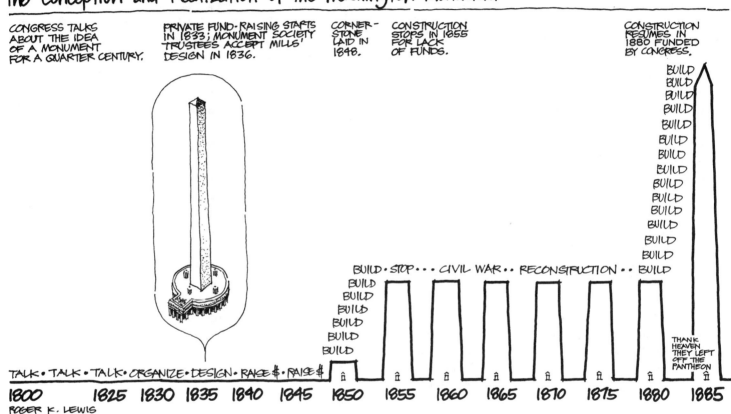

CONGRESS TALKS ABOUT THE IDEA OF A MONUMENT FOR A QUARTER CENTURY.

PRIVATE FUND-RAISING STARTS IN 1833; MONUMENT SOCIETY TRUSTEES ACCEPT MILLS' DESIGN IN 1836.

CORNER-STONE LAID IN 1848.

CONSTRUCTION STOPS IN 1855 FOR LACK OF FUNDS.

CONSTRUCTION RESUMES IN 1880 FUNDED BY CONGRESS.

BUILD BUILD BUILD BUILD BUILD BUILD BUILD BUILD BUILD BUILD BUILD BUILD BUILD BUILD

BUILD • STOP • • • CIVIL WAR • • RECONSTRUCTION • • BUILD

BUILD BUILD BUILD BUILD BUILD BUILD

THANK HEAVEN THEY LEFT OFF THE PANTHEON

TALK • TALK • TALK • ORGANIZE • DESIGN • RAISE $ • RAISE $

1800   1825 1830 1835 1840 1845 1850 1855 1860 1865 1870 1875 1880 1885

ROGER K. LEWIS

301

Except for marketing and financing, investment building and not-for-profit building are similar. An architect must be hired to design the project in accordance with program and budgetary criteria. The budget must reflect anticipated construction costs, plus other expenses: professional fees for architectural, engineering, and other design services; land acquisition costs; construction loan interest and points (if any); furnishings and special equipment; insurance; and project management.

Construction contract bids must be sought and, with architect and sponsor whispering prayers at the bid opening, fall within budget allocations. Otherwise, the sponsor must either obtain supplementary funds or appropriations, never an easy task, or reduce the scope of the project through redesign or program shrinkage. The latter option may require substantial additional effort on the part of the architect and engineers.

Also like investment projects, nonprofit projects can encounter roadblocks or go unrealized. They can become entangled in litigation or be plagued by unforeseen technical problems. Hidden site conditions can crop up, or labor and material shortages can occur, resulting in costly delays as construction prices rise and overhead stretches out.

The Washington Monument is perhaps D.C.'s most graphic example of what can happen. Early in the 19th century, the monument was planned and a monument society was formed to raise funds privately by citizen subscription. Robert Mills prepared the design—a 700-foot obelisk with a "colonnaded pantheon" at its base—but money came in slowly.

In 1848, having collected almost $90,000, the society began construction. Soil conditions forced the monument to slightly higher ground off axis. Seven years later, 150 feet in the air, the monument's growth stopped. Money was running out. In 1855, "Know Nothings" had thrown into the Potomac a block of marble from the Temple of Concord in Rome, a gift of the Pope. Their 1855 caper was to confiscate the monument society's property so that further fund-raising became impossible.

No work was done during the Civil War and for 15 years afterward. In 1876, Congress decided to complete construction at federal expense. The monument was finally dedicated in 1885, 80 years after it was first contemplated, without its pantheon, and at a total cost well beyond the original estimates.

Discussion of the public or institutional development process would be incomplete without consideration of the indispensable building committee normally comprised of organization officials, well-meaning volunteers, experts, and persons of influence or affluence. While commercial development enterprises are almost always guided by the commanding hand and head of a single entrepreneur or general partner, institutions tend to look to their building committees for steerage. If such committees have a wise and decisive chair, then the committee can act effectively in overseeing development tasks.

But sometimes building committees go in several directions at once, become embroiled in internal controversy, adopt contradictory policy, or refuse to make timely decisions. If the chair and project architect cannot mediate satisfactorily to formulate a cohesive vision, a building may emerge that indeed appears to have been designed by a committee of many minds.

Government agencies such as the General Services Administration, the Army Corps of Engineers, or local school boards can also get carried away with their own methodologies, techniques, and managerial strategies, to the detriment of good architecture. In an attempt to dictate and control final project results, they may establish design criteria so rigid that the architectural outcome is effectively prescribed in advance, precluding innovative proposals by designers.

Of course, developers of investment projects can behave similarly, rejecting anything but the most conventional and mundane of designs from a position of safety and advocacy of the tried and true. With either public money at stake in the case of government-sponsored projects, or investors' and lenders' money in the case of privately sponsored projects, these conservative attitudes are somewhat understandable.

Although Washington has its share of conservative and decidedly mediocre architecture, project sponsors and much of their public constituency often realize that buildings can and should do more than just satisfy a single user's immediate space needs. Buildings of a public or quasi-public nature should exemplify architecture's best and serve generations of citizens not yet born.

November 10, 1984

The Home Builders

"Home is where the heart is" goes an old proverb. And although the geographic heart of cities is downtown, most city dwellers would claim their personal residence, not downtown, as the emotional center of their urban universe.

In fact, most city land is occupied by housing. Residential blocks, streets, and neighborhoods contribute significantly to the texture and identity of cities like Washington. But how is this dwelling fabric developed?

Housing developers respond to and influence that most demanding and unpredictable of market targets, the household. The potential market size can number in the thousands, but the share of the market subject to capture may be very small.

While office building or shopping center developers offer square footage that they can market in any quantity and configuration to suit tenants, housing developers produce dwelling units that they must rent or sell one by one. Commercial project developers usually must assemble small parcels of land, subdivided piecemeal in previous decades, into a single developable parcel. Housing developers historically have done the opposite, by subdividing large parcels into ever smaller lots.

The demand for housing is extremely sensitive to highly variable economic conditions: home mortgage interest rates, mortgage loan availability, material and labor costs, and household income. At the same time, patterns of demand for housing depend on locational issues: perceived quality of neighborhoods and schools, availability of shopping, access to utilities and public services (mass transit, police and fire protection, trash pickup, water and sewer hookups).

In Washington, as in most other cities, housing developers have tended to operate in a push-pull fashion with local public planning efforts and infrastructure development. Government builds major roads to serve both current and anticipated needs. Then developers acquire land accessible to the road and utility network and undertake its improvement.

Such improvements are subject to zoning and subdivision regulations that prescribe the type, density, and geometrical parameters of use in residential districts. These include lot sizes, lot widths, yard and setback requirements, lot coverage, building height limits, and parking requirements. Architects, land planners, and engineers lay out the site plan, which, once approved, is transformed into a precisely drawn "record plat." Only after the plat is finally approved and recorded can land subdivision, lot conveyance, and home building occur.

As homes are purchased and community facilities added, neighborhoods become established. Property values and taxes rise, and the market begins again to look for new developments at lower costs accessible to the ever extendable road network.

Eventually, neighborhoods that once seemed suburban become urban. Some may deteriorate or change in socioeco-

305

SURE IT'S A LONG COMMUTE TO DOWNTOWN, BUT THINK HOW MUCH CLOSER YOU ARE TO WEST VIRGINIA!
YEAH, AND IF YOUR HOUSEHOLD INCOME IS BELOW $40,000 PER YEAR, YOU CAN BUY A MOBILE HOME IN WEST VIRGINIA!
MY QUESTION IS... WHO'S GOING TO PUT IN ALL THOSE TREES?
DENSE? IS SHE TALKING ABOUT THE TRAFFIC, THE DEVELOPER, OR THE ARCHITECT?
SOMETHING FOR EVERYONE..... SINGLE-FAMILY HOUSES, TOWNHOUSES, GARDEN APARTMENTS, CONDOS! ALL ON A FEW ACRES OF LAND.... SEEMS PRETTY DENSE THOUGH.....
SINEQUANON... MUST BE A REFERENCE TO AN OLD INDIAN TRIBE.
SINEQUANON ROAD
SINEQUANON UTILITIES
OUTLANDIA
A BIT OF THE CITY BUILT IN THE COUNTRY
ROGER K. LEWIS

nomic character, only to be redeveloped by a new generation of developers through preservation and rehabilitation of older units, or through demolition and complete replacement by a new type of housing.

The home-building industry is immense, fragmented, and localized. There are hundreds of independent housing developers in Washington and tens of thousands in the United States. A few are large organizations like U.S. Home or Ryland, but most are small and somewhat ad hoc in their operations, building only a few units annually.

Small home builders are continually going in and out of business as times and fortunes change. Speculation in housing is an enterprise where someone with limited capital can make or lose a great deal of money relatively quickly, where the freewheeling gambler and prudent investor can both play the same game.

Consider the most familiar types of housing: the single-family detached house; attached housing (duplexes, rowhouses, townhouses); multifamily walk-up housing (lowrise garden apartments); and midrise or highrise elevator housing.

For each type, there are limitless ways to configure units and shape and style buildings. Density (number of dwelling units per acre) is also a critical variable. Higher density can result in lower land costs per dwelling unit and a more urban building fabric, but increased traffic and parking demands.

For example, developers long ago discovered that the three-story walk-up garden apartment building was the cheapest form of housing to build. With one or two prefabricated metal stairs serving 12 apartments (4 per floor), more square footage can be provided per construction dollar than with any other type of housing. But a glance at such projects inside and outside the Capital Beltway reveals landscapes dominated by drives and parking lots, trash dumpsters, and ambiguous open spaces.

The housing developer who builds homes for sale, whatever the physical type, normally uses advertising and real estate bro-

kers to contact and persuade prospective buyers. The developer hopes that he or she did not build too many units for the market to absorb, that affordable mortgages are available, and that costs and selling prices have not risen to a level where buyers are drawn away by stiff competition down the block.

If units remain unsold, the developer must still continue to pay interest on the construction loan, plus other carrying costs—real estate taxes, insurance, utilities, maintenance, and homeowner association or condominium fees. Eventually, when equity pockets are empty, the developer may be forced into a distress sale at discount prices or even foreclosure.

Building housing for sale offers fewer tax shelter benefits than rental housing. But unsubsidized rental housing has become almost impossible to develop, whatever the density or physical type, because development costs have increased much faster than rental levels. This is why most unsubsidized multifamily housing built over the last decade has been condominium apartments for sale, not rent. Rent control, although beneficial to tenants, has further deterred developers from investing in rental housing.

Since the early 1970s, most new rental housing has been developed with government assistance. After the virtual discontinuance of public housing programs (under which local housing authorities acted as the developer), both private and nonprofit sponsors continued to build rental housing for lower-income citizens using interest subsidy or rent subsidy programs.

What made these subsidized projects attractive to private investors was not cash flow, but, rather, high leverage and tax benefits. Low-income rental housing owners could take accelerated depreciation. Moreover, they needed to invest only small amounts of equity cash because most project development costs were covered by the mortgage, sometimes even 100 percent. Mortgage insurance programs underwritten by the Federal Housing Administration made possible these high loan-to-value ratios.

Thus, for several decades, the policy of the federal government has been to use the tax system as a means to achieve both social and economic objectives. Combining urban development, housing, and tax policies, America's post–World War II aim has been to direct growth while serving the needy and tapping the resources of the affluent. Unfortunately, these policies can conflict with credit-tightening monetary policy, which substantially curtails housing industry activity.

Like the developers of commercial real estate and nonprofit projects, housing developers must manage multiple resources and orchestrate the efforts of many people involved in the development process. Whether for one house or a thousand, it is a complex and risky undertaking whose ultimate rewards are never guaranteed, but whose necessity is undeniable.

November 17, 1984

A Development Story ... Tough Start, Happy Ending

Once upon a time, the U.S. Department of Housing and Urban Development (HUD) made lots of low-interest, long-term mortgage loans to nonprofit sponsors for the construction of elderly housing projects—the Section 202 direct loan program. With rental assistance payments under HUD's Section 8 program, nonprofit sponsors could provide housing accommodations for needy elderly tenants at below-market rental levels.

On Maryland's upper Eastern Shore—Cecil, Kent, Queen Anne's, Caroline, and Talbot counties—Upper Shore Aging (USA) managed nutrition and transportation programs for the elderly under a special state charter. In 1977, USA applied for and received a Section 202 fund reservation of $3.75 million to develop 130 units of housing, its first venture into building.

However, USA's approach was unusual. It wanted to distribute the units in six towns—Perryville, Cecilton, Chestertown, Sudlersville, Greensboro, and St. Michaels.

An article about the project published by the Urban Land Institute in its 1983 book, *Housing for a Maturing Population*, noted that "the heart of the sponsor's sociological and political strategy was to develop small, intimate mini-villages in several existing communities to which elderly residents had strong familial, social, and religious ties." But the article also pointed out that "it was obvious to all, and especially to HUD, that this strategy posed serious questions of economic feasibility. Clearly, the most cost-effective and logistically simple plan would have been to construct all 130 units together in a few buildings on one site."

Nevertheless, the sponsor was convinced, and HUD initially agreed, that a typical 130-unit apartment building project would fit poorly into these historic Maryland towns. Detached houses—some humble, some stately—characterize these rural communities. Their streets are lined by homes clad in brick or clapboard siding with porches and gabled roofs, dormers and chimneys, neoclassical cornices, and low garden fences. The fabric of these towns, while venerable and charming, is fragile.

Fortunately, small and affordable sites were available in each town, and all had reasonable access to nearby commercial facilities for convenience shopping.

The architectural challenge was clear. On the one hand, buildings had to be designed to meet stringent, statutorily defined budget limitations and HUD Minimum Property Standards. On the other hand, there was a compelling mandate to create an appropriate esthetic image, one that would be compatible with the existing townscapes and, at the same time, provide an accommodating domestic environment for the elderly.

The design concept envisioned a small, one-story prototype building—a quad—containing four side-by-side, one-bedroom apartments of about 575 square feet each. In turn, quads could be clustered around a kind of village green. The size, geometry, and orientation of the cluster arrangement could respond to varying site conditions in each town.

At all six sites, communal facilities—laundry room, meeting room, manager's office—were required. Sidewalks crisscrossed the landscaped village greens to interconnect quads and communal facilities; walks also led to limited on-site parking and abutting public sidewalks and streets.

The quad was designed to look like a big house. Each of the four apartments, stretching from front to back, had its own porch on the living/dining/kitchen side facing the green. Bedrooms on the opposite side had sliding glass doors leading to side and rear yard areas. A ridged roof,

hipped at the four corners, served to unify visually the overall form of the quad building. In a reversal of customary material usage, and for budgetary reasons, the on-grade porches were framed by brick piers and lintels, while the building proper was veneered with aluminum siding, the color of which could be varied.

A total of 27 quad buildings, plus 5 community buildings, were to be built. Perryville's site necessitated a special, two-story walk-up building. Thus, Upper Shore Aging had to build 33 buildings containing 130 units in six geographically scattered locations, all at the same time. The hope was that by using a repeatable prototype, the economies of standardization would offset the increased costs and inefficiencies of dispersal.

As it turned out, perseverance and extra money, in addition to hope, were needed. For this project came close to dying several deaths before it was realized.

Although the undertaking was conceived by USA and funded by HUD as one project, it had to be treated as six separate projects with six mortgages, six sets of construction documents, six appraisals, six separate initial and final closings—six of

everything. This greatly increased overhead costs and processing time, complicated the scheduling, and magnified design and construction efforts. Further, the scattered-site approach, despite unified ownership, resulted in redundant property management operations at each project site. All of these factors continually threatened to make the project economically unfeasible both to build and manage.

Cost extras, especially for unforeseen sitework, exceeded original budget allocations. Yet HUD balked frequently at allowing contingency funds to be used, and they refused to allow savings to be transferred from site to site or between previously approved line item allocations. For example, Chestertown's project cost $30,000 less than budgeted, but this savings could not be reallocated to cover sitework overruns at Greensboro.

Delays in processing by various governmental authorities continually delayed the start of construction. Labor and material prices were rising monthly, pushing the project's probable construction cost above statutory limits. At one point, when architectural and engineering drawings were nearly completed, the sponsor discovered that it had miscalculated the construction budget. As designed, the project could not be built. Only after the architects, engineers, contractor, and sponsor agreed to make cost-cutting (but concept-conserving) revisions in the design and specifications could the project again proceed—but delayed even further.

When finally completed, $4,009,500 had been spent, approximately $31,000 per unit. This included all development costs: land, construction, architectural and engineering fees, loan interest, permits, insurance, miscellaneous consultants, and general overhead. Only $250,000 above the original 1977 allocation, this 6.7 percent cost increase over a three-year period of high inflation seems remarkable.

Rent-up of the units was almost immediate. Tenant waiting lists were needed. To choose occupants from among the pool of qualified applicants, a locally based selection committee was formed and included citizens and government officials, senior citizen group representatives, clergy, and the developer.

Today, tenants continue to express satisfaction with USA's concept. Although small, apartments seem like "bright little houses" with their separate entrances, big windows, and rooms filled with memorabilia. Residents and visitors enjoy the communal spaces, the intimate village greens shaped by the quads, and the front porches on which they can sit and socialize. Many plant and care for flowers, shrubs, and vegetables.

Passing through town, you might not even notice these small-scale minivillages, the largest of which, at Chestertown, contains 30 units; the smallest, at Sudlersville, contains only 16. Yet densities are relatively high—Sudlersville's four quads, community building, and parking occupy less than an acre.

This project exists only because of the unrelenting persistence of everyone involved. But it was often frustrating. Some officials were so wedded to regulations, comparables, and do-not-trust-anyone thinking that, when faced with an atypical yet meritorious proposal, their first reaction was automatically to say no! Happily, those who believed in yes prevailed.

March 8, 1986

Index